W9-BUS-318

Intellectual Freedom Manual

WITHDRAWN
Tribal Library
Saginaw Chippewa Indian Tribe
7070 E. Broadway
Mt. Pleasant MI 48858

ALA Editions purchases fund advocacy, awareness,
and accreditation programs for library professionals worldwide.

WITHDRAWN

NINTH EDITION

Intellectual Freedom Manual

*Compiled by the Office for Intellectual Freedom
of the American Library Association*

Trina Magi, *Editor*
Martin Garnar, *Assistant Editor*

An imprint of the American Library Association
Chicago 2015

TRINA MAGI is a library professor and reference and instruction librarian at the University of Vermont. She has chaired state and regional intellectual freedom committees, served on the ALA Intellectual Freedom Committee, and published a number of articles on privacy. She has won several awards for her intellectual freedom advocacy.

MARTIN GARNAR is the reference services librarian and professor of library science at Regis University in Denver, CO. Martin also teaches professional ethics, library instruction, and foundations of library and information science for the University of Denver's library and information science program. He has served as chair of the ALA Intellectual Freedom Committee and the Committee on Professional Ethics.

© 2015 by the American Library Association

Extensive effort has gone into ensuring the reliability of the information in this book; however, the publisher makes no warranty, express or implied, with respect to the material contained herein.

This publication provides information about laws related to library operations. This information is not intended as legal advice. If legal advice or expert assistance is required, the services of a competent legal professional should be sought.

ISBNs
978-0-8389-1292-8 (paper)
978-0-8389-1336-9 (PDF)
978-0-8389-1337-6 (ePub)
978-0-8389-1338-3 (Kindle)

Library of Congress Cataloging-in-Publication Data
Intellectual freedom manual / Compiled by the Office for Intellectual Freedom
     of the American Library Association ; Trina Magi, Editor ; Martin Garnar,
     Assistant Editor . — Ninth Edition.
   pages   cm
Includes bibliographical references and index.
ISBN 978-0-8389-1292-8 (print : alk. paper)
     1. Libraries—Censorship—United States—Handbooks, manuals, etc. 2. Intellectual
   freedom—United States—Handbooks, manuals, etc. I. Magi, Trina J. editor. II. Garnar,
   Martin, editor.
Z711.4.I57 2015
025.2'130973—dc23   2014037437

Book design by Kimberly Thornton in the Cardea, Aleo, and Lato typefaces.

♾ This paper meets the requirements of ANSI/NISO Z39.48-1992 (Permanence of Paper).

Printed in the United States of America

19 18 17 16 15   5 4 3 2 1

5

Things You Can Do to Support Intellectual Freedom in Your Library

1. **Create a culture** that supports intellectual freedom by regularly talking about it with users, coworkers, employees, administrators, legislators, and governing bodies. Don't wait for a crisis to educate them about the library profession's principles. Meet with other organizations and individuals in your community, and form partnerships around common interests.

2. **Develop written policies** that support intellectual freedom in the following areas: collection development and resource reconsideration, Internet use, meeting rooms and exhibit spaces, privacy and confidentiality, and user behavior.

3. **Formally adopt these core ALA statements** as policy for your library: *Libraries: An American Value, Library Bill of Rights, Code of Ethics of the American Library Association*, and *The Freedom to Read* statement. Frame and prominently post the *Library Bill of Rights* on the walls and on the library website for users to see.

4. **Consult this manual** to learn about best practices for supporting intellectual freedom, and for tools to respond to concerns and challenges.

5. **Ask for help** if you need it. If you're facing a challenge or concern and need help, contact your state intellectual freedom committee or the American Library Association Office for Intellectual Freedom at (800) 545-2433, ext. 4223.

CONTENTS

Part I: Intellectual Freedom and Libraries

Part II:
Intellectual Freedom Issues
and Best Practices

Part III:
Advocacy and Assistance

For historical information about the creation and revision of many of the documents in this book, please consult the companion publication, *A History of ALA Policy on Intellectual Freedom: A Supplement to the Intellectual Freedom Manual, Ninth Edition.*

ACKNOWLEDGMENTS

Special thanks to:

The librarians who participated in the interviews and usability
testing that led to the reorganization of the manual

The staff of the ALA Office for Intellectual Freedom, especially
Barbara Jones and Deborah Caldwell-Stone, who reviewed
content and contributed new material

All the contributors, for sharing so generously of their time
and expertise

The members of the Intellectual Freedom Committee and its
Privacy Subcommittee, for their review and revision of policies and documents, and to Nanette Perez, who provided staff
support for their work

The members of the Committee on Professional Ethics for their
contribution of a new policy statement on copyright

Patrick Hogan, senior editor, ALA Editions, for his assistance
and support

University of Vermont and Regis University, for supporting sab-
batical leaves of absence for the editor and assistant editor

CONTRIBUTORS

HELEN R. ADAMS, a retired school librarian in Wisconsin, is currently an online instructor for Mansfield University (PA) in the areas of intellectual freedom, privacy, and copyright. A trustee of the Freedom to Read Foundation, she is the author of *Protecting Intellectual Freedom and Privacy in Your School Library* (Libraries Unlimited, 2013).

DEBORAH CALDWELL-STONE is deputy director of the ALA Office for Intellectual Freedom. An attorney by training, she practiced appellate law before state and federal courts in Illinois before joining ALA. She works closely with librarians to address intellectual freedom issues including censorship, the impact of new technologies and the USA PATRIOT Act on privacy, and the use of Internet filters in libraries. She has served as an instructor for the ALA-sponsored Lawyers for Libraries and Law for Librarians training institutes and frequently speaks to library groups around the country.

THERESA CHMARA is an attorney in Washington, DC. She has been a First Amendment lawyer for over twenty years and serves as the general counsel of the Freedom to Read Foundation. She is the author of *Privacy and Confidentiality Issues: A Guide for Libraries and Their Lawyers* (ALA, 2009), a frequent speaker on intellectual freedom issues in libraries, and an instructor for the Lawyers for Libraries training seminars.

ROBERT P. DOYLE is executive director of the Illinois Library Association (ILA). Under his leadership, the association has successfully opposed numerous intellectual freedom legislative challenges. Prior to joining ILA, Doyle was director of the ALA International Relations Office. Currently, he serves as the vice president of the Freedom to Read Foundation and is the author of *Banned Books*.

LORETTA GAFFNEY is a writer, researcher, and instructor living and working in Los Angeles. She defended her dissertation, "The Politics of Reading: Why Libraries Are Targets of Conservative Activism, 1990-2010," in 2012. Gaffney has taught courses on intellectual freedom and young adult literature at the University of Illinois, Dominican University, and UCLA. Her current research projects include school librarians' knowledge and Tea Party-related challenges to libraries.

MARTIN GARNAR is the reference services librarian and professor of library science at Regis University in Denver, CO. Martin also teaches professional ethics, library instruction, and foundations of library and information science for the University of Denver's library and information science program. He has served as chair of the ALA Intellectual Freedom Committee and the Committee on Professional Ethics.

SARAH HOUGHTON is the director of the San Rafael Public Library in California and the author of *Librarian in Black*. She has written and presented about intellectual freedom issues in libraries for over a decade.

BARBARA M. JONES is director of the ALA Office for Intellectual Freedom and executive director of the Freedom to Read Foundation. Before joining ALA, she had a 35-year career in academic and research libraries. She has written numerous articles and books, served on state, national, and international committees, and led workshops in the United States, Africa, Canada, Latin America, Europe, and Asia—all in support of intellectual freedom.

TRINA MAGI is a library professor and reference and instruction librarian at the University of Vermont. She has chaired state and regional intellectual freedom committees, served on the ALA Intellectual Freedom Committee, and published a number of articles on privacy. She has won several awards for her intellectual freedom advocacy.

CANDACE MORGAN retired after forty years as a librarian in public, state, special, and academic libraries. She edited the seventh and eighth editions of the *Intellectual Freedom Manual,* and is currently a trainer and coordinator of "Celebrate the Freedom to Read in Oregon."

KRISTIN PEKOLL is the assistant director at the Office for Intellectual Freedom. Before joining ALA, she worked for twelve years as a public librarian at the West Bend Community Memorial Library in Wisconsin.

NANETTE PEREZ is the program officer for the ALA Office for Intellectual Freedom. In addition to assisting the Intellectual Freedom Committee with its work, she manages Banned Books Week, the national book community's annual celebration of the freedom to read.

CARRIE RUSSELL is director of the Program on Public Access to Information for ALA's Office for Information Technology Policy. She joined ALA in 1999 as the association's copyright specialist after a fourteen-year career as an academic librarian at the University of Arizona.

PAT SCALES is a retired middle- and high-school librarian. She is a free-speech advocate who served on the faculty of Lawyers for Libraries and is the author of *Teaching Banned Books: 12 Guides for Young Readers, Protecting Intellectual Freedom in Your School Library,* and *Books Under Fire: A Hit List of Banned and Challenged Children's Books.* She writes for publications including *School Library Journal* and *BookLinks.* She has served as a member and chair of the ALA Intellectual Freedom Committee.

INTRODUCTION AND USER'S GUIDE

BEGINNING WITH THE first edition published in 1974, the *Intellectual Freedom Manual* has served as an essential reference book for librarians seeking information and guidance in applying the principles of intellectual freedom to library service. It is published under the direction of the American Library Association's Office for Intellectual Freedom. Additional information about intellectual freedom issues can be found on the ALA "Intellectual Freedom" website (www.ala.org/advocacy/intfreedom). **Check the website regularly to find the latest news and to see newly adopted and revised ALA policies.**

Scope

Like previous editions, the ninth edition contains current ALA intellectual freedom policies and guidelines; essays on intellectual freedom issues, principles, and law; and practical help for librarians and trustees.

New to this edition are:

- "Issue at a Glance" pages, which provide a summary of important points related to each intellectual freedom issue
- Information about copyright
- Information about responding to requests from law enforcement
- A step-by-step checklist for responding to challenges to library resources
- An essay about intellectual freedom and young people
- An essay about the law regarding libraries and labeling and rating systems (e.g., Motion Picture Association of America movie ratings)

- Expanded content about developing library policies that support intellectual freedom
- Expanded content about Internet filtering
- An expanded "Glossary of Terms"
- "Prisoners' Right to Read: An Interpretation of the *Library Bill of Rights*," approved by the ALA Council in June 2010, after the last edition of the manual went to press.

Those familiar with previous editions of the manual will note the absence of historical essays related to the various policy statements. These have been updated and published in a separate volume titled *A History of ALA Policy on Intellectual Freedom: A Supplement to the Intellectual Freedom Manual.*

Arrangement

This edition is arranged in a new way. Interviews and usability testing of the *Intellectual Freedom Manual* with librarians revealed the need to reorganize the book. The new topical arrangement and the addition of easy-to-read summaries are intended to help readers find information quickly, especially those readers who are less familiar with the content or are faced with a crisis. Readers who are more familiar with ALA policy statements are encouraged to use the index and "Appendix 3" to quickly identify the location of a particular statement in the manual.

Part I, "Intellectual Freedom and Libraries," provides foundational information. It begins with an essay that defines intellectual freedom and explains how it applies to school, public, and academic libraries. Core intellectual freedom documents of ALA, such as the *Library Bill of Rights,* are presented next, followed by practical information about how to create library policies that support intellectual freedom.

Part II, "Intellectual Freedom Issues and Best Practices," contains nine chapters focusing on intellectual freedom issues: (1) access, (2) censorship, (3) children and youth, (4) collection development, (5) copyright, (6) meeting rooms and exhibit spaces, (7) privacy, (8) requests from law enforcement, and (9) workplace speech. Each chapter begins with a summary called "Issue at a Glance," covering key concepts, points of law, additional resources, tips for various types of libraries, and questions for reflection. "Issue at a Glance" is followed by relevant "Official ALA Policy Statements" (e.g., interpretations of the *Library Bill of Rights*), which articulate the association's principles and best practices. These statements have been developed by ALA committees and ratified by the ALA Council. Finally, each chapter includes "A Deeper Look"—one or more essays expanding on the issue. Many of the "Deeper Look" essays provide information about laws related to library operations. This information is *not* intended as legal advice. If legal advice or expert assistance is required, the services of a competent legal professional should be sought.

Part III, "Advocacy and Assistance," offers practical information about how to communicate about intellectual freedom, work with the media, lobby legislators, get help, and get involved in promoting and defending intellectual freedom.

The appendixes include a "Glossary of Terms," "Selected Bibliography," and a list of official ALA policy statements related to intellectual freedom.

How to Use the Manual

- *Refer to it when developing library policy*—Review "Creating Intellectual Freedom Policies for Your Library" (part I, chapter 3) for guidance in creating five essential intellectual freedom policies.
- *Turn to it for guidance when a question or problem emerges*—Consult the relevant chapter in "Intellectual Freedom Issues and Best Practices" (part II), review the tips in "Communicating about Intellectual Freedom" (part III, chapter 1), and consult "Where to Get Help and Get Involved" (part III, chapter 2) if you need additional help.
- *Use it to orient new employees, volunteers, and trustees*—Ask them to read "What Is Intellectual Freedom?" (part I, chapter 1) and "Core Intellectual Freedom Documents of the American Library Association" (part I, chapter 2).
- *Use it for professional development*—Consider having library staff, volunteers, and trustees read the chapters in "Intellectual Freedom Issues and Best Practices" (part II), and schedule times to discuss the "Questions for Reflection" provided. Some of the questions are easily answered after reading the chapter; others present more difficult ethical challenges that are likely to stimulate interesting discussions.
- *Use it as a textbook in library and information science courses*—Use the "Questions for Reflection" listed at the beginning of each chapter in "Intellectual Freedom Issues and Best Practices" (part II) as writing prompts or to start class discussions. Assign readings from the companion publication, *A History of ALA Policy on Intellectual Freedom:*

A Supplement to the Intellectual Freedom Manual, to help students understand the development and evolution of ALA policy on intellectual freedom.

- *Use it to connect with other librarians and help promote intellectual freedom*—Read "Where to Get Help and Get Involved" (part III, chapter 2) to learn about organizations, committees, programs, and awards that focus on intellectual freedom.

The library profession has a long history of defending and promoting freedom of expression and the freedom to read. It is our hope that librarians and library supporters will find this new edition of the *Intellectual Freedom Manual* a valuable and easy-to-use resource as they continue this important work.

—Trina Magi
Editor, ninth edition

Intellectual Freedom and Libraries

What Is Intellectual Freedom?

Barbara M. Jones

What Does Intellectual Freedom Have to Do with My Academic, School, or Public Library?

Although the term *intellectual freedom* has never been officially defined by the American Library Association, it is used in the library profession primarily to mean the right of every individual to both seek and receive information from all points of view without restriction. Intellectual freedom as a professional practice and as a subject for scholarly research has expanded over the years to include conditions that protect the freedom to read, such as privacy. Intellectual freedom concerns have become global, and while technological change doesn't necessarily change legal opinions and basic principles, it does require librarians to interpret those principles in light of new situations.

The American Library Association promotes and defends intellectual freedom through staff services and resources in the Office for Intellectual Freedom (OIF) and the Freedom to Read Foundation—both almost fifty years old. ALA members have passionately supported intellectual freedom principles, considering them core values that make librarianship "professional" and "ethical." Numerous committees carry out the work, including the Intellectual Freedom Committee and its Privacy Subcommittee, the Committee on Professional Ethics, and the Intellectual Freedom Round Table.

Intellectual freedom is part and parcel of a key official, member-approved document of the American Library Association—the *Library Bill of Rights*—and its interpretations. The *Library Bill of Rights* is based on the First Amendment to the U.S. Constitution, which protects and promotes intellectual freedom through its guarantees of freedoms of speech and press. Although the *Library Bill of Rights* does not have the force of law, it has been cited in court cases, along with the *Code of Ethics of the American Library Association,* as a guide to best practice within the library profession. The *Library Bill of Rights* and its interpretations are reviewed and compiled every few years into the *Intellectual Freedom Manual.*

In general, the First Amendment applies only to publicly funded libraries—school, public, and academic. However, library ethical principles are often used in privately funded libraries to support the freedom to read. One can't imagine a prestigious private university, for example, eschewing academic freedom and still being able to attract the students, faculty, and staff needed to preserve its research excellence and academic reputation.

Until recent years intellectual freedom principles usually focused on keeping access to constitutionally protected content within a library as open, diverse, and barrier-free as possible. This content has included all kinds of speech, from authors' books to authors appearing in person at programs, from community forums to video-game nights for teens. Dedication to these principles endures.

Currently the library profession has extended the focus to user-created content, including such resources as library-sponsored blog posts, teen literary magazines, or items produced using 3-D printers. At date of publication, various ALA committees are studying whether new or revised policy statements will be necessary to accommodate developments in this area. Any such statements adopted after publication of this ninth edition will be posted on the ALA website.

The very best libraries and librarians embody intellectual freedom principles. Promoting the freedom to read in our nation's libraries enriches people's lives, supports them in the workplace, and encourages lifelong learning. Intellectual freedom makes it possible for individuals to discuss the latest best seller in a library book club or to read it privately with nobody looking over their shoulders. Diverse collections encourage all users to read widely and critically and to choose what they want to read next. It enables students to understand all aspects of an issue—scientific, political, or other—to prepare them for college or the workforce. Intellectual freedom empowers young people to make smart decisions and solve real-world problems. Practicing intellectual freedom in a library means offering the community tools and opportunities for civic engagement, including voter registration, health care information, and instructional support for new Americans.

Another way to look at intellectual freedom is to list some of the barriers that limit access to some content. Some barriers are required by law, but some are erected merely for convenience. All should be subject to scrutiny:

- Laws and regulations—federal, state, and local
- Library use policies (e.g., the use of meeting rooms)
- Software filters
- Avoiding controversy by not buying a particular young-adult book or submitting to community pressure to remove video-game night
- Lack of physical accessibility to the library
- Fees or service models that separate wealthy users from the poor

Help!

Most of us feel a real culture shock when we move from our academic programs to our real-world careers. The Office for Intellectual Freedom often receives calls from ALA members who say, "My boss is asking me to violate the *Library Bill of Rights* principles I learned in library school. I am a huge intellectual freedom supporter, but I can't afford to lose my job." All professionals experience this transition from school to the workplace, and each of us is challenged to bridge the gap between theory and practice. This ninth edition of the *Intellectual Freedom Manual* looks so different from prior editions because we want to enable the practicing librarian to find information, advice, and solutions more easily, and to feel grounded in our profession's and association's ethics, ideals, and policies. Sometimes librarians in the field have complained that intellectual freedom principles seem too prescriptive, burdensome, or even punitive. We believe that this new, more practical edition of the manual will change that perception.

There is no doubt that at least once in a librarian's career, an intellectual freedom challenge will emerge. Dealing with these problems—often involving conflicting values of equal importance to the parties involved—is part of being a professional. While sometimes there are clear legal reasons to make a particular policy decision, that is not always the case, and librarians must be prepared to work with this manual, their colleagues, and their common sense to solve the problem.

Also, librarians should look outward to their communities for solutions to disputes. In this problem solving, good communication skills are essential. Experience has shown that many disputes between libraries and their communities could have been dispelled by respectful communication. On the other hand, despite our best efforts some conflicts can turn vicious, and while it is never pleasant, there are resources here to address those situations as well.

Good News

In recent years our experience in the Office for Intellectual Freedom is that many intellectual freedom conflicts have been resolved in favor of the freedom to read, despite the fact that U.S. society has rarely been so divided. Our efforts to promote the freedom to read *do* resonate in our communities. Here are some of the reasons some conflicts have been resolved successfully:

- Librarians and boards have made the connection between censorship and antidemocratic values. As one board member put it: "My son is fighting in Iraq for these values. Why should I as a board member remove a book?"
- Americans do not want intrusive government. Consider the 2013 revelations about government surveillance of cell phone records. People of all political stripes were outraged.
- At the same time that organizations try to censor books, others fight back. In the West Bend, Wisconsin, censorship case, a citizens' group opposing censorship was successful in countering the pro-censorship pressure. Librarians have become much more savvy in using the press and community supporters to their advantage. And journalists, whose profession embraces First Amendment-based ethics, are often on our side. Librarians have learned to frame issues so that even in social situations, we are able to explain intellectual freedom in ways that people can understand and support it.
- In academe, faculty and students need to do their research in an open environment. Censorship of any kind usually meets with objections. While it is true that we are seeing more censorship-related issues in higher education, the tradition of academic freedom is still deeply embedded. Most universities and colleges do not want a reputation of creating barriers to research, access to information, creativity, or scholarly production.

The ALA Office for Intellectual Freedom will help you! We now have hundreds of examples to draw from, and we can work with you to apply our experience to your situation.

Listed below are some of the key intellectual freedom issues currently arising in libraries. They are arranged by library type according to where they most often occur, but issues cross boundaries, so please refer to other sections as indicated.

Academic Libraries

There is an enduring myth that intellectual freedom problems and concerns don't affect academic libraries. Nothing could be further from the truth as this manual goes into publication. The American Association of University Professors (AAUP) Committee A on Academic Freedom, the Association of College and Research Libraries (ACRL) Committee on Professional Values, and the Office for Intellectual Freedom have seen an alarming growth in such concerns in colleges and universities. Unfortunately, there is a dearth of academic research to identify problems or analyze solutions in the academic environment.

A memorable quotation from the famous 1893 University of Wisconsin academic freedom case involving economics professor Richard T. Ely encourages the "continual and fearless sifting and winnowing by which alone the truth can be found." Students and faculty members can "sift and winnow" only if a diversity of ideas is readily available. Students from isolated and/or homogeneous communities use their college experience to immerse themselves in a diversity of opinions, research, and people. This is why it is particularly egregious when states place restrictions on public college libraries' purchasing LGBT books for their collections, as was done in South Carolina. This is tragic, as many young adults "come out" for the first time in college, and reliable information is their support. A colleague at a prominent Mexican university began many years ago to open library meeting rooms to the campus Gay Alliance—the only place it was allowed to meet at that time. Openness should be our goal.

Following are some of the intellectual freedom issues facing academic libraries today:

- *Traditional decorum*—Many academic librarians work with college administrators who view the library as a "traditional," grand space—often at the center of campus—that should not be disturbed by demonstrations, banners, chalked sidewalks, or controversial exhibits. This becomes increasingly chilling as campuses relegate free speech to ever-shrinking spaces. Further, as library content and activity become more interactive, there is an inevitable growth in library noise and group activity such as flash mobs. Librarians must balance such priorities as quiet study space and safety with opportunities for meaningful faculty and student group collaboration.
- *Free speech zones*—Campus administrations are setting aside special "free speech" areas, implying that academic freedom does not exist

in other parts of campus. This is a current strategy for some campus administrations to control controversial speech. Even if the library is a designated free-speech zone, such a limitation potentially chills programs, instruction, services, and collections outside that space, which is now both physical and virtual.

- *Trigger warnings*—Some students and organizations are demanding that course syllabi warn that certain visual images or course texts might be disturbing to those with past traumas. These types of warnings are in direct conflict with the *Library Bill of Rights* interpretations regarding labeling and stigmatizing certain content, and are a threat to the precepts of academic freedom. Trigger warnings on course content could easily spread to demands that the library follow suit.

- *Parental pressure regarding college reading assignments*—Parents have become increasingly concerned about their children's reading habits beyond high school, and campuses are experiencing increased parental monitoring and commenting on syllabi and assignments such as summer reading lists. It is tempting for campus administrators to compromise intellectual freedom to satisfy parents. As colleges welcome a more diverse student body in terms of ethnicity, age, religion, and sex/gender identity and/or expression, this has led to values conflicts.

- *Collection development problems*—Collection development in higher education can easily become an ideological battlefield. Faculty members have asked that books be removed because of the reputation of the author or a perceived lack of quality. Alumni donors have asked that their funds not be used to purchase LGBT materials. Science librarians have been pressured to remove or not purchase books about creationism. *The Protocols of the Elders of Zion* and similar propaganda have been banned from collections because of anti-Semitic content, despite the fact that scholars study anti-Semitism and need examples.

- *Course management software and privacy*—Some course management software can track student reading habits for faculty members who want to monitor what content was read on what date. Such information can be used to affect student grades, despite the fact that this violates student reader privacy (and may well violate state confidentiality statutes), and does not definitively show what a student has read. She may own the book, for example, and not access the online content. Because digital communications is so embedded in higher education courses and research, a privacy audit is a good idea for any campus.

School Libraries

U.S. school libraries are the envy of the world. People in most parts of the world are fighting to get school libraries at the same time that the U.S. library community is rallying to keep them open. School libraries are frequently misunderstood by administrators, boards, and the public. They are viewed narrowly as collection repositories to support the curriculum, but school libraries do so much more.

Professional school librarians teach students how to evaluate information in all formats, including the Internet. Some even teach students what intellectual freedom means and how to protect their right to the freedom to read. Librarians help students learn how to think critically and to become lifelong information consumers. At a time when so many students seek meaningful after-school activities, school libraries can offer manga and video-game clubs. Chicago's Lane Tech High School even has a Fahrenheit 451 Banned Book Club. The exciting agenda and potential for school libraries are reflected in the documents and activities of the American Association of School Librarians (AASL).

Successful school libraries work collaboratively with the community to promote the freedom to read. One school librarian launched a brown-bag-lunch book group for parents to read controversial books. She also worked with a local youth pastor and then was invited to the church's youth groups to discuss controversial young adult books. No book was ever removed from her school's library during her tenure there. Such success stories underscore the potential of school libraries to promote intellectual freedom. What better place for a student to encounter new ideas—some of which may be disturbing—than in the supportive environment of a school library?

Indeed, school libraries do have a particular relationship with the students they serve. In two areas First Amendment rights of minors may be abridged. First, the school administration has substantial discretion in designing the curriculum and can determine that a book is "educationally unsuitable" for a library collection. However, the book can't be removed for ideological reasons related to the content. Second, some states may deem some materials "obscene" for minors, even though they are constitutionally protected for adults. These state statutes are called "harmful to minors" statutes.

Minor students are afforded special privacy rights in the Family Educational Rights and Privacy Act (FERPA), which is covered elsewhere in this manual. At the same time, parents can obtain access to student records until the age of eighteen, compromising privacy rights for young adults.

While school librarians can't act in loco parentis (i.e., in the place of a parent) and are usually subject to curricular mandates, they can work successfully with students, parents, and teachers to support the curriculum and help students find the leisure reading that they want. And yet, time and time again, the Office for Intellectual Freedom has seen court decisions and in loco parentis applied too narrowly—so that the school can avoid legal risk. Annually dozens of books are removed from summer reading lists, classrooms, and libraries for being "age inappropriate," "sexually explicit," or "LGBT-friendly." This, despite the recommendations of reading specialists, the National Council of Teachers of English, and librarians who have been trained to recommend specific books for specific age groups.

In addition to the *Library Bill of Rights* interpretations that support general intellectual freedom principles, some specifically enumerate minors' rights to read and view. Below are some of the intellectual freedom problems faced by school libraries:

- *Filtering the Internet*—Filtering has become one of the most insidious forms of censorship. Some software filters are set on such restrictive settings that it is impossible for high school faculty to teach Advanced Placement (AP) courses or for students to find information about homosexuality or other gender- and sex-related topics—at a time in their lives when they need to know. Often students and faculty do not know what information they are missing! According to a recent report, the filters in today's market either over- or under-filter, and some kids are learning to hack them anyway. The new publication, *Fencing Out Knowledge: Impacts of the Children's Internet Protection Act 10 Years Later,* is a must-read for every school librarian, administrator, or board member.

- *Labeling of content*—School libraries frequently purchase book collections from companies like Accelerated Reader, which apply a formula to determine the grade level for each book. Such labels are used (often mandated) to determine what titles a particular student is allowed or not allowed to read. The impact of this severe barrier to reading was brought home to the Office for Intellectual Freedom by a parent calling for help. Her son, in the gifted and talented class, was not allowed to read books labeled above his grade level. Her friend's son with special needs was not allowed to read a book below his grade level. This kind of stigmatization and invasion of student privacy is humiliating and can promote teasing and bullying.

Children are poorly served by what can be considered a "fast food" solution to book selection—"apps" that label children's books with emoticons such as lips for sexual content, the dollar sign for consumerism, and martini glasses for drinking. Busy parents often turn to these instead of to the reader services librarian. These so-called review tools do not consider the book's content as a whole. When librarians use these tools, they are creating the perception that a professional librarian is unnecessary for book selection. (If an app can do it, why should the school hire a librarian?) This aspect of labeling is misunderstood and will be a major topic of conversation in the years to come, as school districts question the necessity of professional school librarians.

- *Trigger warnings*—See the "Academic Libraries" section above.
- *Course management software and privacy*—See the "Academic Libraries" section.

Public Libraries

As Candace Morgan states in the eighth edition of the *Intellectual Freedom Manual:*

> It is the genius of the American system that we base our liberty on the broadest protection of each individual's rights to free expression and on the corollary right to access the expression of others. It is the genius of the American public library to be an institution dedicated to promoting the exercise of these rights.

The U.S. public library is democracy at work. Everyone in that library's community has access to information with professional guidance and service if requested. The information and services support lifelong learning, personal enrichment and entertainment, getting and keeping a job, the ability to discuss complex topics in a public forum, learning to read, listening to stories, or 3-D printing a prototype widget for a new business idea. The public library levels the playing field for immigrants and refugees who need to learn how to navigate U.S. culture. The public library is for those who can't afford a book collection at home and use their local library for everything from the local paper to Internet access to leisure reading. Teen areas are packed after school for "home" work. Public libraries are the place where exciting new services are rolled out for the public's benefit, as in the Chicago Public Library's new 3-D printer space and its You Media space for teens. These sites can be used by budding entrepreneurs or future rap music composers.

All of the above examples mirror intellectual freedom at its best. But one teen who is scolded for looking at a Center for Disease Control website describing sexually transmitted diseases; one student who can't check out Sherman Alexie's *The Absolutely True Diary of a Part-Time Indian* because it has been banned; one immigrant who is afraid to Google "undocumented immigrants" for fear of government surveillance of his search—these betray the promise of U.S. public libraries.

Public librarians grapple with most of the same intellectual freedom issues as their colleagues in colleges and K–12 schools, but they serve a broader community. Below are some issues encountered most often in public libraries:

- *Filtering the Internet*—See the "School Libraries" section above. The new report, *Fencing Out Knowledge: Impacts of the Children's Internet Protection Act 10 Years Later*, documents just how serious this barrier can be in terms of blocking First Amendment-protected information.
- *Labeling of content*—See the "School Libraries" section.
- *Trigger warnings*—See the "Academic Libraries" section.
- *Meeting spaces*—Public libraries typically offer meeting rooms and auditoriums to the community for everything from piano recitals to community forums on the Affordable Care Act. This manual offers practical advice on how to write policies that ensure a fair and legal way to assign these spaces for your community.
- *Collection policies*—Because public libraries respond to public recommendations for collection titles, they are often in the spotlight for buying multiple copies of books that may not win literary prizes but have a wait list of 400 library users.
- *Service to all ages*—Because public libraries are used by babies, seniors, and all ages in between, they may face controversies in assigning books to the right physical space in the library. Is this an adult or a young adult novel? Should all manga be in the adult section?

    A common issue involves the physical placement, and perhaps segregation, of Internet terminals for adults and youth. Libraries would do well to designate separate spaces for Internet access for minors and adults to avoid controversies about seeing possibly disturbing images (even if constitutionally protected) on the Internet. *Fencing Out Knowledge: Impacts of the Children's Internet Protection Act 10 Years Later*, along with this manual and other professional support from the Office for Intellectual Freedom, will provide the librarian the necessary tools to provide the maximum access to constitutionally protected Internet content that the public has a right to access.

- *Privacy and confidentiality*—All fifty states have library confidentiality statutes or the equivalent thereof. It is crucial that every library employee be acquainted with his state's statute. Most protect public library circulation records. Most do not cover K–12 schools or academic institutions. Libraries can adopt policies that offer greater privacy protection than required by law.

Conclusion

It is our hope that this manual will be a valuable and useful resource for librarians and their supporters as they grapple with these issues and work to preserve and promote the freedom to read. Please also consult the resources listed in the "Selected Bibliography" for additional help.

Core Intellectual Freedom Documents of the American Library Association

Library Bill of Rights

Adopted June 19, 1939, by the ALA Council; amended October 14, 1944; June 18, 1948; February 2, 1961; June 27, 1967; and January 23, 1980; inclusion of "age" reaffirmed January 23, 1996.

> A historical essay about this statement can be found in the publication, *A History of ALA Policy on Intellectual Freedom: A Supplement to the Intellectual Freedom Manual, Ninth Edition.*

THE AMERICAN LIBRARY ASSOCIATION affirms that all libraries are forums for information and ideas, and that the following basic policies should guide their services.

I. Books and other library resources should be provided for the interest, information, and enlightenment of all people of the community the library serves. Materials should not be excluded because of the origin, background, or views of those contributing to their creation.

II. Libraries should provide materials and information presenting all points of view on current and historical issues. Materials should not be proscribed or removed because of partisan or doctrinal disapproval.

III. Libraries should challenge censorship in the fulfillment of their responsibility to provide information and enlightenment.

IV. Libraries should cooperate with all persons and groups concerned with resisting abridgment of free expression and free access to ideas.

V. A person's right to use a library should not be denied or abridged because of origin, age, background, or views.

VI. Libraries which make exhibit spaces and meeting rooms available to the public they serve should make such facilities available on an equitable basis, regardless of the beliefs or affiliations of individuals or groups requesting their use.

> In 1993, the ALA Intellectual Freedom Committee adopted the following statement:
>
> > In the *Library Bill of Rights* and all its Interpretations, it is intended that: "origin" encompasses all the characteristics of individuals that are inherent in the circumstances of their birth; "age" encompasses all the characteristics of individuals that are inherent in their levels of development and maturity; "background" encompasses all the characteristics of individuals that are a result of their life experiences; and "views" encompasses all the opinions and beliefs held and expressed by individuals.
>
> *Note:* This statement was first included in "Access to Library Resources and Services Regardless of Gender or Sexual Orientation—An Interpretation of the *Library Bill of Rights*" in 1993 (now titled "Access to Library Resources and Services Regardless of Sex, Gender Identity, Gender Expression, or Sexual Orientation"; see part II, chapter 1). In 1994 it was included in "Guidelines for the Development and Implementation of Policies, Regulations, and Procedures Affecting Access to Library Materials, Services, and Facilities" (see part I, chapter 3).

I.
Overview
and Core
Documents

Code of Ethics of the American Library Association

Adopted at the 1939 Midwinter Meeting by the ALA Council; amended June 30, 1981; June 28, 1995; and January 22, 2008.

> A historical essay about this statement can be found in the publication, *A History of ALA Policy on Intellectual Freedom: A Supplement to the Intellectual Freedom Manual, Ninth Edition.*

AS MEMBERS OF the American Library Association, we recognize the importance of codifying and making known to the profession and to the general public the ethical principles that guide the work of librarians, other professionals providing information services, library trustees and library staffs.

Ethical dilemmas occur when values are in conflict. The American Library Association *Code of Ethics* states the values to which we are committed, and embodies the ethical responsibilities of the profession in this changing information environment.

We significantly influence or control the selection, organization, preservation, and dissemination of information. In a political system grounded in an informed citizenry, we are members of a profession explicitly committed to intellectual freedom and the freedom of access to information. We have a special obligation to ensure the free flow of information and ideas to present and future generations.

The principles of this code are expressed in broad statements to guide ethical decision making. These statements provide a framework; they cannot and do not dictate conduct to cover particular situations.

I. We provide the highest level of service to all library users through appropriate and usefully organized resources; equitable service policies; equitable access; and accurate, unbiased, and courteous responses to all requests.

II. We uphold the principles of intellectual freedom and resist all efforts to censor library resources.

III. We protect each library user's right to privacy and confidentiality with respect to information sought or received and resources consulted, borrowed, acquired or transmitted.

IV. We respect intellectual property rights and advocate balance between the interests of information users and rights holders.

V. We treat co-workers and other colleagues with respect, fairness, and good faith, and advocate conditions of employment that safeguard the rights and welfare of all employees of our institutions.

VI. We do not advance private interests at the expense of library users, colleagues, or our employing institutions.

VII. We distinguish between our personal convictions and professional duties and do not allow our personal beliefs to interfere with fair representation of the aims of our institutions or the provision of access to their information resources.

VIII. We strive for excellence in the profession by maintaining and enhancing our own knowledge and skills, by encouraging the professional development of co-workers, and by fostering the aspirations of potential members of the profession.

Questions and Answers on Enforcement of the Code of Ethics of the American Library Association

Adopted January 2009 by the ALA Committee on Professional Ethics.

1. What is ALA's procedure to enforce the *Code of Ethics*?

As a voluntary membership organization, ALA does not enforce the *Code of Ethics* for a variety of reasons. As a non-licensing professional society, the ALA would have two possible actions in response to a violation of the *Code of Ethics*:

- Suspend or expel a member from membership, or
- Admonish or censure an individual or institution, publicly or privately.

Because membership in a professional society may affect an individual's career, U.S. anti-trust laws permit punitive action affecting membership:

A. Only for a good cause,
B. Only after affording the member due process.

    A. Good cause will be found to exist only if the member has engaged in conduct which the professional society has a legitimate interest in prohibiting or controlling, which may not be the case with individual infringements of the *Code of Ethics* in particular situations. The federal government would not permit a professional society to suspend or expel a person from membership on grounds of race, gender, anticompetitive motives, personal vendetta, etc.

    B. To meet due process requirements, the accused must have an opportunity to be heard, to be represented by counsel, and to undertake an appeal. Some professional associations have, for example, a mini-trial in front of a panel of judges. In such mini-trials, the panel typically makes a recommendation to the association's board of directors, which makes the final determination on punishment. A separate body must act as appellate reviewers.

Considerations regarding due process:

- Fulfilling the due process requirements is expensive and problematic, because judges must be flown to a central location for the hearing, and the presence of legal counsel is standard.
- Because professional associations do not have investigative arms, they must rely solely on presentations of the complainant and the accused. Often the judges find themselves unable to determine the truth and decline to find in favor of the complainant because the complainant failed to carry the burden of proof.
- Also, the judges, the appellate reviewers, and the association are not covered by the type of immunity enjoyed by federal and state judges. If the judges make a mistake and suspend or expel a member or make a public statement about a member or another individual or institution which is based on faulty determinations, they can be sued individually and collectively for defamation on anti-trust violations.

2. Has ALA had an enforcement procedure in the past?

The enforcement of ALA documents has focused on the *Library Bill of Rights*. After its adoption, some members called for a "policing" effort to publicize censorship problems and bring pressure upon authorities to correct conditions conducive to censorship. After nearly a twenty-year debate, a Program of Action in Support of the *Library Bill of Rights* was adopted. This first Program of Action was developed by the IFC and approved by council. It created a mechanism where complaints about censorship incidents were reported to the Office of Intellectual Freedom and acted upon by the Intellectual Freedom Committee. Under this program, three fact-finding projects were undertaken between 1969 and 1970. The three complaints investigated under the Program of Action made it clear that cases involving intellectual freedom also might raise issues of tenure, academic status, ethical practices, and a variety of other matters. In 1970, a case involving denied employment made it clear that the program only dealt with the *Library Bill of Rights*. The Intellectual Freedom Committee rewrote the Program of Action to allow jurisdiction over all ALA policies on intellectual freedom and tenure. At the 1971 Midwinter meeting, the Library Administrative Division and the Association of College and Research Libraries claimed vested interests in investigations, particularly those involving tenure of academic librarians. A membership group, appointed by the ALA president, presented the Program of Action for Mediation, Arbitration, and Inquiry to Council in June 1971. It was adopted and the first Program of Action rescinded.

The new Program of Action established a Staff Committee on Mediation, Arbitration, and Inquiry (SCMAI), which functioned somewhat as the IFC had under the old document. In addition to intellectual freedom problems, the new committee handled cases involving tenure, professional status, fair employment practices, ethical practices, and due process as set forth in ALA policies. In June 1990, the SCMAI was replaced by the Standing Committee on Review, Inquiry, and Mediation (SCRIM). Lack of funding caused the SCRIM to cease operations in September 1992.

3. What can be done about violations of the *Code of Ethics?*

Libraries are encouraged to adopt the *Code of Ethics* as a policy. With the ALA *Code of Ethics* as a local policy, enforcement moves to the local level. Violations of the *Code of Ethics* may also be a violation of local, state, or federal law. For example, many states have laws regarding confidentiality of library users' records, which is also addressed in Article III of the *Code of Ethics*. In this case, dealing with a violation through the court system would be a possibility. Article V addresses the workplace, another example of where there are many laws to protect the rights and welfare of workers. While an employer or employee in violation of this *Code of Ethics* principle should be accountable, there are many agencies at the state and federal level designated to handle these infractions.

4. How do other professional associations enforce codes of ethics?

Many examples of codes can be found with any Internet search. Websites of organizations with which ALA may have some commonality, though not in all cases, are listed in the web version of this document. Only those organizations with some kind of license or certification that can be withdrawn seem to have enforceable codes. In some cases membership in an organization can be withdrawn, but this may not have major consequences for the individual if membership is not required by the individual's profession.

5. Why have a code of ethics if there is no enforcement?

The answer to this question can be found in the preamble to the principles—

> As members of the American Library Association, we recognize the importance of codifying and making known to the profession and to the general public the ethical principles that guide the work of librarians, other professionals providing information services, library trustees and library staffs.
>
> Ethical dilemmas occur when values are in conflict. The American Library Association *Code of Ethics* states the values to which we are committed, and embodies the ethical responsibilities of the profession in this changing information environment.
>
> We significantly influence or control the selection, organization, preservation, and dissemination of information. In a political system grounded in an informed citizenry, we are members of a profession explicitly committed to intellectual freedom, and the freedom of access to information. We have a special obligation to ensure the free flow of information and ideas to present and future generations.

6. What can I as an individual do to help ensure that the values and the principles of the code are upheld?

The code offers guidelines for responsible behavior and sets forth a common basis for resolving ethical dilemmas encountered in daily practice. You can obtain a copy of the code and post it where you and others in your workplace can see it daily. You can make yourself aware of local, state, or federal laws concerning ethical conduct and how that conduct might be enforced in the workplace. You can also encourage adoption of the code as local policy and advocate for ethics education as a necessary component of staff development. Most importantly, you can make a personal resolution to live daily the values and principles embodied by the code, to engage in an ongoing process of professional growth and ethical self-reflection, and to model ethical behavior and decision-making.

The Freedom to Read

Adopted June 25, 1953, by the ALA Council and the Association of American Publishers Freedom to Read Committee; revised January 28, 1972; January 16, 1991; July 12, 2000; and June 30, 2004. (This statement was originally issued in May 1953 by the Westchester Conference of the American Library Association and the American Book Publishers Council, which in 1970 consolidated with the American Educational Publishers Institute to become the Association of American Publishers.)

> A historical essay about this statement can be found in the publication, *A History of ALA Policy on Intellectual Freedom: A Supplement to the Intellectual Freedom Manual, Ninth Edition.*

THE FREEDOM TO READ is essential to our democracy. It is continuously under attack. Private groups and public authorities in various parts of the country are working to remove or limit access to reading materials, to censor content in schools, to label "controversial" views, to distribute lists of "objectionable" books or authors, and to purge libraries. These actions apparently rise from a view that our national tradition of free expression is no longer valid; that censorship and suppression are needed to counter threats to safety or national security, as well as to avoid the subversion of politics and the corruption of morals. We, as individuals devoted to reading and as librarians and publishers responsible for disseminating ideas, wish to assert the public interest in the preservation of the freedom to read.

Most attempts at suppression rest on a denial of the fundamental premise of democracy: that the ordinary individual, by exercising critical judgment, will select the good and reject the bad. We trust Americans to recognize propaganda and misinformation, and to make their own decisions about what they read and believe. We do not believe they are prepared to sacrifice their heritage of a free press in order to be "protected" against what others think may be bad for them. We believe they still favor free enterprise in ideas and expression.

These efforts at suppression are related to a larger pattern of pressures being brought against education, the press, art and images, films, broadcast media, and the Internet. The problem is not only one of actual censorship. The shadow of fear cast by these pressures leads, we suspect, to an even larger voluntary curtailment of expression by those who seek to avoid controversy or unwelcome scrutiny by government officials.

Such pressure toward conformity is perhaps natural to a time of accelerated change. And yet suppression is never more dangerous than in such a time of social tension. Freedom has given the United States the elasticity to endure strain. Freedom keeps open the path of novel and creative solutions, and enables change to come by choice. Every silencing of a heresy, every enforcement of an orthodoxy, diminishes the toughness and resilience of our society and leaves it the less able to deal with controversy and difference.

Now as always in our history, reading is among our greatest freedoms. The freedom to read and write is almost the only means for making generally available ideas or manners of expression that can initially command only a small audience. The written word is the natural medium for the new idea and the untried voice from which come the original contributions to social growth. It is essential to the extended discussion that serious thought requires, and to the accumulation of knowledge and ideas into organized collections.

We believe that free communication is essential to the preservation of a free society and a creative culture. We believe that these pressures toward conformity present the danger of limiting the range and variety of inquiry and expression on which our democracy and our culture depend. We believe that every American community must jealously guard the freedom to publish and to circulate, in order to preserve its own freedom to read. We believe that publishers and librarians have a profound responsibility to give validity to that freedom to read by making it possible for the readers to choose freely from a variety of offerings.

The freedom to read is guaranteed by the Constitution. Those with faith in free people will stand firm on these constitutional guarantees of essential rights and will exercise the responsibilities that accompany these rights.

We therefore affirm these propositions:

1. *It is in the public interest for publishers and librarians to make available the widest diversity of views and expressions, including those that are unorthodox, unpopular, or considered dangerous by the majority.*

   Creative thought is by definition new, and what is new is different. The bearer of every new thought is a rebel until that idea is refined and tested. Totalitarian systems attempt to maintain themselves in power by the ruthless suppression of any concept that challenges the established orthodoxy. The power of a democratic system to adapt to change is vastly strengthened by the freedom of its citizens to choose widely from among conflicting opinions offered freely to them. To stifle every nonconformist idea at birth would mark the end of the democratic process. Furthermore, only through the constant activity of weighing and selecting can the democratic mind attain the strength demanded by times like these. We need to know not only what we believe but why we believe it.

2. *Publishers, librarians, and booksellers do not need to endorse every idea or presentation they make available. It would conflict with the public interest for them to establish their own political, moral, or aesthetic views as a standard for determining what should be published or circulated.*

Publishers and librarians serve the educational process by helping to make available knowledge and ideas required for the growth of the mind and the increase of learning. They do not foster education by imposing as mentors the patterns of their own thought. The people should have the freedom to read and consider a broader range of ideas than those that may be held by any single librarian or publisher or government or church. It is wrong that what one can read should be confined to what another thinks proper.

3. *It is contrary to the public interest for publishers or librarians to bar access to writings on the basis of the personal history or political affiliations of the author.*

No art or literature can flourish if it is to be measured by the political views or private lives of its creators. No society of free people can flourish that draws up lists of writers to whom it will not listen, whatever they may have to say.

4. *There is no place in our society for efforts to coerce the taste of others, to confine adults to the reading matter deemed suitable for adolescents, or to inhibit the efforts of writers to achieve artistic expression.*

To some, much of modern expression is shocking. But is not much of life itself shocking? We cut off literature at the source if we prevent writers from dealing with the stuff of life. Parents and teachers have a responsibility to prepare the young to meet the diversity of experiences in life to which they will be exposed, as they have a responsibility to help them learn to think critically for themselves. These are affirmative responsibilities, not to be discharged simply by preventing them from reading works for which they are not yet prepared. In these matters values differ, and values cannot be legislated; nor can machinery be devised that will suit the demands of one group without limiting the freedom of others.

5. *It is not in the public interest to force a reader to accept the prejudgment of a label characterizing any expression or its author as subversive or dangerous.*

The ideal of labeling presupposes the existence of individuals or groups with wisdom to determine by authority what is good or bad for others. It presupposes that individuals must be directed in making up their minds about the ideas they examine. But Americans do not need others to do their thinking for them.

6. *It is the responsibility of publishers and librarians, as guardians of the people's freedom to read, to contest encroachments upon that freedom by individuals or groups seeking to impose their own standards or tastes upon the community at large; and by the government whenever it seeks to reduce or deny public access to public information.*

It is inevitable in the give and take of the democratic process that the political, the moral, or the aesthetic concepts of an individual or group will occasionally collide with those of another individual or group. In a free society individuals are free to determine for themselves what they wish to read, and each group is free to determine what it will recommend to its freely associated members. But no group has the right to take the law into its own hands, and to impose its own concept of politics or morality upon other members of a democratic society. Freedom is no freedom if it is accorded only to the accepted and the inoffensive. Further, democratic societies are more safe, free, and creative when the free flow of public information is not restricted by governmental prerogative or self-censorship.

7. *It is the responsibility of publishers and librarians to give full meaning to the freedom to read by providing books that enrich the quality and diversity of thought and expression. By the exercise of this affirmative responsibility, they can demonstrate that the answer to a "bad" book is a good one, the answer to a "bad" idea is a good one.*

The freedom to read is of little consequence when the reader cannot obtain matter fit for that reader's purpose. What is needed is not only the absence of restraint, but the positive provision of opportunity for the people to read the best that has been thought and said. Books are the major channel by which the intellectual inheritance is handed down, and the principal means of its testing and growth. The defense of the freedom to read requires of all publishers and librarians the utmost of their faculties, and deserves of all Americans the fullest of their support.

We state these propositions neither lightly nor as easy generalizations. We here stake out a lofty claim for the value of the written word. We do so because we believe that it is possessed of enormous variety and usefulness, worthy of cherishing and keeping free. We realize that the application of these propositions may mean the dissemination of ideas and manners of expression that are repugnant to many persons. We do not state these propositions in the comfortable belief that what people read is unimportant. We believe rather that what people read is deeply important; that ideas can be dangerous; but that the suppression of ideas is fatal to a democratic society. Freedom itself is a dangerous way of life, but it is ours.

A Joint Statement by:
    American Library Association
    Association of American Publishers

Subsequently endorsed by:
    American Booksellers Foundation for Free Expression
    The Association of American University Presses
    The Children's Book Council
    Freedom to Read Foundation
    National Association of College Stores
    National Coalition Against Censorship
    National Council of Teachers of English
    The Thomas Jefferson Center for the Protection of Free Expression

Libraries: An American Value

Adopted February 3, 1999, by the ALA Council.

A historical essay about this statement can be found in the publication, *A History of ALA Policy on Intellectual Freedom: A Supplement to the Intellectual Freedom Manual, Ninth Edition.*

LIBRARIES IN AMERICA are cornerstones of the communities they serve. Free access to the books, ideas, resources, and information in America's libraries is imperative for education, employment, enjoyment, and self-government.

Libraries are a legacy to each generation, offering the heritage of the past and the promise of the future. To ensure that libraries flourish and have the freedom to promote and protect the public good in the twenty-first century, we believe certain principles must be guaranteed.

To that end, we affirm this contract with the people we serve:

- We defend the constitutional rights of all individuals, including children and teenagers, to use the library's resources and services;
- We value our nation's diversity and strive to reflect that diversity by providing a full spectrum of resources and services to the communities we serve;
- We affirm the responsibility and the right of all parents and guardians to guide their own children's use of the library and its resources and services;
- We connect people and ideas by helping each person select from and effectively use the library's resources;
- We protect each individual's privacy and confidentiality in the use of library resources and services;
- We protect the rights of individuals to express their opinions about library resources and services;
- We celebrate and preserve our democratic society by making available the widest possible range of viewpoints, opinions and ideas, so that all individuals have the opportunity to become lifelong learners—informed, literate, educated, and culturally enriched.

Change is constant, but these principles transcend change and endure in a dynamic technological, social, and political environment.

By embracing these principles, libraries in the United States can contribute to a future that values and protects freedom of speech in a world that celebrates both our similarities and our differences, respects individuals and their beliefs, and holds all persons truly equal and free.

Creating Intellectual Freedom Policies for Your Library

LIBRARIES HAVE A responsibility to meet the information needs of everyone in their communities. To do so, they must promote and protect intellectual freedom. The first step is to develop formal, written library policies and procedures. Once established and adopted by the governing body, policies should be reviewed regularly and updated as needed. The library should ensure that its governing body and all library employees and volunteers, regardless of title, are aware of these policies and receive training in the principles of intellectual freedom and the implementation of policy.

Read This Before You Create or Update Your Policies

When creating policies, librarians need to understand the public forum doctrine and what rights are applicable under the First Amendment. Please read "The Right to Receive Information: Libraries, the First Amendment, and the Public Forum Doctrine" later in this section.

Why Is It Important to Put Policies in Writing?

Well-written, board-approved policies and up-to-date procedures based on those policies achieve several things:

- Encourage stability and continuity in the library's operations while reducing ambiguity and confusion
- Demonstrate that the library is running a businesslike operation
- Give credence to the library's actions

- Inform the community about the library's intent, goals, and aspirations
- Give the public a means to evaluate library performance and show that the library is willing to be held accountable for its decisions
- Help disarm critics, as unfounded accusations seldom prevail when the library's operations are based on policies and procedures that reflect thorough research, sound judgment, and careful planning
- Serve as evidence of the library's normal practices, which can be helpful if the library is sued for enforcing reasonable policies

Essential Library Policies

The following five library policies are essential for supporting intellectual freedom. Libraries may have additional policies to guide their operations.

- Collection Development and Resource Reconsideration
- Internet Use (required by law if the library receives E-rate or LSTA funding)
- Use of Meeting Rooms and Exhibit Spaces
- Privacy and Confidentiality
- User Behavior and Library Use

Guidelines for the Development and Implementation of Policies, Regulations, and Procedures Affecting Access to Library Resources, Services, and Facilities

Adopted June 28, 1994, by the ALA Intellectual Freedom Committee; revised January 19, 2005; and March 29, 2014.

A historical essay about this statement can be found in the publication, *A History of ALA Policy on Intellectual Freedom: A Supplement to the Intellectual Freedom Manual, Ninth Edition.*

THE AMERICAN LIBRARY ASSOCIATION has adopted the *Library Bill of Rights* and interpretations of the *Library Bill of Rights* to provide library governing authorities, librarians and other library staff, and library users with guidelines on how constitutional principles apply to libraries in the United States of America.

Publicly supported libraries exist within the context of a body of law derived from the United States Constitution and appropriate state constitutions, defined by statute, and implemented by regulations, policies, and procedures established by their governing bodies and administrations. These regulations, policies, and procedures establish the mission of the library, define its functions, services, and operations, and ascertain the rights and responsibilities of the individuals served by the library.

Publicly supported library service is based upon the First Amendment right of free expression. The publicly supported library is a governmental entity that provides free, equal, and equitable access to information for all people of the community it serves. When this mission is confirmed in its policies and practices, the library is a designated limited public forum for access to information. When library policies or practices make meeting rooms, exhibit spaces, and/or bulletin boards available for public use, these spaces are designated as limited public forums for the exchange of information.

Because the *Library Bill of Rights* "affirms that all libraries are forums for information and ideas," libraries that are not publicly supported also are encouraged to observe these guidelines as they develop policies, regulations, and procedures.

Libraries adopt administrative policies and procedures regulating the organization and use of library materials, services, and facilities. These policies and procedures affect access and may have the effect of restricting, denying, or creating barriers to access to the library as a public forum, including the library's resources, facilities, and services. Library policies and procedures that impinge upon First Amendment rights are subject to a higher standard of review than may be required in the policies of other public services and facilities.

Because libraries function as limited public forums for access to information, Article V of the *Library Bill of Rights* states: "A person's right to use a library should not be denied or abridged because of origin, age, background, or views." Thus, policies, procedures, or regulations that may result in denying, restricting, or creating physical or economic barriers to access to the library as a limited public forum must be based on a compelling government interest. However, library governing authorities may place reasonable and narrowly drawn restrictions on the time, place, or manner of access to library resources, services, or facilities, provided that such restrictions are not based upon arbitrary distinctions between individuals or classes of individuals. Some examples of such distinctions would be restricting access based on citizenship or immigration status; restricting access for minors to resources routinely provided to adults; restricting access based on financial means or housing status; restricting access based on partisan or doctrinal disapproval of the user's views or of the information the user seeks.

Guidelines

The American Library Association's Intellectual Freedom Committee recommends that publicly supported libraries use the following guidelines, based on constitutional principles, to develop policies, regulations, and procedures. Libraries that are not publicly supported also are encouraged to observe these guidelines as they develop policies, regulations, and procedures.

All library policies, regulations, and procedures should be carefully examined to determine if they may result in denying, restricting, or creating barriers to access. If they may result in such restrictions, they:

1. should be developed and implemented within the legal framework that applies to the library. This includes: the United States Constitution, including the First and Fourteenth Amendments, due process, and equal and equitable treatment under the law; the applicable state constitution; federal and state civil rights legislation; all other applicable federal, state, and local legislation; and applicable case law;

2. should cite statutes or ordinances upon which the authority to make that policy is based, when appropriate;

3. should be developed and implemented within the framework of the *Library Bill of Rights* and its Interpretations;

4. should be based upon the library's mission and objectives;

5. should narrowly tailor prohibitions or restrictions, in the rare instances when they are required, so they are not more restrictive than what is necessary to serve their objectives;

6. should attempt to balance competing interests and avoid favoring the majority at the expense of individual rights, or allowing individual users' rights to interfere materially with the majority's rights to free, equal, and equitable access to library resources, services, and facilities;

7. should avoid arbitrary distinctions between individuals or classes of users, and should not have the effect of denying or abridging a person's right to use library resources, services, or facilities based upon arbitrary distinctions such as origin, age, background, or views;[1]

8. should not target specific users or groups of users based upon an assumption or expectation that such users might engage in behavior that will materially interfere with the achievement of substantial library objectives;

9. must be clearly stated so that a reasonably intelligent person will have fair warning of what is expected;

10. must provide a means of appeal;

11. must be reviewed regularly by the library's governing authority and by its legal counsel;

12. must be communicated clearly and made available in an effective manner to all library users;

13. must be enforced evenhandedly, and not in a manner intended to benefit or disfavor any person or group in an arbitrary or capricious manner;[2]

14. should, if reasonably possible, provide adequate alternative means of access to information for those whose behavior results in the denial or restriction of access to any library resource, service, or facility.

NOTES

1. In the *Library Bill of Rights* and all its interpretations, it is intended that: "origin" encompasses all the characteristics of individuals that are inherent in the circumstances of their birth; "age" encompasses all the characteristics of individuals that are inherent in their levels of development and maturity; "background" encompasses all the characteristics of individuals that are a result of their life experiences; and "views" encompasses all the opinions and beliefs held and expressed by individuals.

2. Libraries should develop an ongoing staff training program designed to foster the understanding of the legal framework and principles underlying library policies and to assist staff in gaining the skill and ability to respond to potentially difficult circumstances in a timely, direct, and open manner. This program should include training to develop empathy and understanding of the social and economic problems of library users.

Creating Policy for Your Library— Collection Development and Resource Reconsideration

THE PRIMARY PURPOSE of a collection development or resource selection policy is to promote the development of a collection based on institutional goals and user needs. The policy serves as the basis of a sound selection program by identifying specific criteria for resources to be added to the collection through purchase, subscription, or donation.

Occasional objections to resources will be made despite the quality of the selection process. The pro-

See also part II, chapter 4, "Collection Development and Management"; and part II, chapter 2, "Censorship, Challenged Resources, and Internet Filtering."

cedure for reconsideration of challenged resources should be clearly stated. The procedure should establish a fair framework for registering complaints while defending the principles of intellectual freedom, library users' right of access, and professional responsibility. Having a well-prepared policy—and following it carefully—will be invaluable should a challenge arise.

Policy Checklist—Collection Development

☐ State the purpose of policy, how often will it be reviewed, and to whom library users should address questions.

☐ Explain how collection development, selection, and maintenance relate to the mission of the library. (For example: "The library serves as a limited public forum for access to the full range of recorded information within the marketplace of ideas. Collection development shall be content-neutral so that the library represents a wide range of viewpoints on subjects of interest.")

☐ Refer to the principles on which the policy is based (e.g., federal and state constitutions and the U.S. Bill of Rights; *Library Bill of Rights* and its interpretations; *The Freedom to Read* statement).

☐ Describe the scope and objectives of the collection. (In school libraries, indicate that the collection exists not only to support the curriculum, but also to meet the extracurricular and recreational needs of the students. For example: "The objective of the collection is to make available to the faculty and students a collection of materials that will enrich and support the curriculum, meet the educational needs of the students and the faculty, and support the intellectual growth, personal development, individual interests, and recreational needs of students.")

☐ Identify the persons (using position titles, not names) who have authority to make selection decisions.

☐ Identify the criteria used in selection. Examples include artistic or literary excellence, appropriateness to level of user, authenticity, interest, cost, technical criteria such as quality of sound in audio materials, suitability of format for library use, representation of minority points of view, relation to the existing collection, timeliness or permanence, prizes or awards received, etc.

  – Include criteria that are relevant to the library's mission and goals.
  – Do not require that all criteria be met.
  – Explain how the library will treat donated resources and specify that such resources will be subject to the same selection criteria as resources the library purchases.

☐ Identify the resources consulted in making selection decisions. If the library routinely purchases items on specific best-seller lists, this should be included in policy. (Beware of *requiring* reviews.)

☐ Explain the manner in which controversial resources will be considered for selection. For example, the policy might state: "Individual items that may be controversial or offensive to some users or staff may be selected if their inclusion will contribute to the range of viewpoints in the collection as a whole and the effectiveness of the library's ability to serve the community."

☐ Explain how users can request that resources be added to the collection.

☐ Explain how the collection is maintained through activities such as discarding, binding materials, or transferring to other formats.

☐ Explain how resources will be arranged in the library, and indicate that prejudicial labels will not be used.

Policy Checklist—Reconsideration of Challenged Resources

☐ Recognize and respect users' right to question selection decisions.

☐ Outline the procedure for handling complaints about resources, describing every step from the initial response through the highest appeal (see part II, chapter 2, "Censorship, Challenged Resources, and Internet Filtering"). Indicate that the procedure applies regardless of the source of the challenge (library user, library staff member, faculty member, administrator, trustee or board member, community member, elected official, or government employee).

☐ Create a "Request for Reconsideration" form, asking why the challenger believes the resource does not meet selection criteria and what action he requests. (See "Sample Form: Request for Reconsideration of Library Resources" in part II, chapter 2.)

☐ State that challenged resources will be evaluated using the criteria in the selection policy and that they will remain in place during the reconsideration process.

☐ If a committee is used, be informed about your state's open meeting and public records laws as they apply to staff committees making policy-related decisions or recommendations.

☐ Provide a decision letter to the user indicating how to appeal the decision. The letter should refer directly to the user's request; it should not be a form letter.

Creating Policy for Your Library— Internet Use

ANY LIBRARY THAT provides public access to the Internet should have an Internet use policy. All libraries that receive E-rate or LSTA grant funding for Internet access are *required* to have policies.

> See also part II, chapter 2, "Censorship, Challenged Resources, and Internet Filtering."

Policy Checklist—Internet Use

Note: The Children's Internet Protection Act (CIPA) and the Neighborhood Children's Internet Protection Act (NCIPA) impose particular policy requirements on both public and school libraries that are not addressed by these guidelines. If your library is subject to these laws, you should consult the law and legal counsel to ensure that your policies conform to the law.

- ☐ State the purpose of policy, how often will it be reviewed, and to whom library users should address questions.
- ☐ Explain how access to the Internet relates to the mission of the library.
- ☐ Refer to the principles on which the policy is based (e.g., federal and state constitutions and the U.S. Bill of Rights; *Library Bill of Rights* and its interpretations; *The Freedom to Read* statement).
- ☐ Include a disclaimer stating that the library is not responsible for Internet content.
- ☐ Outline the library's procedures for use of the Internet, covering details such as reservations and time limits.
- ☐ State user rights and responsibilities. Advise users to follow federal, state, and local laws on the use of the Internet.
- ☐ State that the library prohibits the use of library equipment to access material that is obscene, child pornography, or, in the case of minors, harmful to minors (as defined in state law). (Note that "child pornography" and "obscenity" are legal terms describing material that is not protected by the First Amendment. "Pornography," however, is not a legal term and is defined by people in different ways. Not all pornography is obscene and illegal. See Appendix 1, "Glossary of Terms.")
- ☐ Explain how the library works to protect the privacy of people using public terminals.
- ☐ Explain how the library protects the confidentiality of records that identify individual users and link them to search strategies, sites accessed, or data about information they sought or retrieved.
- ☐ Inform users about the consequences if procedures are not followed.

- [ ] Alert parents to guidelines relating to minor library users and be clear that it is the parents, and not library employees, who are responsible for monitoring their children's Internet activity.
- [ ] Where filters are used, the policy must give notice of that fact and include procedures for disabling filters for adults when the adult asks for disabling. The policy also should include a procedure for unblocking specific sites for minors as long as those sites are neither obscene, harmful to minors, or child pornography.
- [ ] Post the policy in a clear and conspicuous manner.
- [ ] Apply the policy consistently and objectively.
- [ ] Provide an appeal mechanism, even if informal.

Creating Policy for Your Library— Use of Meeting Rooms and Exhibit Spaces

LIBRARIES SHOULD DEVELOP and publish policy statements governing the use of meeting rooms, display cases, exhibit spaces, and any other facilities they make available to their users.

See also: part II, chapter 6, "Meeting Rooms, Exhibit Spaces, and Programs."

Policy Checklist—Meeting Rooms and Exhibit Spaces

- [ ] State the purpose of policy, how often it will be reviewed, and to whom library users should address questions.
- [ ] Explain how providing access to meeting rooms and exhibit spaces relates to the mission of the library.
- [ ] Refer to the principles on which the policy is based (e.g., federal and state constitutions and U.S. Bill of Rights; *Library Bill of Rights* and its interpretations; *The Freedom to Read* statement).
- [ ] Describe the facility with particularity and define who is eligible to use the facility.
- [ ] State any rules concerning the time, place, or manner of use. Rules must not pertain to the content of a meeting or to the beliefs or affiliations of the sponsors. The policy should not prohibit the use of meeting rooms by religious organizations or exclude users based upon their religious beliefs or the content of their speech. Numerous court decisions have established that libraries may not discriminate against religious organizations when providing access to meeting rooms.
- [ ] Provide a means of appealing a decision to deny access to the library's facilities.

Creating Policy for Your Library—Privacy and Confidentiality

A WELL-DEFINED PRIVACY policy communicates the library's commitment to protecting users' personally identifiable information, tells library users how their information is used, and explains under what circumstances personally identifiable information might be disclosed to third parties.

In addition to the privacy policy, the library should consider developing a records management plan that identifies the types of records kept by the library, sets forth retention schedules for those records, and establishes procedures for the purging or destruction of the records when mandated by the schedule. The library also should develop procedures for employees and volunteers to follow in responding to outside inquiries concerning user records, including inquiries coming from law enforcement agents. Such procedures should explain how records are preserved when the library is given notice that the records are subject to legal process or evidence of a crime.

See also: part II, chapter 7, "Privacy and Confidentiality"; part II, chapter 8, "Visits and Requests from Law Enforcement"; and "Privacy Tool Kit," available at www.ala.org/advocacy/privacyconfidentiality/toolkitsprivacy/privacy

Policy Checklist—Privacy and Confidentiality

☐ State the purpose of the policy, how often it will be reviewed, and to whom library users should address questions.

☐ Explain how protecting user privacy and confidentiality relates to the mission of the library.

☐ Refer to the principles on which the library's commitment to protecting privacy is based (e.g., federal and state constitutions and the U.S. Bill of Rights; *Library Bill of Rights* and its interpretations; *Code of Ethics of the American Library Association*; *The Freedom to Read* statement).

☐ Refer to any federal, state, and local laws that impact library privacy policy. State library confidentiality statutes may impose special or additional duties on libraries and their employees. State laws and local ordinances addressing open records and records management and the state Freedom of Information Act also must be considered when drafting policies concerning records retention and access to records. (To date, no statute or regulation requires a library to adopt particular data retention practices or to reconfigure its processes or systems to collect information. State and local laws may impose other duties on public libraries subject to their jurisdiction.)

☐ List the personally identifiable information that will be protected (e.g., circulation and registration records; in-person, telephone, chat, or text reference requests; hold, recall, reserve, and interlibrary loan requests; server and client computer logs).

☐ Include statements about the library's commitment to do the following:

- Limit the degree to which personally identifiable information is monitored, collected, disclosed, and distributed. (For example, user information will be disclosed to third parties only in response to a properly executed court order.)

- Notify users whenever the library collects their personally identifiable information and give them the right to see information collected about them by the library.

- Avoid creating unnecessary records, including non-text records such as video recordings.

- Avoid library practices and procedures that place personally identifiable information on public view (e.g., postcard renewal notices; self-service "hold" shelves that reveal users' identities; stating reserve requests or interlibrary loan titles on voice-mail messages that may be heard by other household members; positioning staff terminals so that the public can read the screens).

- Require that user records remain on a local server and not be exported to the cloud or a third-party server.

- Avoid retaining records that are not needed for efficient operation of the library, including data-related logs, digital records, vendor-collected data, and system backups.

- Ensure that contracts and licenses reflect library policies and legal obligations concerning privacy.

- Regularly purge personally identifiable information, including personally identifiable information associated with library resource use, material circulation history, and security/surveillance tapes and logs. ("Purging" does not imply wholesale destruction of records. Statistical information, library usage data permanently stripped of personally identifiable information, and historical documents can and should be retained to aid library administration and preservation of the historical record.)

- Employ policies addressing records management, retention, and purging throughout the institution, including information technology departments and off-site locations.

– Keep personally identifiable information secure and ensure it is accessed only by authorized library staff.
– Notify users about any data breaches that occur.

☐ Post the policy in a clear and conspicuous manner.

Creating Policy for Your Library— User Behavior and Library Use

These guidelines, officially titled "Guidelines for the Development of Policies and Procedures regarding User Behavior and Library Usage," were adopted January 24, 1993, by the ALA Intellectual Freedom Committee; revised November 17, 2000; January 19, 2005; and March 29, 2014.

See also "The Law Regarding Access to the Library: User-Behavior Rules" in part II, chapter 1.

LIBRARIES ARE FACED with problems of user behavior that must be addressed to ensure the effective delivery of service and full access to facilities. Library governing bodies should approach the regulation of user behavior within the framework of the *Code of Ethics of the American Library Association,* the *Library Bill of Rights,* and the law, including local and state statutes, constitutional standards under the First and Fourteenth Amendments, due process, and equal and equitable treatment under the law.

A historical essay about this statement can be found in the publication, *A History of ALA Policy on Intellectual Freedom: A Supplement to the Intellectual Freedom Manual, Ninth Edition.*

There is a significant government interest in maintaining a library environment that is conducive to all users' exercise of their constitutionally protected right to receive information. This significant interest authorizes publicly supported libraries to maintain a safe and healthy environment in which library users and staff can be free from harassment, intimidation, and threats to their safety and well-being. Libraries should provide appropriate safeguards against such behavior and enforce policies and procedures addressing that behavior when it occurs. Since the *Library Bill of Rights* "affirms that all libraries are forums for information and ideas," all libraries are encouraged to observe these guidelines as they develop policies, regulations and procedures.

In order to protect all library users' right of access to library facilities, to ensure the safety of users and staff, and to protect library resources and facilities from damage, the library's governing authority may impose reasonable restrictions on the time, place, or manner of library access.

Policy Checklist—User Behavior and Library Use

The American Library Association's Intellectual Freedom Committee recommends that publicly supported libraries use the following guidelines, based upon constitutional principles, to develop policies and procedures governing the use of library facilities:

- [ ] Libraries are advised to rely upon existing legislation and law enforcement mechanisms as the primary means of controlling behavior that involves public safety, criminal behavior, or other issues covered by existing local, state, or federal statutes. In many instances, this legal framework may be sufficient to provide the library with the necessary tools to maintain order.

- [ ] If the library's governing body chooses to write its own policies and procedures regarding user behavior or access to library facilities, services, and resources, the policies should cite statutes or ordinances upon which the authority to make those policies is based.

- [ ] Library policies and procedures governing the use of library facilities should be carefully examined to ensure that they embody the principles expressed in the *Library Bill of Rights*.

- [ ] Reasonable and narrowly drawn policies and procedures designed to prohibit interference with use of the facilities and services by others, or to prohibit activities inconsistent with achievement of the library's mission statement and objectives, are acceptable.

- [ ] Such policies and the attendant implementing procedures should be reviewed frequently and updated as needed by the library's legal counsel for compliance with federal and state constitutional requirements, federal and state civil rights legislation, all other applicable federal and state legislation, and applicable case law.

- [ ] Every effort should be made to respond to potentially difficult circumstances of user behavior in a timely, direct, and open manner. Common sense, reason, and sensitivity should be used to resolve issues in a constructive and positive manner without escalation.

- [ ] Libraries should develop an ongoing staff training program based upon their user behavior policy. This program should include training to develop empathy and understanding of the social and economic problems of some library users.

☐ Policies and regulations that impose restrictions on library access:

- should apply only to those activities that materially interfere with the public's right of access to library facilities, the safety of users and staff, and the protection of library resources and facilities;
- should narrowly tailor prohibitions or restrictions so that they are not more restrictive than needed to serve their objectives;
- should not be used to limit library users' access to constitutionally protected speech that may be considered controversial or objectionable;
- should attempt to balance competing interests and avoid favoring the majority at the expense of individual rights, or allowing individual users' rights or beliefs to supersede those of the majority of library users;
- should be based solely upon actual behavior and not upon arbitrary distinctions between individuals or classes of individuals. Policies should not target specific users or groups of users based upon an assumption or expectation that such users might engage in behaviors that could disrupt library service;
- should not restrict access to the library by persons who merely inspire the anger or annoyance of others. Policies based upon appearance or behavior that is merely annoying, or that merely generates negative subjective reactions from others, do not meet the necessary standard. Such policies should employ a reasonable, objective standard based on the behavior itself;
- must provide a clear description of the behavior that is prohibited and the various enforcement measures in place so that a reasonably intelligent person will have both due process and fair warning; this description must be continuously and clearly communicated in an effective manner to all library users;
- to the extent possible, should not leave those affected without adequate alternative means of access to information in the library;
- must be enforced evenhandedly, and not in a manner intended to benefit or disfavor any person or group in an arbitrary or capricious manner.

The user behaviors addressed in these guidelines are the result of a wide variety of individual and societal conditions. Libraries should take advantage of the expertise of local social service agencies, advocacy groups, mental health professionals, law enforcement officials, and other community resources to develop community strategies for addressing the needs of a diverse population.

The Right to Receive Information

Libraries, the First Amendment, and the Public Forum Doctrine

Theresa Chmara

WHEN WE THINK about the exercise of First Amendment rights, we usually think of the person giving a speech, the group passing out pamphlets, or the organization carrying picket signs or banners. In the public library context, however, we need to think about the library user not as speech giver or sign holder but as a person entitled under the First Amendment to receive information or access to the facility. When creating policies regarding user-behavior rules, access to resources, and use of meeting rooms and exhibit spaces, librarians need to understand what rights are applicable under the First Amendment. This requires an evaluation of general First Amendment principles and public forum doctrine.

To Learn More...

For more information about how First Amendment principles and the public forum doctrine apply to library operations and policies, please see the following:

"The Law Regarding Access to the Library: User-Behavior Rules," part II, chapter 1.

"The Law Regarding Access to Library Resources: Removal of Materials," part II, chapter 2.

"The Law Regarding Minors' First Amendment Rights to Access Information," part II, chapter 3.

"The Law Regarding Access to Meeting Rooms and Exhibit Spaces," part II, chapter 6.

General First Amendment Principles

It is well established that the right to receive information is a corollary to the First Amendment right to speak. The Supreme Court first addressed the right to receive information in *Martin v. Struthers*.[1] This 1943 decision upheld the right of residents in a company town to receive pamphlets from a person going door to door. The court held that "the right of freedom of speech and press has broad scope . . . This freedom embraces the right to distribute literature, and necessarily protects the right to receive it." In its subsequent opinion in *Griswold v. Connecticut*,[2] the court identified "the right to receive, the right to read and freedom of inquiry" among the rights protected by the First Amendment. In 1965, Justice William Brennan elaborated on these rights:

> The protection of the Bill of Rights goes beyond the specific guarantees to protect from Congressional abridgment those equally fundamental personal rights necessary to make the express guarantees fully meaningful. I think the right to receive publications is such a fundamental right.

Does the First Amendment Apply to Your Library?

The First Amendment applies only to the government and publicly funded agencies. It does not apply to private entities. The extent to which it applies to a public agency—whether a public library, public school library, or academic library that is part of a public institution—will depend on the context and application of the public forum doctrine.

Because the mission of public libraries is to serve the larger community, courts have imposed stricter standards on restrictions to access and required greater access to information and the library facility in those institutions. Public schools and universities—including their libraries— serve defined communities of students and employees, rather than the general public. As a result, they generally are considered nonpublic forums. They may have greater latitude to impose restrictions on access consistent with their missions. Students' access to resources and the removal of materials in public schools and public academic libraries, however, are matters still subject to the First Amendment.

Any institution that opens its facility to the public for the use of its space could be considered a limited or designated forum for that purpose and would have to meet the more stringent First Amendment standard applicable to that type of forum. Also, any library that participates in the Federal Depository Library Program (FDLP) must provide free access to FDLP information resources in all formats to any member of the general public without any impediments.

All libraries, public or private, are encouraged to adopt policies supporting intellectual freedom and reflecting the principles expressed in the *Library Bill of Rights*.

> The dissemination of ideas can accomplish nothing if otherwise willing addressees are not free to receive and consider them. It would be a barren marketplace of ideas that had only sellers and no buyers.[3]

Minors also have rights under the First Amendment, although they are not as broad as the rights of adults, particularly in the school context. In *Board of Education v. Pico,* the Supreme Court considered whether a local school board violated the Constitution by removing books from a school library and in doing so held unequivocally that "the right to receive ideas is a necessary predicate to the recipient's meaningful exercise of his own rights of speech, press, and political freedom."[4]

More recently, the Supreme Court held in *Reno v. American Civil Liberties Union* that "the CDA [Communications Decency Act] lacks the precision that the First Amendment requires when a statute regulates the content of speech" because "in order to deny minors access to potentially harmful speech, the CDA effectively suppresses a large amount of speech that adults have a constitutional right to receive and to address to one another."[5] The analysis of what the right to receive information means must begin with an exploration of the library as a public forum.

Public Forum Doctrine

There are three types of forums: (1) traditional public forums, (2) designated or limited public forums, and (3) nonpublic forums. Traditional public forums are locations such as streets, parks, or sidewalks that "have immemorially been held in trust for the use of the public and, time out of mind, have been used for purposes of assembly, communicating thoughts between citizens, and discussing public questions."[6] If the government creates restrictions that are content-based in a traditional public forum, its actions will be reviewed for constitutionality by a *strict scrutiny* standard. Under strict scrutiny, the restriction will be deemed unconstitutional unless the government can demonstrate that the restriction is necessary to achieve a compelling government interest and the restriction is narrowly tailored to achieve that interest.[7]

Of course, governments may impose valid time, place, and manner restrictions even in a traditional public forum provided that the regulations are content-neutral, narrowly tailored to serve a significant government interest, and leave open ample channels of communication.[8] For example, time, place, and manner restrictions may regulate hours of operation, disruptions in the library, costs for copying, time limits on use of materials or library services, removal of damaged books, capacity for use of meeting rooms, sign-up procedures for use of library meeting rooms, and limits on the number of days that an exhibit space may be used. Such restrictions must be content-neutral, objectively defined, and consistently applied.

A designated or limited public forum is "property that the State has opened for expressive activity by part or all of the public."[9] Courts have held that "the government does not create a [designated] public forum by inaction or by permitting limited discourse, but only by intentionally opening a nontraditional public forum for public discourse."[10] In determining whether a place that is not a traditional public forum has become a designated or limited public forum, courts will look to the "policy and practice of the government to ascertain whether it intended to designate a place not traditionally open to assembly and debate as a public forum."[11] Once a court determines that a government entity has created a designated or limited public forum, any content-based restrictions will be evaluated to determine if the government has a compelling interest for the restriction and whether the restriction is narrowly tailored to achieve that interest.[12]

A nonpublic forum is government property that has been reserved for its intended purposes even if used for communication. For example, a public library might utilize a meeting room in its facility for its own purposes without allowing any use of the room by the public. Thus, the room would be used for staff meetings, library reading group meetings, children's story hours conducted by staff, or meetings of the Friends of the Library. Although the meeting room is used for communication purposes by the library, it remains a nonpublic forum. The Supreme Court has held that "control over access to a non-public forum can be based on subject matter and speaker identity so long as the distinctions drawn are reasonable in light of the purpose served by the forum and are viewpoint neutral."[13]

Generally, courts will look to the policy of the entity, the practice of use of the forum, and "its compatibility with expressive activity."[14] Courts will evaluate specific factors in determining what type of forum has been created by the government, such as (1) whether there is a written policy, (2) whether it is applied consistently, (3) whether the policy is based on subjective or overly general criteria, (4) the selectivity of the criteria used to determine access, and (5) consistency with the principal function of the forum.[15]

Court precedents demonstrate that both a library's policies and its practices will determine the type of forum it has created. Specific application of these principles demonstrates further that different considerations apply in the context of the distinct services provided to library users by these public libraries. In general, courts have held that publicly funded libraries are designated or limited forums for the receipt of information.

NOTES

1. *Martin v. Struthers,* 319 U.S. 141 (1943).

2. *Griswold v. Connecticut,* 381 U.S. 479 (1965).

3. *Lamont v. Postmaster General,* 381 U.S. 301 (1965).

4. *Board of Education v. Pico,* 457 U.S. 853, 867 (1982).

5. *Reno v. American Civil Liberties Union,* 521 U.S. 844, 876 (1997).

6. *Perry Education Association v. Perry Local Educators' Association,* 460 U.S. 37, 45 (1983) (quoting *Hague v. CIO,* 307 U.S. 496, 515 (1939)).

7. *Perry,* 460 U.S. at 45; *Widmar v. Vincent,* 454 U.S. 263, 269-70 (1981).

8. *Perry,* 460 U.S. at 45.

9. *International Soc. for Krishna Consciousness, Inc. v. Lee,* 505 U.S. 672, 678 (1992).

10. *Cornelius v. NAACP Legal Defense & Ed. Fund, Inc.,* 473 U.S. 788, 802 (1985); *see also Arkansas Educ. Television Com'n v. Forbes,* 523 U.S. 666, 677 (1998) (holding that designated public forums are created by "purposeful government action").

11. *Cornelius,* 473 U.S. at 802.

12. *Arkansas Educ.,* 523 U.S. at 677.

13. *Cornelius,* 473 U.S. at 806.

14. *Id.* at 802.

15. *Hopper v. City of Pasco,* 241 F.3d 1067 (9th Cir.), *cert. denied,* 534 U.S. 951 (2001) (holding that the city violated the First Amendment when it denied artists access to a city hall display area); *see also Planned Parenthood/Chicago Area v. Chicago Transit Authority,* 767 F.2d 1225 (7th Cir. 1985) (concluding that the city violated the First Amendment when it denied a nonprofit group access to advertising space on transit authority vehicles).

Intellectual Freedom Issues and Best Practices

Access to Library Resources and Services

ISSUE AT A GLANCE

Key Concepts

- Library resources and services should be provided for the interest, information, and enlightenment of all people in the community the library serves.
- Libraries should strive to provide free, unrestricted, and unfiltered access to library resources and services—including the Internet— for all people in their user communities, regardless of origin, background, disability, age, reading level, economic status, housing status, views, sex, gender identity, gender expression, or sexual orientation.
- When examining terms or conditions attached to library funding, including private gifts, librarians and governing bodies should reject any restrictions that limit equal and equitable access to information.

What Is Meant by "Origin," "Age," "Background," and "Views"?

In 1993 the ALA Intellectual Freedom Committee adopted the following statement:

In the *Library Bill of Rights* and all its interpretations, it is intended that: "origin" encompasses all the characteristics of individuals that are inherent in the circumstances of their birth; "age" encompasses all the characteristics of individuals that are inherent in their levels of development and maturity; "background" encompasses all the characteristics of individuals that are a result of their life experiences; and "views" encompasses all the opinions and beliefs held and expressed by individuals.

What Does the Law Say?

- The First Amendment to the Constitution mandates the right of all persons to free expression and the corollary right to receive the constitutionally protected expression of others.
- As government-owned and government-funded institutions, public libraries, public schools, and public universities and colleges are state actors, whose activities are controlled by the First Amendment to the Constitution. (See part I, chapter 4, "The Right to Receive Information: Libraries, the First Amendment, and the Public Forum Doctrine.")
- Private libraries and private schools, universities and colleges not controlled or funded by the government are private actors not subject to the First Amendment (though private institutions may become subject to government regulation by accepting government funding or by agreeing to comply with government accreditation standards). Private libraries and educational institutions can protect free expression and academic freedom through private policy or contract.
- Private institutions have the right to close their libraries to the general public, but are not required to do so. All libraries, public or private, designated by Title 44 of the U.S. Code as government depository libraries, must make their government information collections open to the general public.

Creating Policy for Your Library

- Consider formally adopting the *Library Bill of Rights* (see part 1, chapter 2) as policy for your library. It contains statements that support access to library resources by a diversity of people.
- Be sure you have policies outlining your procedures and rules for accessing library resources (see part I, chapter 3). Policies regarding the use of the library and its services should be (1) written, (2) objective, (3) consistently and equitably enforced without regard to the identity or beliefs of the user, and (4) reasonable and related to library use. If enforcement of the policy denies a user's request or results in a sanction or the denial of access to the library or one of its resources, the policy should provide for an appeal mechanism.

Especially for Academic Libraries

- Because they are unique, expensive, and often fragile, special collections materials are often kept in closed stacks. As long as the motive is to ensure that these materials survive for library users in future years, this action is consistent with the intellectual freedom principle of ensuring access.

Especially for Public Libraries

- Placing materials in a "children's room" or "young adult section" does not constitute restricting access, as long as all library users are able to access all collections of the library.

Especially for School Libraries

- Systems that apply particular age, grade, or developmental levels should not be used to restrict access for students who wish to read above or below their official levels. Labels that identify a resource as having a particular reading level should not be placed on the outside of the book, as they may stigmatize those reading books at lower levels and encourage students to self-censor their reading.
- Overly restrictive Internet filtering affects students' access to information including constitutionally protected speech (see *Fencing Out Knowledge: Impacts of the Children's Internet Protection Act 10 Years Later,* www.ala.org/offices/sites/ala.org.offices/files/content/oitp/publications/issuebriefs/cipa_report.pdf).

To Learn More

- Visit the ALA "Intellectual Freedom" website (www.ala.org/advocacy/intfreedom) for links to information about access issues.

Questions for Reflection

- How is access to information and services an intellectual freedom issue?
- What strategies can you use to reach out to underserved populations in your community?
- What kinds of restrictions on library use are permissible? Why?
- How does the "digital divide" relate to intellectual freedom?

II.1
Access

OFFICIAL ALA POLICY STATEMENTS

Access to Digital Information, Services, and Networks

An Interpretation of the *Library Bill of Rights*

Adopted January 24, 1996, by the ALA Council; amended January 19, 2005; and July 15, 2009.

A historical essay about this statement can be found in the publication, *A History of ALA Policy on Intellectual Freedom: A Supplement to the Intellectual Freedom Manual, Ninth Edition.*

Introduction

FREEDOM OF EXPRESSION is an inalienable human right and the foundation for self-government. Freedom of expression encompasses the freedom of speech and the corollary right to receive information.[1] Libraries and librarians protect and promote these rights regardless of the format or technology employed to create and disseminate information.

The American Library Association expresses the fundamental principles of librarianship in its *Code of Ethics* as well as in the *Library Bill of Rights* and its Interpretations. These principles guide librarians and library governing bodies in addressing issues of intellectual freedom that arise when the library provides access to digital information, services, and networks.

Libraries empower users by offering opportunities both for accessing the broadest range of information created by others and for creating and sharing information. Digital resources enhance the ability of libraries to fulfill this responsibility.

Libraries should regularly review issues arising from digital creation, distribution, retrieval, and archiving of information in the context of constitutional principles and ALA policies so that fundamental and traditional tenets of librarianship are upheld. Although digital information flows across boundaries and barriers despite attempts by individuals, governments, and private entities to channel or control it, many people lack access or capability to use or create digital information effectively.

In making decisions about how to offer access to digital information, services, and networks, each library should consider intellectual freedom principles in the context of its mission, goals, objectives, cooperative agreements, and the needs of the entire community it serves.

The Rights of Users

All library system and network policies, procedures, or regulations relating to digital information and services should be scrutinized for potential violation of user rights. User policies should be developed according to the policies and guidelines established by the American Library Association, including "Guidelines for the Development and Implementation of Policies, Regulations, and Procedures Affecting Access to Library Materials, Services, and Facilities."

Users' access should not be restricted or denied for expressing, receiving, creating, or participating in constitutionally protected speech. If access is restricted or denied for behavioral or other reasons, users should be provided due process, including, but not limited to, formal notice and a means of appeal.

Information retrieved, utilized, or created digitally is constitutionally protected unless determined otherwise by a court of competent jurisdiction. These rights extend to minors as well as adults ("Access to Library Resources and Services for Minors," "Access to Resources and Services in the School Library," and "Minors and Internet Activity").[2] Libraries should use technology to enhance, not deny, digital access. Users have the right to be free of unreasonable limitations or conditions set by libraries, librarians, system administrators, vendors, network service providers, or others. Contracts, agreements, and licenses entered into by libraries on behalf of their users should not violate this right. Libraries should provide library users the training and assistance necessary to find, evaluate, and use information effectively.

Users have both the right of confidentiality and the right of privacy. The library should uphold these rights by policy, procedure, and practice in accordance with "Privacy: An Interpretation of the *Library Bill of Rights*" and "Advocating for Intellectual Freedom: An Interpretation of the *Library Bill of Rights.*"

Equity of Access

The digital environment provides expanding opportunities for everyone to participate in the information society, but individuals may face serious barriers to access.

Digital information, services, and networks provided directly or indirectly by the library should be equally, readily, and equitably accessible to all library users. American Library Association policies oppose the charging of user fees for the provision of information services by libraries that receive support from public funds (B.4.2 "Free Access to Information"; B.2.1.14 "Economic Barriers to Information Access"; B.3.1 "Diversity: Policy Objectives";

B.8.10 "Library Services for the Poor: Policy Objectives"). All libraries should develop policies concerning access to digital information that are consistent with ALA's policies and guidelines, including "Economic Barriers to Information Access: An Interpretation of the *Library Bill of Rights*," "Guidelines for the Development and Implementation of Policies, Regulations, and Procedures Affecting Access to Library Materials, Services, and Facilities," and "Services to Persons with Disabilities: An Interpretation of the *Library Bill of Rights*."

Information Resources and Access

Libraries, acting within their mission and objectives, must support access to information on all subjects that serve the needs or interests of each user, regardless of the user's age or the content of the material. In order to preserve the cultural record and to prevent the loss of information, libraries may need to expand their selection or collection development policies to ensure preservation, in appropriate formats, of information obtained digitally. Libraries have an obligation to provide access to government information available in digital format.

Providing connections to global information, services, and networks is not the same as selecting and purchasing materials for a library collection. Libraries and librarians should not deny or limit access to digital information because of its allegedly controversial content or because of a librarian's personal beliefs or fear of confrontation. Furthermore, libraries and librarians should not deny access to digital information solely on the grounds that it is perceived to lack value. Parents and legal guardians who are concerned about their children's use of digital resources should provide guidance to their own children. Some information accessed digitally may not meet a library's selection or collection development policy. It is, therefore, left to each user to determine what is appropriate.

Publicly funded libraries have a legal obligation to provide access to constitutionally protected information. Federal, state, county, municipal, local, or library governing bodies sometimes require the use of Internet filters or other technological measures that block access to constitutionally protected information, contrary to the *Library Bill of Rights* (ALA Policy Manual, B.2.1.17, "Resolution on the Use of Filtering Software in Libraries"). If a library uses a technological measure that blocks access to information, it should be set at the least restrictive level in order to minimize the blocking of constitutionally protected speech. Adults retain the right to access all constitutionally protected information and to ask for the technological measure to be disabled in a timely manner. Minors also retain the right to access constitutionally protected information and, at the minimum, have the right to ask

II. 1
Access

the library or librarian to provide access to erroneously blocked information in a timely manner. Libraries and librarians have an obligation to inform users of these rights and to provide the means to exercise these rights.[3]

Digital resources provide unprecedented opportunities to expand the scope of information available to users. Libraries and librarians should provide access to information presenting all points of view. The provision of access does not imply sponsorship or endorsement. These principles pertain to digital resources as much as they do to the more traditional sources of information in libraries ("Diversity in Collection Development").

NOTES

1. *Martin v. Struthers,* 319 U.S. 141 (1943); *Lamont v. Postmaster General,* 381 U.S. 301 (1965); *Susan Nevelow Mart, "The Right to Receive Information,"* 95 *Law Library Journal* 2 (2003).

2. *Tinker v. Des Moines Independent Community School District,* 393 U.S. 503 (1969); *Board of Education, Island Trees Union Free School District No. 26 v. Pico,* 457 U.S. 853 (1982); *American Amusement Machine Association v. Teri Kendrick,* 244 F.3d 954 (7th Cir. 2001); *cert. denied,* 534 U.S. 994 (2001).

3. "If some libraries do not have the capacity to unblock specific Web sites or to disable the filter or if it is shown that an adult user's election to view constitutionally protected Internet material is burdened in some other substantial way, that would be the subject for an as-applied challenge, not the facial challenge made in this case." *United States et al. v. American Library Association,* 539 U.S. 194 (2003) (Justice Kennedy, concurring).

Access to Library Resources and Services Regardless of Sex, Gender Identity, Gender Expression, or Sexual Orientation
An Interpretation of the *Library Bill of Rights*

Adopted June 30, 1993, by the ALA Council; amended July 12, 2000; June 30, 2004; and July 2, 2008.

AMERICAN LIBRARIES EXIST and function within the context of a body of laws derived from the United States Constitution and the First Amendment. The *Library Bill of Rights* embodies the basic policies that guide libraries in the provision of services, materials, and programs.

A historical essay about this statement can be found in the publication, *A History of ALA Policy on Intellectual Freedom: A Supplement to the Intellectual Freedom Manual, Ninth Edition.*

In the preamble to its *Library Bill of Rights,* the American Library Association affirms that all libraries are forums for information and ideas. This concept of forum and its accompanying principle of *inclusiveness* pervade all six articles of the *Library Bill of Rights.*

The American Library Association stringently and unequivocally maintains that libraries and librarians have an obligation to resist efforts that systematically exclude materials dealing with any subject matter, including sex, gender identity, gender expression, or sexual orientation:

- Article I of the *Library Bill of Rights* states that "Materials should not be excluded because of the origin, background, or views of those contributing to their creation." The association affirms that books and other materials coming from gay, lesbian, bisexual, and/or transgendered presses, gay, lesbian, bisexual, and/or transgendered authors or other creators, and materials regardless of format or services dealing with gay, lesbian, bisexual, and/or transgendered life are protected by the *Library Bill of Rights.* Librarians are obligated by the *Library Bill of Rights* to endeavor to select materials without regard to the sex, gender identity, or sexual orientation of their creators by using the criteria identified in their written, approved selection policies (ALA policy B.2.1.5).

- Article II maintains that "Libraries should provide materials and information presenting all points of view on current and historical issues. Materials should not be proscribed or removed because of partisan or doctrinal disapproval." Library services, materials, and programs representing diverse points of view on sex, gender identity, gender expression, or sexual orientation should be considered for purchase and inclusion in library collections and programs (ALA policies B.2.1.1, B.2.1.9, and B.2.1.11). The association affirms that attempts to proscribe or remove materials dealing with gay, lesbian, bisexual, and/or transgendered life without regard to the written, approved selection policy violate this tenet and constitute censorship.

- Articles III and IV mandate that libraries "challenge censorship" and cooperate with those "resisting abridgement of free expression and free access to ideas."

- Article V holds that "A person's right to use a library should not be denied or abridged because of origin, age, background, or views." In the *Library Bill of Rights* and all its interpretations, it is intended that "origin" encompasses all the characteristics of individuals that are inherent in the circumstances of their birth; "age" encompasses all the characteristics of individuals that are inherent in their levels of development and maturity; "background" encompasses all the characteristics of individuals that are a result of their life experiences; and "views" encompasses all the opinions and beliefs held and expressed by individuals. Therefore, Article V of the *Library Bill of Rights* mandates that library services, materials, and programs be available to all members of the community the library serves, without regard to sex, gender identity, gender expression, or sexual orientation. This includes providing youth with comprehensive sex education literature (ALA policy B.8.6.2).

- Article VI maintains that "Libraries which make exhibit spaces and meeting rooms available to the public they serve should make such facilities available on an equitable basis, regardless of the beliefs or affiliations of individuals or groups requesting their use." This protection extends to all groups and members of the community the library serves, without regard to sex, gender identity, gender expression, or sexual orientation.

The American Library Association holds that any attempt, be it legal or extra-legal, to regulate or suppress library services, materials, or programs must be resisted in order that protected expression is not abridged. Librarians have a professional obligation to ensure that all library users have free and equal access to the entire range of library services, materials, and programs. Therefore, the association strongly opposes any effort to limit access to information and ideas. The association also encourages librarians to proactively support the First Amendment rights of all library users, regardless of sex, gender identity, gender expression, or sexual orientation.

Economic Barriers to Information Access
An Interpretation of the *Library Bill of Rights*

Adopted June 30, 1993, by the ALA Council.

A historical essay about this statement can be found in the publication, *A History of ALA Policy on Intellectual Freedom: A Supplement to the Intellectual Freedom Manual, Ninth Edition.*

A DEMOCRACY PRESUPPOSES an informed citizenry. The First Amendment mandates the right of all persons to free expression, and the corollary right to receive the constitutionally protected expression of others. The publicly supported library provides free, equal, and equitable access to information for all people of the community the library serves. While the roles, goals and objectives of publicly supported libraries may differ, they share this common mission.

The library's essential mission must remain the first consideration for librarians and governing bodies faced with economic pressures and competition for funding. In support of this mission, the American Library Association has enumerated certain principles of library services in the *Library Bill of Rights*.

Principles Governing Fines, Fees, and User Charges

Article I of the *Library Bill of Rights* states:

> Books and other library resources should be provided for the interest, information, and enlightenment of all people of the community the library serves.

Article V of the *Library Bill of Rights* states:

> A person's right to use a library should not be denied or abridged because of origin, age, background, or views.

The American Library Association opposes the charging of user fees for the provision of information by all libraries and information services that receive their major support from public funds. All information resources that are provided directly or indirectly by the library, regardless of technology, format, or methods of delivery, should be readily, equally and equitably accessible to all library users.

Libraries that adhere to these principles systematically monitor their programs of service for potential barriers to access and strive to eliminate such barriers when they occur. All library policies and procedures, particularly those involving fines, fees, or other user charges, should be scrutinized for potential barriers to access. All services should be designed and implemented with care, so as not to infringe on or interfere with the provision or delivery of information and resources for all users. Services should be reevaluated regularly to ensure that the library's basic mission remains uncompromised.

Librarians and governing bodies should look for alternative models and methods of library administration that minimize distinctions among users based on their economic status or financial condition. They should resist the temptation to impose user fees to alleviate financial pressures, at long-term cost to institutional integrity and public confidence in libraries.

Library services that involve the provision of information, regardless of format, technology, or method of delivery, should be made available to all library users on an equal and equitable basis. Charging fees for the use of library collections, services, programs, or facilities that were purchased with public funds raises barriers to access. Such fees effectively abridge or deny access for some members of the community because they reinforce distinctions among users based on their ability and willingness to pay.

Principles Governing Conditions of Funding

Article II of the *Library Bill of Rights* states:

> Materials should not be proscribed or removed because of partisan or doctrinal disapproval.

Article III of the *Library Bill of Rights* states:

> Libraries should challenge censorship in the fulfillment of their responsibility to provide information and enlightenment.

Article IV of the *Library Bill of Rights* states:

> Libraries should cooperate with all persons and groups concerned with resisting abridgment of free expression and free access to ideas.

The American Library Association opposes any legislative or regulatory attempt to impose content restrictions on library resources, or to limit user access to information, as a condition of funding for publicly supported libraries and information services.

The First Amendment guarantee of freedom of expression is violated when the right to receive that expression is subject to arbitrary restrictions based on content.

Librarians and governing bodies should examine carefully any terms or conditions attached to library funding and should oppose attempts to limit through such conditions full and equal access to information because of content. This principle applies equally to private gifts or bequests and to public funds. In particular, librarians and governing bodies have an obligation to reject such restrictions when the effect of the restriction is to limit equal and equitable access to information.

Librarians and governing bodies should cooperate with all efforts to create a community consensus that publicly supported libraries require funding unfettered by restrictions. Such a consensus supports the library mission to provide the free and unrestricted exchange of information and ideas necessary to a functioning democracy.

The association's historic position in this regard is stated clearly in a number of association policies: B.4.2 "Free Access to Information," B.5.2 "Financing of Libraries," 51.2 "Equal Access to Library Service," 51.3 "Intellectual Freedom," B.2 "Intellectual Freedom Policies," B.11.1 "Policy Objectives," and B.8.10 "Library Services for the Poor."

Intellectual Freedom Principles for Academic Libraries

An Interpretation of the *Library Bill of Rights*

Approved June 29, 1999, by the ACRL Board of Directors; adopted July 12, 2000, by the ALA Council; amended July 1, 2014.

> A historical essay about this statement can be found in the publication, *A History of ALA Policy on Intellectual Freedom: A Supplement to the Intellectual Freedom Manual, Ninth Edition.*

A STRONG INTELLECTUAL freedom perspective is critical to the development of academic library collections, services, and instruction that dispassionately meet the education and research needs of a college or university community. The purpose of this statement is to outline how and where intellectual freedom principles fit into an academic library setting, thereby raising consciousness of the intellectual freedom context within which academic librarians work. The following principles should be reflected in all relevant library policy documents.

1. The general principles set forth in the *Library Bill of Rights* form an indispensable framework for building collections, services, and policies that serve the entire academic community.
2. The privacy of library users is and must be inviolable. Policies should be in place that maintains [*sic*] confidentiality of library borrowing records and of other information relating to personal use of library information and services.
3. The development of library collections in support of an institution's instruction and research programs should transcend the personal values of the selector. In the interests of research and learning, it is essential that collections contain materials representing a variety of perspectives on subjects that may be considered controversial.

4. Preservation and replacement efforts should ensure that balance in library materials is maintained and that controversial materials are not removed from the collections through theft, loss, mutilation, or normal wear and tear. There should be alertness to efforts by special interest groups to bias a collection though systematic theft or mutilation.

5. Licensing agreements should be consistent with the *Library Bill of Rights,* and should maximize access.

6. Open and unfiltered access to the Internet should be conveniently available to the academic community in a college or university library. Content filtering devices and content-based restrictions are a contradiction of the academic library mission to further research and learning through exposure to the broadest possible range of ideas and information. Such restrictions are a fundamental violation of intellectual freedom in academic libraries.

7. Freedom of information and of creative expression should be reflected in library exhibits and in all relevant library policy documents.

8. Library meeting rooms, research carrels, exhibit spaces, and other facilities should be available to the academic community regardless of research being pursued or subject being discussed. Any restrictions made necessary because of limited availability of space should be based on need, as reflected in library policy, rather than on content of research or discussion.

9. Whenever possible, library services should be available without charge in order to encourage inquiry. Where charges are necessary, a free or low-cost alternative (e.g., downloading to disc rather than printing) should be available when possible.

10. A service philosophy should be promoted that affords equal access to information for all in the academic community with no discrimination on the basis of race, age, values, gender, sexual orientation, gender identity, cultural or ethnic background, physical, sensory, cognitive or learning disability, economic status, religious beliefs, or views.

11. A procedure ensuring due process should be in place to deal with requests by those within and outside the academic community for removal or addition of library resources, exhibits, or services.

12. It is recommended that this statement of principle be endorsed by appropriate institutional governing bodies, including the faculty senate or similar instrument of faculty governance.

Prisoners' Right to Read

An Interpretation of the *Library Bill of Rights*

Adopted June 29, 2010, by the ALA Council; amended July 1, 2014.

A historical essay about this statement can be found in the publication, *A History of ALA Policy on Intellectual Freedom: A Supplement to the Intellectual Freedom Manual, Ninth Edition.*

THE AMERICAN LIBRARY Association asserts a compelling public interest in the preservation of intellectual freedom for individuals of any age held in jails, prisons, detention facilities, juvenile facilities, immigration facilities, prison work camps and segregated units within any facility. As Supreme Court Justice Thurgood Marshall wrote in *Procunier v. Martinez* (416 U.S. 428 [1974]):

> When the prison gates slam behind an inmate, he does not lose his human quality; his mind does not become closed to ideas; his intellect does not cease to feed on a free and open interchange of opinions; his yearning for self-respect does not end; nor is his quest for self-realization concluded. If anything, the needs for identity and self-respect are more compelling in the dehumanizing prison environment.

Participation in a democratic society requires unfettered access to current social, political, economic, cultural, scientific, and religious information. Information and ideas available outside the prison are essential to prisoners for a successful transition to freedom. Learning to be free requires access to a wide range of knowledge, and suppression of ideas does not prepare the incarcerated of any age for life in a free society. Even those individuals that a lawful society chooses to imprison permanently deserve access to information, to literature, and to a window on the world. Censorship is a process of exclusion by which authority rejects specific points of view. That material contains unpopular views or even repugnant content does not provide justification for censorship. Unlike censorship, selection is a process of inclusion that involves the search for resources, regardless of format, that represent diversity and a broad spectrum of ideas. The correctional library collection should reflect the needs of its community.

Libraries and librarians serving individuals in correctional facilities may be required by federal, state, or local laws; administrative rules of parent agencies; or court decisions to prohibit material that instructs, incites, or advocates criminal action or bodily harm or is a violation of the law. Only those items that present an actual compelling and imminent risk to safety and security should be restricted. Although these limits restrict the range of resources available, the extent of limitation should be minimized by adherence to the American Library Association's *Library Bill of Rights* and its interpretations.

These principles should guide all library services provided to prisoners:

- Collection management should be governed by written policy, mutually agreed upon by librarians and correctional agency administrators, in accordance with the *Library Bill of Rights,* its Interpretations, and other ALA intellectual freedom documents.
- Correctional libraries should have written procedures for addressing challenges to library resources, including a policy-based description of the disqualifying features, in accordance with "Challenged Resources" and other relevant intellectual freedom documents.
- Correctional librarians should select resources that reflect the demographic composition, information needs, interests, and diverse cultural values of the confined communities they serve.
- Correctional librarians should be allowed to purchase resources that meet written selection criteria and provide for the multi-faceted needs of their populations without prior correctional agency review. They should be allowed to acquire resources from a wide range of sources in order to ensure a broad and diverse collection. Correctional librarians should not be limited to purchasing from a list of approved resources.
- Age is not a reason for censorship. Incarcerated children and youth should have access to a wide range of library resources, as stated in "Access to Library Resources and Services for Minors."
- Correctional librarians should make all reasonable efforts to provide sufficient resources to meet the information and recreational needs of prisoners who speak languages other than English.
- Equitable access to information should be provided for persons with disabilities as outlined in "Services to Persons with Disabilities."
- Media or materials with non-traditional bindings should not be prohibited unless they present an actual compelling and imminent risk to safety and security.
- Resources with sexual content should not be banned unless they violate state and federal law.
- Correctional libraries should provide access to computers and the Internet.

When free people, through judicial procedure, segregate some of their own, they incur the responsibility to provide humane treatment and essential rights. Among these is the right to read. The right to choose what to read is deeply important, and the suppression of ideas is fatal to a democratic society. The denial of the right to read, to write, and to think—to intellectual freedom—diminishes the human spirit of those segregated from society. Those who cherish their full freedom and rights should work to guarantee that the right to intellectual freedom is extended to all incarcerated individuals.

Restricted Access to Library Materials
An Interpretation of the *Library Bill of Rights*

Adopted February 2, 1973, by the ALA Council; amended July 1, 1981; July 3, 1991; July 12, 2000; June 30, 2004; January 28, 2009; and July 1, 2014.

A historical essay about this statement can be found in the publication, *A History of ALA Policy on Intellectual Freedom: A Supplement to the Intellectual Freedom Manual, Ninth Edition.*

LIBRARIES ARE A traditional forum for the open exchange of information. Restricting access to library materials violates the basic tenets of the American Library Association's *Library Bill of Rights.*

Some libraries block access to certain materials by placing physical or virtual barriers between the user and those materials. For example, materials are sometimes labeled for content or placed in a "locked case," "adults only," "restricted shelf," or "high-demand" collection. Access to certain materials is sometimes restricted to protect them from theft or mutilation, or because of statutory authority or institutional mandate.

In some libraries, access is restricted based on computerized reading management programs that assign reading levels to books and/or users and limit choices to titles on the program's reading list. Titles not on the reading management list have been removed from the collection in some school libraries. Organizing collections by reading management program level, ability, grade, or age level is another example of restricted access. Even though the chronological age or grade level of users is not representative of their information needs or total reading abilities, users may feel inhibited from selecting resources located in areas that do not correspond to their assigned characteristics.

Physical restrictions and content filtering of library resources and services may generate psychological, service, or language skills barriers to access as well. Because restricted materials often deal with controversial, unusual, or sensitive subjects, having to ask a library worker for access to them may be embarrassing or inhibiting for patrons desiring access. Even when a title is listed in the catalog with a reference to its restricted status, a barrier is placed between the patron and the publication. (See also "Labeling and Rating Systems.") Because restricted materials often feature information that some people consider objectionable, potential library users may be predisposed to think of labeled and filtered resources as objectionable and be discouraged from asking for access to them.

Federal and some state statutes require libraries that accept specific types of federal and/or state funding to install content filters that limit access to Internet resources for minors and adults. Internet filters are [*sic*] applied to Internet resources in some libraries may prevent users from finding targeted categories of information, much of which is constitutionally protected. The use of Internet filters must be addressed through library policies and procedures to ensure that users receive information and that filters do not prevent users from exercising their First Amendment rights. Users have the right to unfiltered access to constitutionally protected information. (See also "Access to Digital Information, Services, and Networks.")

Library policies that restrict access to resources for any reason must be carefully formulated and administered to ensure they do not violate established principles of intellectual freedom. This caution is reflected in ALA policies, such as "Evaluating Library Collections," "Access to Library Services and Resources for Minors," "Preservation Policy," and the ACRL "Code of Ethics for Special Collections Librarians."

Donated resources require special consideration. In keeping with the "Joint Statement on Access" of the American Library Association and Society of American Archivists, libraries should avoid accepting donor agreements or entering into contracts that impose permanent restrictions on special collections. As stated in the "Joint Statement on Access," it is the responsibility of a library with such collections "to make available original research materials in its possession on equal terms of access."

A primary goal of the library profession is to facilitate access to all points of view on current and historical issues. All proposals for restricted access should be carefully scrutinized to ensure that the purpose is not to suppress a viewpoint or to place a barrier between users and content. Libraries must maintain policies and procedures that serve the diverse needs of their users and protect the First Amendment right to receive information.

Services to Persons with Disabilities
An Interpretation of the *Library Bill of Rights*

Adopted January 28, 2009, by the ALA Council.

THE AMERICAN LIBRARY Association recognizes that persons with disabilities are a large and often neglected part of society. In addition to many personal challenges, some persons with disabilities face economic inequity, illiteracy, cultural isolation, and discrimination in education, employment, and the broad range of societal activities. The library plays a catalytic role in their lives by facilitating their full participation in society.

A historical essay about this statement can be found in the publication, *A History of ALA Policy on Intellectual Freedom: A Supplement to the Intellectual Freedom Manual, Ninth Edition.*

The First Amendment to the U.S. Constitution mandates the right of all persons to free expression and the corollary right to receive the constitutionally protected expression of others. A person's right to use the library should not be denied or abridged because of disabilities. The library has the responsibility to provide materials "for the interest, information, and enlightenment of all people of the community the library serves." (See also the *Library Bill of Rights*.) When information in libraries is not presented in formats that are accessible to all users, discriminatory barriers are created.

Library staff should be proactive in reaching out to persons with disabilities and facilitating provision of resources and services. Library staff also should be aware of the available technologies and how to assist all users with library technology. All library resources should be available in formats accessible by persons of all ages with different abilities. These materials must not be restricted by any presuppositions about information needs, interests, or capacity for understanding. The library should offer different, necessary modes of access to the same content using equipment, electronics, or software. All information resources provided directly or indirectly by the library, regardless of technology, format, or method of delivery, should be readily, equally and equitably accessible to all library users. Libraries should make every effort to support the needs of their users with disabilities, and when necessary, should seek financial or other assistance to do so.

ALA recognizes that providing specialized services often requires retention of extensive patron records, such as a user's transaction histories. Libraries assume responsibility for protecting the confidentiality of all personally identifiable information entrusted to them to perform services.

II. 1
Access

Libraries should provide training opportunities for all staff and volunteers in order to sensitize them to issues affecting persons with disabilities and to teach effective techniques for providing services for users with disabilities and for working with colleagues with disabilities.

Libraries should use strategies based upon the principles of universal design to ensure that library facilities, policies, services, and resources meet the needs of all users. Libraries should provide a clear path for persons with disabilities to request accommodations that will enable them to participate fully in library programs and services. Further, libraries and schools should work with persons with disabilities, agencies, organizations, and vendors to integrate assistive technology into their facilities and services to meet the needs of persons with a broad range of disabilities, including learning, mobility, sensory, and developmental disabilities.

The preamble to the *Library Bill of Rights* states, "all libraries are forums for information and ideas." By removing the physical, technological, and procedural barriers to accessing those forums, libraries promote the full inclusion of persons with disabilities into our society.

The Universal Right to Free Expression
An Interpretation of the *Library Bill of Rights*

Adopted January 16, 1991, by the ALA Council; amended July 1, 2014.

A historical essay about this statement can be found in the publication, *A History of ALA Policy on Intellectual Freedom: A Supplement to the Intellectual Freedom Manual, Ninth Edition.*

FREEDOM OF EXPRESSION is an inalienable human right and the foundation for self-government. Freedom of expression encompasses the freedoms of speech, press, religion, assembly, and association, and the corollary right to receive information without interference and without compromising personal privacy.

The American Library Association endorses this principle, which is also set forth in the Universal Declaration of Human Rights, adopted by the United Nations General Assembly. The Preamble of this document states that ". . . recognition of the inherent dignity and of the equal and inalienable rights of all members of the human family is the foundation of freedom, justice, and peace in the world . . ." and ". . . the advent of a world in which human beings shall enjoy freedom of speech and belief and freedom from fear and want has been proclaimed as the highest aspiration of the common people. . . ."

Article 12 of this document states:

> No one shall be subjected to arbitrary interference with his privacy, family, home or correspondence, nor to attacks upon his honor or reputation. Everyone has the right to the protection of the law against such interference or attacks.

Article 18 of this document states:

> Everyone has the right to freedom of thought, conscience and religion; this right includes freedom to change his religion or belief, and freedom, either alone or in community with others and in public or private, to manifest his religion or belief in teaching, practice, worship and observance.

Article 19 states:

> Everyone has the right to freedom of opinion and expression; this right includes freedom to hold opinions without interference and to seek, receive and impart information and ideas through any media regardless of frontiers.

Article 20 states:

> 1. Everyone has the right to freedom of peaceful assembly and association.
> 2. No one may be compelled to belong to an association.

On December 18, 2013, the United Nations General Assembly adopted a resolution reaffirming that the right to personal privacy applies to the use of communications technology and digital records, and requiring the governments of member nations to "respect and protect" the privacy rights of individuals.

We affirm our belief that these are inalienable rights of every person, regardless of origin, age, background, or views. We embody our professional commitment to these principles in the *Library Bill of Rights* and *Code of Ethics,* as adopted by the American Library Association.

We maintain that these are universal principles and should be applied by libraries and librarians throughout the world. The American Library Association's policy on International Relations reflects these objectives: ". . . to encourage the exchange, dissemination, and access to information and the unrestricted flow of library materials in all formats throughout the world."

We know that censorship, ignorance, and manipulation are the tools of tyrants and profiteers. We support the principles of net neutrality, transparency, and accountability. We maintain that both government and corporate efforts to suppress, manipulate, or intercept personal communications and search queries with minimal oversight or accountability, and without user consent, is oppressive and discriminatory. The technological ability of commercial and government interests to engage in the massive collection and aggregation of personally identifiable information without due process and transparency is an abuse of the public trust and inimical to privacy and free expression. We believe that everyone benefits when each individual is treated with respect, and ideas and information are freely shared, openly debated, and vigorously tested in the market of public experience.

The American Library Association is unswerving in its commitment to human rights, but cherishes a particular commitment to privacy and free expression; the two are inseparably linked and inextricably entwined with the professional practice of librarianship. We believe that the rights of privacy and free expression are not derived from any claim of political, racial, economic, or cultural hegemony. These rights are inherent in every individual. They cannot be surrendered or subordinated, nor can they be denied, by the decree of any government, or corporate interest. True justice and equality depend upon the constant exercise of these rights.

We recognize the power of information and ideas to inspire justice, to restore freedom and dignity to the exploited and oppressed, to change the hearts and minds of the oppressors, and to offer opportunities for a better life to all people.

Courageous people, in difficult and dangerous circumstances throughout human history, have demonstrated that freedom lives in the human heart and cries out for justice even in the face of threats, enslavement, imprisonment, torture, exile, and death. We draw inspiration from their example. They challenge us to remain steadfast in our most basic professional responsibility to promote and defend the rights of privacy and free expression.

There is no good censorship. Any effort to restrict free expression and the free flow of information through any media and regardless of frontiers aids discrimination and oppression. Fighting oppression with censorship is self-defeating. There is no meaningful freedom for the individual without personal privacy. A society that does not respect the privacy of the individual will be blind to the erosion of its rights and liberties.

Threats to the privacy and freedom of expression of any person anywhere are threats to the privacy and freedom of all people everywhere. Violations of these human rights have been recorded in virtually every country and society across the globe. Vigilance in protecting these rights is our best defense.

In response to these violations, we affirm these principles:

The American Library Association opposes any use of governmental prerogative that leads to the intimidation of individuals that prevents them from exercising their rights to hold opinions without interference, and to seek, receive, and impart information and ideas. We urge libraries and librarians everywhere to resist such abuse of governmental power, and to support those against whom such governmental power has been employed.

The American Library Association condemns any governmental effort to involve libraries and librarians in restrictions on the right of any individual to hold opinions without interference, and to seek, receive, and impart information and ideas. Such restrictions, whether enforced by statutes or regulations, contractual stipulations, or voluntary agreements, pervert the function of the library and violate the professional responsibilities of librarians.

The American Library Association rejects censorship in any form. Any action that denies the inalienable human rights of individuals only damages the will to resist oppression, strengthens the hand of the oppressor, and undermines the cause of justice.

The American Library Association will not abrogate these principles. We believe that censorship corrupts the cause of justice, and contributes to the demise of freedom.

A DEEPER LOOK

The Law Regarding Access to the Library: User-Behavior Rules

Theresa Chmara

COURTS GENERALLY HAVE held that the public library is a designated or limited public forum for the receipt of information. Restrictions on access to the library itself must, therefore, be evaluated with First Amendment principles in mind. This critical issue was first considered in the case of *Kreimer v. Bureau of Police for the Town of Morristown.*[1] Richard Kreimer, a homeless man, was banned from the public library in Morristown, New Jersey, for disrupting library users and because his personal hygiene was offensive to other users. He sued the library in federal court. The Third Circuit appellate court held unequivocally that the First Amendment protects the right to receive information and "includes the right to some level of access to a public library, the quintessential locus of the receipt of information."[2]

> **What's a "Public Forum"?**
>
> This essay uses the term *public forum*. To learn more about what that means and how it applies to libraries, please read part I, chapter 4, "The Right to Receive Information: Libraries, the First Amendment, and the Public Forum Doctrine." (p.43)

The appellate court emphasized, however, that public libraries are quintessential designated or limited public forums for *access to information*, but not, unless specifically authorized by the library, for engaging in other types of expressive activities (such as making speeches or distributing pamphlets). The court found that the Morristown Library had "intentionally opened the Library to the public" for "specified purposes: reading, studying, using the Library materials."[3] The court thus held that the library has the right to establish reasonable rules governing library use and that the library's power to regulate user behavior is *not* limited to cases of "actual disruption." The court held specifically that libraries may regulate non-expressive activity designed to promote safety or efficient access to materials. Importantly, the *Kreimer* case settled before the court had an opportunity to apply these general principles to the particular facts of the case and determine whether the Morristown rules were applied in a constitutional manner to Richard Kreimer.[4]

The principles established by the *Kreimer* case have been applied and expanded by numerous courts. Critically, however, a restriction upheld as constitutional in one library setting may not necessarily be upheld in another. In each case, the courts will evaluate whether the particular library had a compelling need for the restriction in light of its particular mission.

The cases demonstrate the types of issues raised by restrictions on access. For example, in *Brinkmeier v. City of Freeport,* a library user was served with a notice prohibiting him from entering the library on the ground that he had harassed a library employee in a location removed from the library premises.[5] Relying on *Kreimer,* the district court held that library users have a First Amendment right to access the public library but that the right has some limits. The court held that Freeport's policy against harassment was unreasonable for the following reasons: (1) it was unwritten and broadly stated, (2) there was no definition of terms such as "harassing" and "intimidation," (3) the expulsion was not tied to use of the library by other users or employees, (4) the policy did not have geographical limitations in that it seemed to apply to conduct occurring outside the library, and (5) there was no formal or informal procedure for challenging denial of access to the library.[6] Of course, the library employee would have recourse to other remedies, such as applying for a stay-away order through the courts that would prevent the person harassing her from approaching her anywhere, including her place of employment.

Similarly, in *Armstrong v. District of Columbia Public Library,* a user's exclusion from the library on the ground that his appearance was "objectionable" was deemed unconstitutional.[7] The district court held that the standard was unconstitutionally vague and overbroad: "It threatens to compromise access to information and ideas found within the Library's limited public forum by directly precluding, or otherwise discouraging, use of the D.C. Public Library system by persons that Library staff, in their discretion, find objectionable."[8] The court also held that the appearance rule violated the user's due process rights: "Not only does the vague appearance regulation increase the risk of discriminatory decisions regarding library access, its arbitrary nature and application prevents the type of uniform decision-making required to provide fair notice of what hygiene conditions will be prohibited."[9]

By contrast, the court will uphold exclusions where the rules are objective and precisely defined and the library offers some process, formal or informal, for appeal. For example, in *Neinast v. Board of Trustees,* a court upheld the constitutionality of evicting a barefoot user from library premises.[10] The district court held that the library was a limited public forum but that the shoe requirement was constitutional: "The shoe requirement is a valid, content-neutral regulation that promotes communication of the written word in a safe and sanitary condition" because "as evidenced by various incident reports, the Library's floor sometimes contains feces, semen, blood, and broken glass, all of which pose a significant danger to barefoot individuals."[11] The Sixth Circuit appellate court affirmed the trial court's decision, concluding that the shoe requirement was narrowly drawn to achieve the goal of protecting barefoot users from harm that might come to them from materials found on the library floors and to protect the library itself from the potential of lawsuits and litigation costs if sued by a user for injuries sustained while barefoot.[12]

Thus, when crafting policies on use of the public library and its various services, library officials must ensure that the policies are (1) written, (2) objective, (3) consistently enforced, (4) reasonable and related to library use, and (5) accompanied by an appeal mechanism, even if that mechanism is informal.

NOTES

1. *Kreimer v. Bureau of Police for the Town of Morristown,* 958 F.2d 1242 (3d Cir. 1992).

2. *Id.* at 1255.

3. *Id.* at 1259-60.

4. In examining constitutional challenges, a court must determine if a restriction is facially unconstitutional or unconstitutional as applied. A statute will be deemed facially unconstitutional if it could never be applied in a constitutional manner. If a statute is facially constitutional, then a court examines whether it has been applied in an unconstitutional manner to the complaining party.

5. *Brinkmeier v. City of Freeport* (Case No. 93C 20039), 1993 U.S. Dist. Lexis 9255 (N.D. Ill. July 2, 1993).

6. *Id.;* see also *Wayfield v. Town of Tisbury,* 925 F. Supp. 880, 884-85 (D. Mass. 1996) (holding that a library card was a type of license giving its holder access to the library, deprivation of which infringed upon a liberty or property right requiring the library to provide due process before imposing restrictions on the right to enter the library).

7. *Armstrong v. District of Columbia Public Library,* 154 F. Supp. 2d 67, 75 (D.D.C. 2001).

8. *Id.* at 79.

9. *Id.* at 81.

10. *Neinast v. Board of Trustees,* 190 F. Supp. 2d 1040 (S.D. Ohio 2002), *aff'd,* 346 F.3d 585 (6th Cir. 2003), *cert. denied,* 541 U.S. 990 (2004).

11. *Id.* at 1044.

12. *Neinast v. Board of Trustees,* 346 F.3d 585 (6th Cir. 2003), *cert. denied,* 541 U.S. 990 (2004); *see also People v. Taylor,* 630 N.Y.S.2d 625, 164 Misc. 2d 868 (N.Y. Sup. Ct. 1995) (upholding the conviction for trespass of a user who

violated a ban against playing cards and board games in the library after being unsuccessful in his attempt to have the library lift its ban and despite being requested by the director of the library and three police officers to abide by the library rules).

Censorship, Challenged Resources, and Internet Filtering

ISSUE AT A GLANCE

Key Concepts

- Individuals have a right to express their opinions about library resources and services.
- Libraries should select resources according to their collection development policies, and they should have formal procedures for reconsideration of challenged resources. Challenged resources should remain in the collection during the reconsideration process, and resources that meet the criteria for selection should not be removed.
- Resources should not be removed from the collection because of partisan or doctrinal disapproval or because of the origin, background, or views of the author(s) or creator(s).
- The use of Internet filters to block constitutionally protected speech, including content on social networking and gaming sites, compromises First Amendment freedoms and the core values of librarianship. Internet safety for children and adults is best addressed through educational programs that teach people how to find and evaluate information.

Need help handling a challenge?

- Contact the intellectual freedom committee of your state or regional library association. Consult the ALA Office for "Intellectual Freedom" website (www.ala.org/oif) for contact information.
- Contact the ALA Office for Intellectual Freedom at (800) 545–2433, ext. 4223.

Please Report Challenges to ALA

- Use the reporting form at www.ala.org/bbooks/challengedmaterials/reporting.
- All information is kept confidential. ALA reports information about challenges only in aggregate or after the challenge has been reported in the press.

What Does the Law Say?

- The U. S. Constitution protects free expression and the corollary right to receive the constitutionally protected expression of others. The Supreme Court has held that the Bill of Rights of the U.S. Constitution requires a procedure to examine critically all challenged expression before it can be suppressed.
- Libraries that do not receive funding for Internet access through the E-rate discount program or LSTA grants are not subject to the Children's Internet Protection Act and are not required to use Internet filters. No library is required to seek or accept such funding.
- "Pornography" is *not* a legal term. It is frequently used to refer to materials that are sexually explicit or considered by some to be objectionable, but often those materials are protected by the First Amendment. In contrast, "obscenity" and "child pornography" *are* terms of law, and materials so designated by a court of law are not protected by the First Amendment. "Harmful to minors" is a legal term identifying sexually themed materials that are constitutionally protected for adults but are restricted for minors. (Please see the "Glossary of Terms" for definitions.)

Creating Policy for Your Library

- Consider formally adopting the *Library Bill of Rights* and the *Code of Ethics of the American Library Association* as policy for your library (see part I, chapter 2). They contain statements about resisting censorship and not removing materials based on partisan or doctrinal disapproval.
- Be sure you have a collection development policy that covers resources in all formats, including online resources and websites, and that you follow it (see part I, chapter 3).
- In your collection development policy, include a procedure for reconsideration of challenged resources (see part I, chapter 3).

Especially for Academic Libraries

- Academic libraries are sometimes pressured to remove resources that are considered "unscholarly," "pseudoscience," or offensive to groups (e.g., Holocaust denial literature). Academic libraries usually include these holdings for the purpose of studying the controversy or for the historical record.
- See also "Intellectual Freedom Principles for Academic Libraries" in part II, chapter 1.

Especially for Public Libraries

- As challenges often start at the front desk or in the shelves, it's important that all staff members understand the library's reconsideration policy and know the proper procedures for responding to a library user's concerns. It's also important to educate the library's governing body about the process and why public libraries include materials that may be considered controversial.

Especially for School Libraries

- The courts have distinguished between a school board's control over materials used in the curriculum (used by all students) and those within the school library collection, which is a "marketplace of ideas" (*Right to Read Defense Committee v. School Committee of the City of Chelsea*). If a resource has been selected using a school's collection development policy, it should not be removed without due process.
- School libraries should guard against filtering the Internet beyond the requirements of CIPA and state law and thereby restricting students' access to constitutionally protected resources. School districts should have a process for unblocking sites that do not include images that are obscene, child pornography, or defined by a court of law as "harmful to minors."
- Public school libraries should guard against "viewpoint discrimination," the act of favoring or promoting materials that advance a particular point of view on a potentially controversial topic. School libraries should provide access to resources that present a range of views on such topics.

To Learn More

- Visit the ALA "Intellectual Freedom" website (www.ala.org/advocacy/ intfreedom) for links to information about censorship, challenges, Internet filtering, and banned books.
- For a list of state Internet filtering laws, see www.ncsl.org/research/ telecommunications-and-information-technology/state-internet -filtering-laws.aspx.
- Read *Fencing Out Knowledge: Impacts of the Children's Internet Protection Act 10 Years Later,* Kristin Batch, ALA Office for Information Technology Policy and ALA Office for Intellectual Freedom, 2014, available at www.ala.org/offices/sites/ala.org.offices/files/content/ oitp/publications/issuebriefs/cipa_report.pdf.

Questions for Reflection

- What are the steps in your reconsideration process? How frequently is the process reviewed with staff?
- How does Internet filtering differ from making selection decisions for library materials?
- The author of a popular and controversial nonfiction book admits to falsifying some of her data. You have multiple copies in your collection. What do you do?

OFFICIAL ALA POLICY STATEMENTS

Challenged Resources
An Interpretation of the *Library Bill of Rights*

Formerly titled "Challenged Materials—An Interpretation of the Library Bill of Rights." *Adopted June 25, 1971, by the ALA Council; amended July 1, 1981; January 10, 1990; January 28, 2009; and July 1, 2014.*

A historical essay about this statement can be found in the publication, *A History of ALA Policy on Intellectual Freedom: A Supplement to the Intellectual Freedom Manual, Ninth Edition.*

LIBRARIES: AN AMERICAN VALUE states, "We protect the rights of individuals to express their opinions about library resources and services." The American Library Association declares as a matter of firm principle that it is the responsibility of every library to have a clearly defined written policy for collection development that includes a procedure for review of challenged resources. Collection development applies to print and media resources or formats in the physical collection. It also applies to digital resources such as databases, e-books and other downloadable and streaming media.

Content filtering is not equivalent to collection development. Content filtering is exclusive, not inclusive, and cannot effectively curate content or mediate access to resources available on the Internet. This should be addressed separately in the library's acceptable use policy. These policies reflect the American Library Association's *Library Bill of Rights* and are approved by the appropriate governing authority.

Challenged resources should remain in the collection and accessible during the review process. The *Library Bill of Rights* states in Article I that "Materials should not be excluded because of the origin, background, or views of those contributing to their creation," and in Article II, that "Materials should not be proscribed or removed because of partisan or doctrinal disapproval." Freedom of expression is protected by the Constitution of the United States, but constitutionally protected expression is often separated from unprotected expression only by a dim and uncertain line. The Supreme Court has held that the Constitution requires a procedure designed to examine critically all challenged expression before it can be suppressed.[1] This procedure should be open, transparent, and conform to all applicable open meeting and public records laws. Resources that meet the criteria for selection and inclusion within the collection should not be removed.

Therefore, any attempt, be it legal or extra-legal,[2] to regulate or suppress resources in libraries must be closely scrutinized to the end that protected expression is not abridged.

NOTES

1. *Bantam Books, Inc. v. Sullivan*, 372 U.S. 58 (1963).

2. "Extra-legal" refers to actions that are not regulated or sanctioned by law. These can include attempts to remove or suppress materials by library staff and library board members that circumvent the library's collection development policy, or actions taken by elected officials or library board members outside the established legal process for making legislative or board decisions. "Legal process" includes challenges to library materials initiated and conducted pursuant to the library's collection development policy, actions taken by legislative bodies or library boards during official sessions or meetings, or litigation undertaken in courts of law with jurisdiction over the library and the library's governing body.

Expurgation of Library Resources
An Interpretation of the *Library Bill of Rights*

Formerly titled "Expurgation of Library Materials—An Interpretation of the Library Bill of Rights.*" Adopted February 2, 1973, by the ALA Council; amended July 1, 1981; January 10, 1990; July 2, 2008; and July 1, 2014.*

A historical essay about this statement can be found in the publication, *A History of ALA Policy on Intellectual Freedom: A Supplement to the Intellectual Freedom Manual, Ninth Edition.*

EXPURGATING LIBRARY RESOURCES is a violation of the American Library Association's *Library Bill of Rights*. Expurgation as defined by this interpretation includes any deletion, excision, alteration, editing, or obliteration of any part of a library resource by administrators, employees, governing authorities, parent institutions (if any), or third party vendors when done for the purposes of censorship. Such action stands in violation of Articles I, II, and III of the *Library Bill of Rights*, which state that "Materials should not be excluded because of the origin, background, or views of those contributing to their creation," "Materials should not be proscribed or removed because of partisan or doctrinal disapproval," and "Libraries should challenge censorship in the fulfillment of their responsibility to provide information and enlightenment."

The act of expurgation denies access to the complete work and the entire spectrum of ideas that the work is intended to express. This is censorship. Expurgation based on the premise that certain portions of a work may be harmful to minors is equally a violation of the *Library Bill of Rights.*

Expurgation without permission from the rights holder may violate the copyright provisions of the United States Code.

The decision of rights holders to alter or expurgate future versions of a work does not impose a duty on librarians to alter or expurgate earlier versions of a work. Librarians should resist such requests in the interest of historical preservation and opposition to censorship. Furthermore, librarians oppose expurgation of resources available through licensed collections. Expurgation of any library resource imposes a restriction, without regard to the rights and desires of all library users, by limiting access to ideas and information.

A DEEPER LOOK

How to Respond to Challenges and Concerns about Library Resources

Kristin Pekoll and Helen R. Adams

LIBRARIES ARE THE only place dedicated to serving the information needs of everyone in the community. As such, they collect and make available a wide variety of information resources representing the range of human thought and experience. With such a wide spectrum of ideas and information available, it is inevitable that people will occasionally encounter resources they believe to be offensive or inappropriate. They may complain and request that such resources be removed. Below are step-by-step suggestions about how to respond.

A historical essay about this statement can be found in the publication, *A History of ALA Policy on Intellectual Freedom: A Supplement to the Intellectual Freedom Manual, Ninth Edition.*

These suggestions are not enough, however. Every library should have a collection development policy approved by its governing body. In addition to outlining the process and criteria for selecting resources, the policy should describe the procedure the library staff will follow when a user requests that a resource be reconsidered. (See part I, chapter 3, for guidelines about writing policy.) Having a policy and procedure in place will help library staff deal confidently and fairly with users who express concerns.

What Is a Challenge?

A challenge is an attempt to remove or restrict resources, based on the objections of a person or group. Challenges do not simply involve a person expressing a point of view; rather, they are an attempt to remove material from the curriculum or library, thereby restricting the access of others. Challenges sometimes lead to censorship.

In 1986 the ALA Intellectual Freedom Committee developed definitions to clarify terminology associated with challenges, and revised those definitions in 2014. Please see the "challenges" entry in the "Glossary of Terms" for definitions of the following:

- Expression of concern/oral complaint
- Challenge
- Request for reconsideration
- Public challenge
- Censorship

Throughout the process, it is critically important that library workers remain calm, respectful, and courteous. There is no reason to become defensive when a complaint is made. Not only is this counterproductive, but it runs counter to library efforts to encourage user involvement.

If the library has no collection development policy with a review process, affirm the principles of intellectual freedom found in the *Library Bill of Rights* as you respond to the challenge. Two relevant ALA documents to read are "Challenged Resources: An Interpretation of the *Library Bill of Rights*" (see part II, chapter 2) and "Access to Library Resources and Services for Minors: An Interpretation of the *Library Bill of Rights*" (see part II, chapter 3).

All challenges, regardless of the source, should be handled in the same way and in accordance with policy. Do not make exceptions in the reconsideration process based on whether the challenge is submitted by a member of the public or by a library worker or volunteer.

Oral Complaints and Expressions of Concern

Oral complaints can occur at any time. Library workers and educators who receive such expressions of concern should courteously refer them to the person responsible for responding to concerns, who should take the following steps:

1. Acknowledge that every person has the right to question library resources, and a library user with a complaint should feel confident that her concerns will be taken seriously. Listen thoughtfully and respectfully. Try to elicit the specific reason for her concern, whether she has read the entire work or only parts, and the specific action she would like library staff to take.

Seeking Support and Reporting Challenges

Challenges can be stressful. Find a loyal personal friend or colleague with whom you can discuss the situation confidentially and not be concerned that your words will be repeated to others. Avoid blogs and discussion lists where it is easy for communication to fall into the wrong hands or for misinformation to spread.

Call the American Library Association's Office for Intellectual Freedom (even if you're not a member of ALA) at (800) 545–2433, ext. 4223. Dedicated, experienced professionals are available weekdays by phone from 8:30 to 4:30 (Central time) or any time by e-mail. In addition to listening, OIF staff can provide advice, strategies, book reviews, and letters of support to school boards and library authorities. The office also maintains a confidential database of challenges to track trends and responses.

You may also consider contacting your state library association's intellectual freedom committee and other local library groups. OIF has contacts in state intellectual freedom organizations and can provide contact information for other resources in your state.

2. Do not make promises of taking action or appear to agree with the individual. Instead, offer assistance in finding something else that would better meet the person's needs.

3. If the person requests the item be removed from the library's collection, explain that although the individual may be offended by the library resource, others may not have the same perspective. Describe how library materials are selected. Libraries have diverse collections with materials from many points of view, and a library's mission is to provide access to information for all users. All library users have the First Amendment right to borrow, read, view, and listen to library resources.

4. If the individual is concerned about a children's or young adult resource, explain that parents and guardians play the major role in guiding their children's or wards' reading and library use. Often a person's concern about a children's or young adult book involves a desire to "protect all children" by removing that item from the collection or restricting access to it. Explain that each family has the right to determine which library materials are acceptable for its children and must accord the same right to other parents.

5. Many expressions of concern end after the individual has had an opportunity to express personal feelings about a library resource. The person only wanted to be heard and have his opinions acknowledged. No further action is needed. If this is the case, thank the person for his interest, make notes about the conversation, and file them for future reference. Additionally, report the conversation to the library director or principal.

6. If the concerned individual is not satisfied during the discussion and wants the item removed, explain the formal reconsideration process and its time line. Often persons who have a concern would like immediate action and are not aware of the length of time this procedure takes. State what your policy says about the availability of the material during the reconsideration process. Best practice is that the material under reconsideration will not be removed from use or have access restricted pending completion of the process.

7. Provide a copy of the library's collection development policy and reconsideration form. Stress that no action is taken unless the form is fully completed, signed (identifying the individual or group), and submitted. Explain that the submission of a completed form will trigger the formal reconsideration process, and that the document will become part of the public record.

8. After the conversation, make notes about the conversation, date them, and retain the information to provide background in the event that a request for formal reconsideration form is filed. Remember that all such notes become part of the record of the reconsideration process and may become public records.

9. Keep your director or principal informed of any concerns expressed, whether you feel they have been successfully resolved or not. Knowing that a concern was expressed helps that individual respond knowledgeably if the concerned person contacts her.

When the Reconsideration Process Is Subverted or Undermined

If after discussing the legal and ethical reasons for following the reconsideration process, the principal or library director does not follow policy and removes the challenged resource (or one about which a concern has been raised), how far should a librarian go to defend a library resource?

This is a personal, ethical decision, and the librarian must weigh what else can be done. If the director or principal is adamant, the librarian may be forced to evaluate the risk of retaliation from his supervisor or losing a job against the merits of continuing to oppose censorship by a supervisor. After considering the situation carefully, he may come to acknowledge that he has done all that is possible at this time, or he may decide that taking a principled stand is better for him.

The process can also be compromised if the concerned individual or group goes around the policy structure to speak directly to a higher authority such as an alderman, school superintendent, or school board members. Although the public official or school administrator should remind the challenger that there is a review process in place, this does not always occur.

Working with the Media

At any time, others may become aware of a library challenge, from word of mouth about a verbal complaint, from a blog by the individual or group who filed the challenge, or from a board agenda posted publicly in the community. The concerned individual(s) may use the media to share their viewpoint and attempt to sway public opinion. Rumors and opinions can escalate a challenge into a media wildfire.

In these circumstances, it is important that the library or school district speak with one official voice: the library director, principal, superintendent, or other designated spokesperson. Everyone else on the library or school staff should decline to make statements or answer questions and should refer media inquiries to the spokesperson. The common talking point for all libraries involved in a challenge is the freedom to read and access to information.

When appropriate, as the challenge becomes public, library and school district administrators may seek the support of local media. Informing local civic organizations of the facts and enlisting their support may counter negative, one-sided media coverage with moderate, tempered discussion. See part III, chapter 1, for more information about working with the media and dealing with controversy and negative publicity.

Formal Written Requests for Reconsideration

If the library receives a completed reconsideration form, the person or group designated in library policy to handle challenges should take the following steps:

1. Respond quickly to the individual, acknowledging that the formal reconsideration request has been received, restating the steps in the process, and reviewing the time line.

2. Review the complaint carefully. Was the form completed by an individual with personal concerns or a person representing a group? Look at the reason(s) for the challenge. Has the individual read the entire resource or only specified parts? What action is the person requesting? Does the person seek to have the resource removed from the collection, restricted (e.g., requiring minors to provide written permission from a parent or guardian), reclassified and moved to a different location (e.g., young-adult to adult section or middle school to high school library), or another action such as labeling the book to alert potential readers (e.g., "sexually explicit" or "mature")?

3. Prepare a one-page document overviewing for the library director or the school's principal/superintendent the book's title, summary of the plot or content, selection criteria met by the resource, list of positive reviews, awards received, and a brief summary of the recon-

sideration process.[1] For your knowledge, it is helpful to determine how often the resource has been checked out and how many libraries in the local area, the school district, or the state own the resource.

4. Meet with the library director or the school's principal to discuss the challenge and how to proceed. Review the reconsideration process with him to ensure that the board-approved policy is followed. If an administrator is tempted to acquiesce to a demand to remove a library resource without due process, explain the legal and ethical issues involved. Circumventing policy may put a school district or library in legal jeopardy of a lawsuit if a library resource is removed without following the official reconsideration process.[2] Such action also sends the message that the policy does not matter, and it is easy to remove a resource from a library—a message that can easily spread. The *Code of Ethics of the American Library Association* directs library professionals to "uphold the principles of intellectual freedom and resist all efforts to censor library resources."[3]

5. Follow your library's reconsideration procedure exactly, even if it seems outdated, redundant, or incorrect. The procedure can be updated later. The review process must be transparent and objective, and should include the following general steps. (Review the boxes that follow this list of steps for more detail about how challenges are typically handled in public, school, and academic libraries.)

   - Read or reread the book or listen to or view the work in question.
   - Determine if the resource meets the selection criteria in the library's collection development policy.
   - Decide whether or not the resource will be retained.
   - Send a written letter informing the person of the decision. Address the letter to the individual; do not use an impersonal form letter. Explain how she may appeal the decision if desired, and inform her that appealing the decision will require disclosing the complaint on the agenda of the entity that handles appeals, and in other documents.

6. Update staff in your library or school about the reconsideration process, but be aware of the potential for open records requests. Keep personal opinions and emotional responses out of all official communications. Paper and electronic documents can be obtained and viewed by anyone who submits a request through the proper channels. If you have questions, check with the library's legal counsel.

7. When the final decision about the questioned resource has been made, keep a record of the event, and report the result to the ALA Office for Intellectual Freedom using its Online Challenge Reporting Form, available at www.ala.org/bbooks/challengedmaterials/reporting. OIF will keep confidential the details of the challenge, using the information only for statistical purposes.

If You Hold a Public Hearing . . .

If a challenge rises to the level of an appeal, your library's reconsideration process may or may not call for a public hearing by your governing board as part of the appeal process. If it does, the following tips may be helpful.

Before the Hearing:

- Brief members of the governing body on:
    - The library collection development policy
    - How the library has responded to the challenge and the decision made
    - Policies and procedures (including open meeting laws) that should be followed

- Have all members of the governing body read, view, or listen to the challenged resource in its entirety.

- Decide ahead of time on the length of the hearing and set definite beginning and ending times.

- Announce the hearing well in advance.

- Prepare a news release covering the facts, and make it available to media representatives who attend or ask questions, along with a copy of the *Library Bill of Rights* and your library's collection development policy. It is important that the media and the public understand that the library's decisions are not arbitrary, but based on a great deal of work, thought, and consultation.

- Seek support from ally groups and individuals who can speak in support of the freedom to read, view, and listen, or who can send written expressions of support (e.g., attorneys, educators, students, librarians, ministers, people from the media, your state intellectual freedom committee, local colleges and universities, educational groups).

At the Hearing:

- Distribute copies of the *Library Bill of Rights* and your library's collection development policy.

- Ask people who wish to speak to sign in.

- Have the chair of the board preside. At the beginning of the hearing, she should explain the process the governing body will follow and when it will issue its decision.

- Have individuals speak in the order they signed in, and appoint a timekeeper to limit each speaker to a specific amount of time. If you allow participants to speak a second time, do so only after everyone who has registered has had an opportunity to speak.

8. After the challenge is completed, reflect on what was accomplished. For example, if the resource was retained in the collection, users still have access to the information or fiction book. Did you learn something that can be applied to the next challenge? Did you garner new allies? Should lines of communication with civic, religious, educational, or political bodies of the community, and local media be strengthened? Can this experience be used as the basis for library advocacy to the entire community? Also, analyze the reconsideration process for weaknesses and omissions and create a list of possible changes that would improve the process. Meet with the library director or the principal to discuss whether the timing is right for revising the policy.

ADDITIONAL INFORMATION FOR PUBLIC LIBRARIES

The library's collection development and reconsideration policy determines who reviews the challenge. For example, the objections may be reviewed by the librarian(s) in charge of the collection or the director, depending on the size of the library. Some library procedures include a formal meeting with the individual, while others take the reconsideration form as explanation enough. The policy generally outlines the basis for review and designates the position or group that makes the decision and informs the initiator of the challenge by letter. The letter should include the decision and information on the library's appeal process.

If the individual decides to appeal, the item should be placed on the board meeting agenda, and the user should be informed of the date, time, and place of the meeting. Librarians should consult with their attorneys for advice about how to comply with open meeting laws. The board should receive documentation to review before the meeting, including the original written complaint, an overview of the item being challenged (summary, location in the library, reviews, recommended lists, circulation statistics, and local, system, and state ownership details), the librarian's initial decision, and the letter to the library user informing him of the initial decision. Encourage the board to review the challenged item in its entirety. Offer to obtain copies for anyone who would like to review the resource prior to the public hearing. The board will review and debate the original decision and may or may not invite comment from the user and/or the public according to library procedures. In most cases, the library board's decision is final.

ADDITIONAL INFORMATION FOR SCHOOL LIBRARIES

When a fully completed reconsideration form is received, the principal will assemble a reconsideration committee to review the challenged resource. To assist the committee's work, the librarian should provide a copy of the challenged resource to each committee member, information about the resource (reviews, recommended lists, awards received, how it meets collection development policy selection criteria), and a copy of the form completed by the individual initiating the challenge. The committee should discuss and weigh the merits and deficiencies of the work in relation to its intended educational, recreational, personal, or extracurricular purposes and use by students and make a written decision to the superintendent to retain, remove, or move the challenged work to another level. The concerned individual will receive a copy of the reconsideration committee's written decision (usually sent by the superintendent, principal, or other administrator who served on the reconsideration committee), and if not satisfied, she may appeal the decision to the school board.

If there is an appeal, the school board will make the final decision on the disposition of the challenged work at a board meeting. The person bringing the challenge will be informed of the date, time, and place. Prior to the special meeting, the superintendent should review with board members their role and responsibilities. Each should receive a packet of information that includes a copy of the work (or an opportunity to review it), the selection and reconsideration policy, a summary of the work's content, reviews, recommended lists, awards received, an analysis of how the work meets collection development policy selection criteria, the reconsideration form, the written decision of the reconsideration committee, and the letter informing the individual of the committee's decision. During its special meeting, the board will review and discuss the reconsideration committee's decision and may invite the individual who submitted the challenge to speak. Additionally, the board may invite public comments, depending on its reconsideration process. Board members will reach a decision, which is final, concluding the reconsideration of the library resource. The superintendent will notify the individual formally by letter of the school board's decision.

ADDITIONAL INFORMATION FOR ACADEMIC LIBRARIES

Academic libraries should have written policies for handling requests from administrators, faculty and staff members, students, parents, alumni, donors, legislators, or board members to remove books or block access to controversial content. Such requests should be submitted to the team of people that makes collection development decisions. That team should evaluate the material to determine if it meets the collection development criteria and issue a written response to the person making the request. The response should include information about the library's appeal process. In academic libraries, appeals are usually handled by the library dean or director.

Book challenges in an academic library are not likely to be about immorality or sexually explicit images. They are likely to be arguments that a particular work is too popular, that it is offensive to women or another group, that the content is not scholarly and is therefore inappropriate for academic research, or that its conclusions are scientifically incorrect or inaccurate. Academic librarians should be aware that the excuse of "unscholarly" may be used to challenge the presence of controversial content in the library. As in public and school libraries, the collection should contain various viewpoints so that library users may learn about and examine them.

NOTES

1. Gail Dickinson, "The Challenges of CHALLENGES: What to Do?" *School Library Media Activities Monthly* 23, no. 6 (February 2007): 22, Academic Search Complete, EBSCO*host*.

2. Ibid.

3. American Library Association, *Code of Ethics of the American Library Association*, last modified January 22, 2008, www.ala.org/advocacy/proethics/codeofethics/codeethics.

Sample Form

Request for Reconsideration of Library Resources

[In this space, identify who has authorized use of this form (e.g., your library director, board of trustees, board of education, etc.) and to whom the form should be returned.

Example: The school board of Mainstream County, U.S.A., has delegated the responsibility for selection and evaluation of library/educational resources to the school library media specialist/curriculum committee, and has established reconsideration procedures to address concerns about those resources. Completion of this form is the first step in those procedures. If you wish to request reconsideration of school or library resources, please return the completed form to the Coordinator of Library Media Resources, Mainstream School Dist., 1 Mainstream Plaza, Anytown, U.S.A. Please note that this form may become part of the public record.]

Name _____ Date_____

Address _____ City _____

State _____ Zip Code _____ Phone _____

Do you represent self? _____ Organization? _____

Resource on which you are commenting:

_____ Book _____Textbook _____ Video _____ Display _____Magazine

_____ Library Program _____ Audio Recording _____ Newspaper

_____ Electronic Information/Network (please specify)

_____ Other _____

Title of the resource _____

Author/producer of the resource _____

What brought this resource to your attention? _____

Have you examined the entire resource? _____

What concerns you about the resource? (Use other side or additional pages if necessary.) _____

Are there resource(s) you suggest to provide additional information and/or other viewpoints on this topic? _____

Engaging with Organized Groups

Barbara M. Jones and Deborah Caldwell-Stone

ORGANIZATIONS SUPPORTING OR detracting from ALA's intellectual freedom agenda are a blessing and a challenge.

Oppositional Groups

As a reflection of the fractured U.S. political discourse, opposition toward many intellectual freedom policies and activities has grown increasingly intense and even vicious. Some groups may insert themselves into the library's board and other open public meetings not for the purpose of solving a problem democratically, but to disrupt the proceedings or to seek publicity. This is a shock to many librarians who are accustomed to the principles of civic engagement or other means to conduct business. In the same way, the press may approach the library with a preconceived agenda, particularly during "sweeps week," and may not be interested in accuracy or fair representation of all sides of a dispute.

In this increasingly difficult environment, libraries should remember the following:

- Ideally, your library has cultivated allies such as elected officials and a "Friends of the Library" group before a crisis. It is also important to rally supporters such as parents who oppose censorship, to counter oppositional groups. Long-term relations with local government and civic leaders will pay off. Do not "write off" groups or individuals you assume will disagree with the library's policies. For example, because of their strong beliefs about individualism, some fundamentalist clergy and libertarians will support libraries facing challenges.
- Develop a set of talking points for the controversy at hand and make sure that everyone in your organization uses it for the press and at community meetings. Most often it is best to have one designated spokesperson speak to the press and handle outside inquiries. Be positive in your message—that libraries are precious community resources for *all*. Mention some of the successful programs sponsored by your library.
- Sometimes oppositional groups use the very values we cherish to disrupt the library. While library open meetings should reflect the democratic values we promote in our services, there is a point at which disruption may be a crime. If your library experiences such disrup-

II.2
Censorship,
Challenges,
& Internet
Filtering

tion during meetings or in the library itself, you should consult your attorney or local law enforcement. Library policies should communicate what conduct is allowed and what is not—and the consequences for breaking the rules.

See also part III, chapter 1, "Communicating about Intellectual Freedom."

Coalitions

Because intellectual freedom issues have grown in complexity and scope, and because not-for-profit organizational resources are slim, it is essential that groups with the same concerns about free expression collaborate whenever possible. But it takes time and patience, because no two organizations share exactly the same beliefs and priorities. Here are some recommendations to promote cordial and effective relationships within a coalition:

- Before entering a coalition, make sure your own library's mission and focus are clear. There will be some "bottom line" values from which your organization will not depart, and there will be other areas in which compromise and collaboration are possible. Look for the common ground that makes the coalition valuable. Each organization must retain its own identity while at the same time working together with others. It may be necessary at some point to clarify differences in a written document.
- Ensure that any actions within the coalition will not compromise your professional ethical code or values. For example, the ALA Office for Intellectual Freedom, in keeping with the *Code of Ethics of the American Library Association,* assures confidentiality in all transactions with librarians calling for assistance. Other groups may not have the same stricture. Or, we often collaborate with organizations holding somewhat differing views on copyright issues. This means that for some advocacy campaigns, one or the other party may choose not to participate in a particular coalition activity.
- Communicate frequently with coalition partners. In any transactions with the press or the general public, it is crucial that joint press releases, letters, blog posts, or website messages are agreed upon by all parties.

See also part III, chapter 2, "Where to Get Help and Get Involved."

The Law Regarding Access to Library Resources: Removal of Materials

Theresa Chmara

FROM TIME TO time, library users, staff, or community members may raise concerns about the type of information that can be accessed in the library. Decisions to remove materials from a publicly funded library raise serious constitutional concerns.

In *Board of Education v. Pico,* the Supreme Court considered whether a local school board unconstitutionally removed books from a school library. The court acknowledged that local school boards have broad discretion to manage school affairs and make decisions regarding curriculum issues but held that the school board's broad discretion over matters of curriculum is misplaced where it ventures "into the school library and the regime of voluntary inquiry that there holds sway."[1] The court held that "if petitioners *intended* by their removal decision to deny respondents access to ideas with which petitioners disagreed, and if this intent was the decisive factor in petitioner's decision, then petitioners have exercised their discretion in violation of the Constitution."[2]

> **What's a "Public Forum"?**
>
> This essay uses the term *public forum.* To learn more about what that means and how it applies to libraries, please read part I, chapter 4, "The Right to Receive Information: Libraries, the First Amendment, and the Public Forum Doctrine." (p.43)

The principles established by *Pico* have been applied and expanded by numerous courts. Courts have permitted removal of books in the school library context only if the material is "educationally unsuitable" or "pervasively vulgar." In *Case v. Unified School District No. 233,* a federal district court held that a high school in Olathe, Kansas, violated the First Amendment by removing *Annie on My Mind* from the school library.[3] Although the book had been in the general collection of the library since the early 1980s, the school board argued that the book was educationally unsuitable. Applying *Pico,* the district court held that the school board's action was unconstitutional because the substantial motivation in their removal decision was "their own disagreement with the ideas expressed in the book."[4] The court's holding of improper motivation was based on several factors: (1) during the trial, many school board members stated expressly that they voted to remove the book because it "glorified homosexuality" and they believed that homosexuality was "unhealthy" or "sinful"; (2) the school board failed to consider other, less restrictive alternatives to complete removal; and (3) the school board disregarded its own established review procedures.[5]

In *American Civil Liberties Union of Florida v. Miami-Dade School Board,* the Eleventh Circuit upheld the school board's removal of a picture book on Cuba on the ground that the book was factually inaccurate because it failed to provide additional details about the subject matter.[6] The district court had concluded that the removal decision was politically motivated,[7] but the appellate court disagreed. School board members defended their removal decision by arguing that the books were offensive to some members of the Cuban community and educationally unsuitable because they are viewpoint-neutral and do not include detailed facts about Cuba's totalitarian dictatorship. The American Civil Liberties Union (ACLU) expert noted, however, that the "alleged omissions are appropriate omissions given the age level and purpose for which the book is intended."[8]

The determination of whether a decision to censor materials is based on educational suitability or political motivation will be a fact-based inquiry in every instance and will require testimony from educational experts on the question of suitability. The reach of the decision in the Miami-Dade case is thus limited to that case alone. The inquiry in a censorship case focuses on "motivation," and each court faced with that inquiry must determine if the particular school board or government entity removed particular books based on their own viewpoints or objective educational concerns. The Eleventh Circuit's conclusion that the school board did not engage in politically motivated censorship therefore would not preclude another court from finding in a different situation that removal of the same books in another library was unconstitutional viewpoint discrimination.

Censorship issues related to library materials also arise in the public library context. In *Sund v. City of Wichita Falls,* the city council passed a resolution that required a public library director to remove books from the children's section and place them in the sections designated for adult books if presented with a petition signed by 300 library cardholders requesting such removal.[9] This mechanism was used to remove two books dealing with homosexuality: *Daddy's Roommate* and *Heather Has Two Mommies.* The court held that the library is a limited public forum (conceded by both parties) and that the books could not be constitutionally removed from the children's room based on the petitioners' disagreement with the content and views expressed in those books. The court found the removal to be unconstitutional despite the fact that the books were not removed entirely from the library premises because "the burdens on Plaintiffs' First Amendment rights imposed by the Resolution are nonetheless constitutionally objectionable."[10] The court held that the removal placed significant burdens on the ability of children and their parents to find the books while browsing in the children's section of the library.

That principle was demonstrated as well in *Counts v. Cedarville School District*, when the school district removed *Harry Potter* books from general circulation in the school library and permitted students access to them only with parental permission.[11] Parents in the school district sued the school board, alleging that their child's rights were violated by the removal of the books from the open shelves of the library. The district court agreed, holding that the minor's rights were violated by the removal of the books from the school library shelves because the books were "stigmatized."[12] The court held, moreover, that having to request the books from a librarian placed a burden on the minor's exercise of her First Amendment rights. The court also held that it was irrelevant that the minor plaintiff had the books at home or otherwise had access to the books because it violated her rights to burden her ability to access them at her school library. Finally, the court held that the school board did not allege a sufficient justification for the removal of the books in that there was no evidence to support the claim that the books would promote disobedience, disrespect for authority, or disruption in the school.

Cases such as *Case* and *Counts* also demonstrate the importance of following library policies and procedures for reviewing requests for reconsideration of library resources. The *Counts* case began when a parent of two children in the Cedarville School District filed a complaint arguing that *Harry Potter and the Sorcerer's Stone* should be removed from the library. Following procedures for resolving challenges to library materials, the library committee, a committee of fifteen reviewers, reviewed the book and concluded unanimously that the book should remain in the library. The Cedarville School Board—including several members who had not even read the book—then ignored that decision and ordered the removal of all of the books in the *Harry Potter* series. In *Case* and *Counts,* the courts specifically relied on the failure to follow procedures as an indication of improper motivation.

The key factors in determining whether a resource has been removed unconstitutionally in a school library context will focus on whether the removal decision was based on improper motivation, such as disagreement with the ideas expressed in the resource, or objectively on the educational suitability of the resource.

In the context of a public library, which generally is considered to be a limited or designated public forum, government officials must meet an even more exacting standard to support removal of materials. Unless the material has been found by a court to be obscenity, child pornography, or material deemed "harmful to minors," any content-based decision to remove material from the public library will be deemed unconstitutional unless the government can demonstrate that the removal meets the standard of strict scrutiny. Strict scrutiny requires evidence that the restriction is necessary to achieve a compelling government interest and is narrowly tailored to achieve that interest.[13]

NOTES

II.2
Censorship,
Challenges,
& Internet
Filtering

1. *Board of Education v. Pico,* 457 U.S. 853, 869 (1982).

2. *Id.* at 871; see also *Campbell v. St. Tammany Parish School Board,* 64 F.3d 184, 190 (5th Cir. 1995) (holding that in determining whether a school board unconstitutionally removed *Voodoo and Hoodoo,* a history of Louisiana customs related to voodoo, "the key inquiry . . . is the school official's substantial motivation in arriving at the removal decision").

3. *Case v. Unified School District No. 233,* 908 F. Supp. 864 (D. Kan. 1995).

4. *Id.* at 875.

5. *Id.* at 874.

6. *American Civil Liberties Union of Florida v. Miami-Dade School Board,* 557 F.3d 1177 (11th Cir. 2009).

7. *American Civil Liberties Union of Florida v. Miami-Dade School Board,* 439 F. Supp. 2d 1242 (S.D. Fla. 2006).

8. *Id.*

9. *Sund v. City of Wichita Falls,* 121 F. Supp. 2d 530 (N.D. Tex. 2000).

10. *Id.* at 549.

11. *Counts v. Cedarville School District,* 295 F. Supp. 2d 996 (W.D. Ark. 2003).

12. *Id.* at 999.

13. *Perry Education Association v. Perry Local Educators' Association,* 460 U.S. 37, 45 (1983); see also part I, chapter 4, for a discussion of the public forum doctrine and its applicability in the context of the public library.

Internet Filtering and Intellectual Freedom

Part 1: Do I Have to Use an Internet Filter in My Library?

Deborah Caldwell-Stone

IN A REMARKABLE unanimous decision in *Reno v. American Civil Liberties Union,* the Supreme Court declared that the Internet, as a medium of communication, is entitled to the First Amendment's highest protection and that persons using the Internet enjoy the same rights to publish information and receive information as do those who use print media.[1] Because the First Amendment applies without restriction to all material published on, or provided through, the Internet, the American Library Association does not recommend the use of filters to block access to constitutionally protected speech on computers located in publicly funded libraries.

In the wake of the Supreme Court's decision, Congress responded to public concerns about children's and teens' access to sexually explicit content on the Internet by passing laws aimed at regulating minors' access to materials not constitutionally protected for them. Among these laws is the Children's Internet Protection Act.[2]

The Children's Internet Protection Act

CIPA places restrictions on the use of funding for Internet access available through the Universal Service E-rate discount program and the Library Services and Technology Act (LSTA). Public schools and libraries accepting these funds are subject to CIPA and must certify that the institution has adopted an Internet safety policy that includes use of a "technology protection measure"—filtering or blocking software—to keep adults from accessing visual images online that are obscene or child pornography. The filtering software must also block minors' access to images that are "harmful to minors," that is, sexually explicit images that adults have a legal right to access but are lacking any serious literary, artistic, political, or scientific value for minors.

CIPA

The Children's Internet Protection Act (CIPA)—and its requirement to use filtering software—applies *only* to the schools and libraries that choose to accept federal E-rate discounts or LSTA grants for their Internet access. There is no requirement that a school or library accept these federal funds.

CIPA's authority to regulate Internet filtering policies in public schools and public libraries draws on the power of Congress to attach requirements to the funds it distributes. Because there is no requirement that a school or library accept federal funds, CIPA applies only to the schools and libraries that choose to accept E-rate discounts or LSTA grants for their Internet access.

Institutions subject to CIPA's mandate must place filters on all computers owned by the school or library, including those computers used by staff. A librarian or other staff person authorized by the institution may disable the filter or unblock a website for an adult user to enable access for bona fide research or for any other lawful purpose. A librarian may also unblock, for users of all ages, appropriate sites that are wrongfully blocked by the filtering software.

Schools and libraries obligated to comply with CIPA must adopt a written Internet safety policy that addresses the online safety of minors. Before adopting the policy, the institution must hold, after reasonable notice, at least one public hearing or meeting to address the proposed policy. Schools are also required to establish a policy that addresses educating students about appropriate online behavior, including cyberbullying and interacting with others on social networking websites and in chat rooms.

CIPA does not require schools or libraries to block online text, nor does it authorize blocking access to controversial or unorthodox ideas or political viewpoints. Guidance issued by the Federal Communications Commission (FCC), the agency charged with enforcing CIPA, states that online social media sites like Facebook and YouTube do not fall into one of the categories of content that must be blocked under CIPA, and that these sites should not be considered "harmful to minors" under the law.[3] Additionally, CIPA does not authorize or require the adoption of software or other tools to track individual users' web-surfing habits.

Legal Challenge: *United States v. American Library Association*[4]

In 2001, the American Library Association and the Freedom to Read Foundation joined with library users to file a lawsuit challenging the constitutionality of the Children's Internet Protection Act on behalf of public librarians and public library users.[5] Initially, a three-judge panel of the Eastern District of Pennsylvania unanimously held that CIPA violated library users' First Amendment rights.[6] The government appealed that decision, and on June 23, 2003, a sharply divided Supreme Court issued a plurality decision upholding the law. (A plurality decision is issued when no majority of justices back a particular legal opinion but when a majority of justices do agree on the ultimate outcome of the case.)

The plurality—represented by three different opinions—ruled that the First Amendment does not prohibit Congress from requiring public libraries—as a condition of receiving federal funding—to use software filters to control what library users and staff access online via library computers, as long as adults aged seventeen and older could request that the filters be disabled without needing to explain their request. The justices' reliance on the disabling provisions as a cure for any violation of the First Amendment was based on the U.S. solicitor general's position that CIPA allows librarians to unblock or disable filters for adults without any explanation.

While the various opinions issued by the Supreme Court justices in the decision offer different rationales for upholding the law, the clear consensus of the court is that the ability of adult library users to gain access to constitutionally protected speech on the Internet is important to the constitutional use of Internet filters.

Liability for Blocking Constitutionally Protected Content

Both libraries and school boards have been sued in recent years for blocking constitutionally protected content or failing to disable their Internet filters at the request of adults.[7] In one case, a school board was required to pay $125,000 in legal fees to the ACLU when the court found that the school board had violated students' First Amendment rights by blocking students' access to websites affirming civil rights for the lesbian, gay, bisexual, and transgender (LGBT) communities while white-listing sites advocating against civil rights for LGBT persons and promoting "ex-gay" ministries.[8]

While each lawsuit addressed unique facts and circumstances, taken together these lawsuits demonstrate that libraries do not enjoy unlimited discretion when filtering Internet content. In particular, libraries should not employ filters to engage in unconstitutional censorship such as viewpoint discrimination or the deliberate suppression of ideas. Libraries that use filters to block constitutionally protected material, or deliberately block access to controversial content, or fail to implement an effective unblocking policy risk facing similar lawsuits. Libraries considering the use of filtering software should consult their legal counsel.

Liability for Unfiltered Access

The sole court decision to address this issue has ruled that libraries are not responsible for the content that users access through the library's computers connected to the Internet. In *Kathleen R. v. City of Livermore,* the plaintiff sued the City of Livermore for failing to block Internet content after her son downloaded images at a Livermore Public Library that she found inappropriate.[9] The California Court of Appeals held that the library was not legally liable to the parent or her child. It identified three reasons for rejecting the mother's claims:

- Section 230 of the federal Communications Decency Act provides libraries and other Internet service providers immunity from lawsuits seeking to hold them liable for any content published or created by a third party and accessed through the Internet.
- Public libraries do not have a special duty to protect minors from harmful materials on the Internet, as libraries do not have a custodial or other special relationship with minor users. Moreover, the mere provision of Internet access does not imply that libraries are providing minors access to obscene or harmful to minors materials or child pornography.
- The parent could not claim that the library had a policy of providing obscene pornography to minors because the library's existing Internet use policy prohibited the use of its computers for illegal purposes, warned users that controversial material is available on the Internet, and informed parents that the library does not supervise minors' use of the Internet.

The result in *Kathleen R. v. City of Livermore* emphasizes the importance of having a comprehensive Internet use policy for the library.

State Laws and Internet Filtering

Many states have enacted laws that address issues of Internet access, filtering and intellectual freedom in libraries. Make sure to consult your state's legal code for any relevant laws pertaining to library Internet access and policies, including those mandating the use of Internet filters. Many of these laws apply differently to public libraries than to school libraries. The National Council of State Legislatures maintains a frequently updated website at www.ncsl.org containing information about state laws regulating Internet use or access.

I'm being required to install an Internet filter. What should I do?

Deborah Caldwell-Stone and Sarah Houghton

HERE ARE STEPS that libraries and schools subject to CIPA can take to minimize the negative impact of filters. With or without the use of filters, libraries should implement a good education and communication program that informs users of all ages about effective searching, identity protection, and managing access to unwanted materials.

1. *Exercise care in choosing filtering software.* Select filtering software that is transparent in its classification system and that allows the library to fine-tune the categories of content that are blocked. Also, ensure that people, not just automated algorithms, regularly review and analyze the software's blocking criteria. It is important to understand the vendor's philosophy about content filtering. Some vendors are affiliated with religious organizations or espouse particular partisan or doctrinal views. Favor vendors who do not design their software to advance their own values. Additionally, be sure that the library can switch off or opt out of viewpoint- or content-based blocking criteria that may run afoul of the First Amendment. Especially important is the use of accurate categories for illegal content such as obscenity or child pornography. Broad categories such as "pornography," which is not defined by law and is interpreted in many different ways, may sweep up much constitutionally protected material and should be avoided.

2. *Exercise care in installing and maintaining the software.* When installing the filtering software, adjust blacklist criteria to minimize the blocking of constitutionally protected speech. Establish a clear, transparent, and timely process for reviewing and revising blocking criteria as requested by users, and for unblocking constitutionally protected content system-wide. Library staff should be able to disable or unblock the technology at workstations and/or move the user to an unfiltered station as needed.

3. *Develop a well-crafted Internet use policy.* CIPA requires libraries to write and adopt Internet use policies that address minors' safety online and incorporate use of a "technology protection measure." Involve your trustees, legal counsel, and library staff in the writing process, and encourage public participation when creating policies that address public access to information. Ensure that the guidelines, rules, and procedures are reasonable, nondiscriminatory, view-

point-neutral restrictions on Internet access and computer facilities. Once adopted, policies should be easily available for review, and all staff should be trained in appropriate implementation. The policy should advise Internet users of their rights and responsibilities. It should also describe unacceptable behaviors, what the penalties are for violations, and how to appeal a decision imposing a penalty. It should also include a clear, transparent, and timely procedure for asking that the filter be disabled and that constitutionally protected content be unblocked. (See also part I, chapter 3.)

4. *Employ and promote filtering alternatives.* Careful arrangement of computer stations, designated areas for families and children, and the use of privacy screens or devices can protect user privacy and create a comfortable environment for all library users.

5. *Conduct a cost-benefit analysis.* Keep track of all the costs associated with filtering, including the purchase of the filtering software, the cost of support and maintenance, server or network slowdown cost, staff time devoted to training, staff time devoted to unblocking or blocking sites, and costs related to communicating about the library's filtering procedures. You may discover that you actually lose money when you choose to filter, and that it would be more cost-effective to forgo federal funding through E-rate and LSTA and offer unfiltered access. In school settings, keep track of instances where filters have interfered with teachers' ability to teach and students' ability to learn.

NOTES

1. *Reno v. American Civil Liberties Union*, 521 U.S. 844 (1997).

2. Children's Internet Protection Act, P.L. 106–554 (2000), codified at 47 U.S.C. § 254(h)(5) and 20 U.S.C. § 9134(f).

3. FCC Report and Order 11–125, August 21, 2011 (Report and Regulations Implementing CIPA).

4. *United States v. American Library Association*, 539 U.S. 194 (2003).

5. The lawsuit did not address schools or school libraries, as none of the plaintiffs had standing to challenge CIPA on behalf of local school boards.

6. *American Library Association v. United States*, 201 F. Supp. 2d 401 (E.D. Pa. 2002).

7. *Bradburn, et al. v. North Central Regional Library District* (E.D. Wash. 2012); *PFLAG v. Camdenton R-III School District*, 853 F. Supp. 2d 88 (W.D. Mo 2012); and *Hunter v. Salem Public Library* (E.D. Mo. 2013).

8. *PFLAG v. Camdenton R-III School District* (Id.).

9. *Kathleen R. v. City of Livermore*, 87 Cal. App. 4th 684 (2001).

Internet Filtering and Intellectual Freedom
Part 2: Do Filters Really Work?

Sarah Houghton

OF PARAMOUNT INTELLECTUAL freedom concern to libraries is the methodology behind how content is classified in filtering software. Filters on the market today employ artificial intelligence, image recognition, and complex algorithms. Yet with all of these advanced tools and techniques, filters still cannot successfully evaluate and determine the actual content, context, and intent of text, still images, audio, or video. As a result, filter performance is highly variable.

Filters function by analyzing and making a determination about content based on the domain, IP address, keyword, file type, pixel analysis, number and types of links, and other information. Filtering products generally start with a list of domains (website addresses) and IP addresses (where those websites are hosted) and add into the equation some element of the content (trigger words, phrases, file types, etc.).

Products that filter based on domains and IP addresses typically use a search engine to run searches for trigger words or phrases, such as "sex videos." That results list is then run through an algorithm that creates a blacklist of blocked pages, domains, or IPs for the targeted subject matter. Some companies have a staff member spot-check the auto-generated list for errors, but many have no human intervention at all. These domain blacklists generally include 250,000–2,000,000 domains or IP addresses, which are then blocked by the filtering software unless otherwise overridden by staff.

Filtering companies fiercely protect their automated classification processes, white lists, and blacklists. These lists are considered trade secrets and are never made publicly available to their customers. Filtering software companies do not tell their customers the algorithms used or specific sites they block in each category. As a result, no one can know what is being blocked and why without extensive testing and trial and error.

The accuracy of filters is key to the discussion of how Internet filters work. All filters overblock (incorrectly blocking something unobjectionable) and underblock (incorrectly allowing something objectionable). The question is: how much do they do of both, and is that failure rate an acceptable cost?

In studies of filter accuracy from 2001 to 2008 (interestingly, no studies have been published since), the average accuracy success rating of all the tests combined is approximately 78 percent. This means that on average, 78 percent of the time, the filtering software did what it was supposed to do based on its internal rule set. Bear in mind that these studies generally measure only text content. Only one study examined filtering efficacy on images.[1]

The most recent studies done from 2007 to 2008 show a nominally higher accuracy percentage—approximately 83 percent—but the number of studies is limited and therefore leaves a larger margin of error. While filters may be getting a little better with age and development, the software is still wrong at least 17 percent of the time for text content, and wrong 54 percent of the time for image content (you could literally flip a coin and get better accuracy).[2] Constitutionally protected content is routinely overblocked in the simple, cheap Internet filters as well as in the complex and more expensive filters.

Most filtering products identify categories of content, which allows libraries (or the companies who set the defaults) to block sites providing information about one side of a political or social issue. One click can block "non-traditional religious sites" or "pro-gay sites." Websites for the National Organization for Women; Parents, Families, & Friends of Lesbians and Gays; the Quakers; and other organizations are routinely blocked by filters.

Content may be underblocked as well. It is increasingly easy to fool filters, especially with multimedia content. The software is simply not sophisticated enough to make the context-sensitive judgment calls that human beings can make. Website creators, particularly those devoted to adult entertainment and sexually explicit material, have become exceedingly expert at working around filters. Rotating IP addresses and domains, using referral and pass-through sites, and using poor or misleading metadata on multimedia are some of the techniques employed. Some filters use pixel color analysis—what percentage of pixels, and in what configuration—in an attempt to determine if an image contains skin tone. But what is a skin tone pixel? Dark- and light-complexioned individuals, as well as individuals with an above-average amount of body hair, can fool the filters into thinking they aren't looking at naked humans.

In our increasingly multilingual communities, it's also important to realize that the majority of filtering products filter in English only. The mechanisms for analyzing keywords, URLs, and text cannot cope with other languages. Therefore, Spanish- or Russian-language sexually explicit sites are much more easily accessed than their English equivalents. In short, just because there is a filter on a computer does not mean that no sexually explicit material will get through. In fact, it's likely that it will.

The mission of libraries is to provide a broad array of information to a diverse community. By using software generally developed for home use where parents can enforce their views on their children, librarians find themselves violating that mission because the software by design limits information access. The lesson that the poor performance of filters teaches library Internet users is this: when you come to the library, your Internet use is going to often be blocked, so either don't use our Internet access, figure out a way to get around it, or get used to seeing a sub-par stunted version of the actual Internet. As information professionals, are these the lessons we want to be teaching our communities?

NOTES

1. Sarah Houghton-Jan and the San José Public Library, *Internet Filtering Software Tests: Barracuda, CyberPatrol, FilterGate, & WebSense,* April 2, 2008, librarian inblack.net/librarianinblack/wp-content/uploads/2015/03/SJPL-Filtering -Tests.pdf.

2. Paul Resnick, "Exhibit D: Declaration of Resnick," February 4, 2008, http:// filteringfacts.files.wordpress.com/2008/02/bradburn_04_05_08_resnick _report.pdf.

Internet Filtering and Intellectual Freedom
Part 3: How Does Filtering Affect Intellectual Freedom?

Sarah Houghton

INTERNET FILTERING IS one of the most pervasive and recurring intellectual freedom challenges worldwide. For some libraries, and indeed some entire countries, there is no question of whether or not to filter—filters are simply mandated by the government. In the United States, however, there is still at least a cursory nod to intellectual freedom and privacy from our governing agencies. Filtering in the United States is currently tied to optional and tempting library funding, namely federal LSTA and E-rate grants and also some state funding.

A divisive issue in libraries, the question of content filtering is central to our communities' future information access. Content filtering involves values of a fundamental nature, so any solution results in parties feeling that they are giving up something of profound importance.

In the view of ALA and many librarians, content filters are antithetical to the mission of the library to provide free and open access to all legal information. Filters intentionally block access to information, much of it constitutionally protected by the First Amendment. Internet filters restrict free speech. Four of the six statements of principle in the American Library Association's *Library Bill of Rights* are relevant to Internet filtering:

- Materials should not be excluded because of the origin, background, or views of those contributing to their creation.
- Libraries should challenge censorship in the fulfillment of their responsibility to provide information and enlightenment.
- Libraries should cooperate with all persons and groups concerned with resisting abridgment of free expression and free access to ideas.
- A person's right to use a library should not be denied or abridged because of origin, age, background, or views.[1]

Filtering the Internet for any group of library users is incompatible with the core professional values articulated in the ALA *Library Bill of Rights*. Filters exclude material, censor information, and abridge free access to ideas.

The ALA Intellectual Freedom Committee's "Statement on Library Use of Filtering Software" clearly states the outcome of the 1997 United States Supreme Court case *Reno, Attorney General of the United States, et al. v. American Civil Liberties Union et al.*:

> For libraries, the most critical holding of the Supreme Court is that libraries that make content available on the Internet can continue to do so with the same Constitutional protections that apply to the books on libraries' shelves. . . . The Court recognized the importance of enabling individuals to receive speech from the entire world and to speak to the entire world. Libraries provide those opportunities to many who would not otherwise have them. The Supreme Court's decision protects that access.[2]

A key issue in discussions about Internet filtering in libraries is the idea of "selection versus censorship." Some courts and librarians contend that installing filters is equal to library selection of materials, or collection development decisions in which each library has the right to make those selection decisions and they do not violate First Amendment rights as a result. This is a fallacious argument that misinterprets the principles of collection development in libraries. Installing filters on your public access library computers is like outsourcing to a single company all collection development, with that one entity making all collection decisions about what is immediately accessible and what is not. Of greater concern is that the process of selection for

II. 2
Censorship,
Challenges,
& Internet
Filtering

what sites are blocked is predominantly automated by a computer script. Installing a filter is like entrusting the entirety of your collection development to a single proprietary, black-box, artificial intelligence that uses private rating schemes.

Another issue to consider is the "Big Brother" factor. Libraries must consider the effect filters will have on their users, who may behave differently if they feel they are being watched. Users may avoid accessing sites they think might be blocked, worrying that their use is being tracked. At libraries that filter, library users report being too embarrassed to ask for a site to be unblocked, believing the library has already deemed what they want to be unsavory. We must ask ourselves: how many of our library customers walk away without the information they need?

Libraries supported by public funding are governmental institutions and subject to the First Amendment, which forbids libraries from censoring or restricting information based on content or viewpoint. Filtering software unquestionably blocks information protected by the First Amendment. Legal information is blocked, inevitably, putting libraries at legal risk for overblocking. Instead of using filters in libraries to restrict access, librarians, parents, and thoughtful individuals in our communities should work together to find ways to educate, prepare, and support our community members as digital citizens.

NOTES

1. American Library Association, *Library Bill of Rights,* adopted June 19, 1939; amended Oct. 14, 1944; June 18, 1948; Feb. 2, 1961; June 27, 1967; and Jan. 23, 1980; inclusion of "age" reaffirmed January 23, 1996, www.ala.org/advocacy/intfreedom/librarybill.

2. American Library Association, Intellectual Freedom Committee, "Statement on Library Use of Filtering Software," adopted July 1, 1997; rev. November 17, 2000, www.ala.org/advocacy/intfreedom/statementspols/statementlibrary.

Internet Filtering and Intellectual Freedom
Part 4: What Are School Libraries Doing?

Helen R. Adams

THE CHILDREN'S INTERNET Protection Act was implemented in schools in 2001. It requires schools receiving E-rate discounts for Internet access to certify that they have board-approved Internet safety policies that include "technology protection measures," commonly called "filters." The filtering technology must be installed on all computers used by minors and adults to access the Internet. The intention of using filters is to protect minors from viewing images of child pornography, obscenity, or material considered "harmful to minors" as defined under federal law.

Anecdotal evidence indicates that in many districts, misinterpretation of CIPA's filtering requirements has caused a stranglehold approach with filters overblocking much constitutionally protected instructional content, affecting information access and ultimately students' learning opportunities. Fearing complaints or litigation by parents whose children may have seen inappropriate material on a school computer, nervous school administrators have chosen to err on the side of overprotection, thereby filtering online content far beyond the intent of the law.

To determine the extent of filtering in schools, in 2012 the American Association of School Librarians (AASL) added questions about filtering to its annual School Libraries Count! national longitudinal survey. Survey data from 4,385 respondents revealed that in 98 percent of schools Internet content is filtered through multiple means:

- 94 percent use filtering software.
- 87 percent have adopted an acceptable use policy.
- 73 percent supervise students when they are online.

School librarians reported that in 73 percent of schools there was no differentiation in filtering levels based on the age of students, with content for kindergarten students and high school seniors being filtered at the same level.[1]

The most heavily blocked content are social networking sites (88 percent), IM/online chat (74 percent), online games (69 percent), and video services such as YouTube (66 percent). Wholesale blocking of these categories of content is *not* required by CIPA. In schools where students may bring their personal devices to school, 51 percent use some type of filtering for these devices, with 48 percent also relying on acceptable use policies, 47 percent requiring students to log on to a school network, and 28 percent calling on classroom teachers to give permission and monitor use.[2]

Filters routinely overblock legitimate educational websites, and 92 percent of respondents said that they can request wrongly filtered sites be made accessible. Responsiveness to their requests varies greatly. Unblocking may take a few hours (27 percent of schools), one to two days (35 percent), between two and four days (17 percent), or one week or longer (20 percent).[3] Time lags in unblocking lawful academic content create nightmare situations for teachers trying to use websites for student instruction and for students using filtered school Internet access to conduct personal or assignment-related research.

How Restrictive Filtering Affects Students

Although 50 percent of AASL survey takers noted that filters lessened online distractions and 34 percent reported that they decreased the need for monitoring, the results illustrate that librarians find restrictive filtering to be inconsistent with best practices for access to information and advancing digital citizenship.[4] Respondents indicated that filtering has a negative impact on student learning by (1) inhibiting student research (52 percent), (2) failing to recognize "the social aspects of learning" (42 percent), and (3) discouraging online collaboration opportunities (25 percent).[5]

The Internet is a treasure trove of interactive, collaborative learning opportunities, but its promise goes unfulfilled where filters are too restrictive. Although CIPA now requires school districts accepting E-rate funding to educate K–12 students about chat rooms, social media sites, and cyberbullying, instruction is not entirely productive if students have no opportunities for guided practice to test their skills unhampered by filters blocking useful content.

Twenty-first-century learners need to develop multiple literacies. As global citizens, they will be both consumers of information and creators of new content, collaborating and sharing knowledge online. Restrictive filters close off their freedom of expression and do not allow authentic educational experiences.

Homeless students or those living in poverty face challenging disadvantages in school, and filtering adds another obstacle. Economically secure students with personal computers and Internet access at home avoid the filters and complete their research and assignments outside heavily filtered school environments. Unfortunately, impoverished children and young adults are forced to rely on restrictive filtered Internet access in schools or use public libraries, if they are accessible. Internet access at the public library may be as heavily filtered as at the school library.

Many students have legitimate needs for information that filters often block. For example, for students who are questioning their gender identities, finding accurate information in a confidential manner is crucial. Some filters display only one side of an issue. LGBT viewpoint discrimination in filtering was the basis for a 2009 lawsuit filed against two school districts in Tennessee (*Franks v. Metropolitan Board of Education*). Although settled out of court, the filtering company was forced to open pro-LGBT websites for student use. Previously only anti-gay sites were available. A second lawsuit addressing the same issue, *PFLAG v. Camdenton R-III School District*, resulted in a court decision stating that viewpoint discrimination in filtering violates the First Amendment rights of students.

Ironically, a law designed to protect students online is now affecting their learning and personal expression in negative and unequal ways. The Department of Education's National Technology Plan stated it well: "Ensuring student safety on the Internet is a critical concern, but many filters designed to protect students also block access to legitimate learning content and such tools as blogs, wikis, and social networks that have the potential to support student learning and engagement."[6]

What Can School Librarians Do?

Given the current environment, school librarians must determine how to lessen the impact of filters. Librarians can help administrators understand the negative effect of restrictive filters by gathering real-life examples from teachers in all disciplines and grade levels to demonstrate how aggressive filtering affects their lesson plans, instruction, and ability to meet state academic standards. This reporting may need to be repeated in varying formats until ingrained inaccurate interpretations about CIPA's requirements can be altered.

After the librarian's data have gathered support, he can advocate for school-wide strategies to do the following:

- Reduce filtering to a minimal level that satisfies CIPA's requirements but does not restrict the instructional and learning environment.
- Develop K-12 students' digital citizenship through integrated instruction about appropriate online behavior, including the ethical and

responsible use of social networking sites and awareness of cyber-bullying.

- Create a proactive, board-approved "responsible use" policy reflecting students' rights and corresponding accountability.
- Educate staff about evaluation of online resources and the effective academic use of digital tools that engage students, promote critical thinking, and support collaborative projects.
- Protect minors' First Amendment rights by establishing a system to unblock websites that do not present images that are obscene, child pornography, or material harmful to minors.[7]
- Establish a collegial culture where educators collaboratively seek, post, and use carefully selected curricular, recreational, and extracurricular links and electronic subscription resources through classroom and library web pages.
- Inform parents and community members about the positive aspects of interactive online learning.

Finally, school librarians can organize activities for AASL's Banned Websites Awareness Day (BWAD), observed annually during Banned Books Week. On a national scale, BWAD draws attention to overly restrictive filtering of useful educational websites, the academic value of social media tools, and the impact of filtering on student learning. Check the AASL website for activities and resources.

NOTES

1. American Association of School Librarians, "AASL Executive Summary: Filtering in Schools," October 2012, www.ala.org/aasl/research/slc/2012/ filtering.
2. Ibid., 3–4.
3. Ibid., 3.
4. Ibid.
5. Ibid.
6. Tina Barseghian, "Straight from the DOE: Dispelling Myths about Blocked Sites," http://blogs.kqed.org/mindshift/2011/04/straight-from-the-doe-facts -about-blocking-sites-in-schools.
7. Theresa Chmara, "Minors' First Amendment Rights: CIPA & School Libraries," *Knowledge Quest* 39, no. 1 (2010): 21, Academic Search Complete, EBSCO*host*.

Children
and Youth

ISSUE AT A GLANCE

Key Concepts

- The needs and interests of library users must be determined on an individual basis. Librarians cannot predict what resources will best fulfill the needs and interests of users based on a single criterion such as chronological age, education level, literacy skills, or legal emancipation. Therefore, a person's right to use the library and its resources should not be denied or restricted on the basis of these criteria.
- Lack of access to information can be harmful to minors. Teaching young people how to evaluate information and make decisions about the content they view supports healthy and safe growth into adulthood.
- Librarians and library governing bodies cannot assume the role of parents (in loco parentis). Rather, they should maintain that only parents and guardians have the right and responsibility to deter-

For More Information about Minors and the Library

See also the following sections of the *Intellectual Freedom Manual*:

"Access to Library Resources and Services" (part II, chapter 1)

"Censorship, Challenged Resources, and Internet Filtering" (part II, chapter 2)

"Collection Development and Management" (part II, chapter 4)

"Privacy and Confidentiality" (part II, chapter 7)

mine their children's—and only their children's—access to library resources.

What Does the Law Say?

- Children and young adults unquestionably possess First Amendment rights, including the right to receive information and those unenumerated rights, such as the right to privacy, that make the exercise of First Amendment rights meaningful.
- The right of parents or guardians to access their minor children's public library and public school library records varies from state to state. Consult the law in your state. Parents' and guardians' access to their minor children's school library records is also governed by the Family Educational Rights and Privacy Act.

Creating Policy for Your Library

- Consider formally adopting the *Library Bill of Rights* (see part I, chapter 2) as policy for your library. It contains statements about people's right to use a library regardless of age.

Especially for Academic Libraries

- To date, no court has imposed a duty on college and university libraries to supervise the intellectual activities of legal minors who are using the library, either as students or visitors. However, academic libraries should have Internet use policies outlining the guidelines for Internet use, prohibiting the use of computers for illegal purposes, and informing parents that the parents, and not library employees, are responsible for monitoring their children's activity.

Especially for Public Libraries

- Placing materials in a "children's room" or "young adult section" does not constitute restricting access, as long as all library users are able to access all collections of the library.

Especially for School Libraries

- Because school libraries may be the only place for minors to access information, restrictions on access (including filtering of Internet content) should be as minimal as possible, and teaching information literacy skills is of the utmost importance.
- Many schools are required to install Internet filters, either because they accept federal E-rate funds or because it is mandated by state law. Such schools should have a procedure to permit access to sites that are mistakenly blocked.

To Learn More

- Visit the ALA "Intellectual Freedom" website (www.ala.org/advocacy/intfreedom).
- Visit the websites of these organizations:
    - American Association of School Librarians (www.ala.org/aasl)
    - Association for Library Service to Children (www.ala.org/alsc)
    - Cooperative Children's Book Center (ccbc.education.wisc.edu/freedom/whatif/default.asp)
    - Public Library Association (www.ala.org/pla)
    - Young Adult Library Services Association (www.ala.org/yalsa)

- Read *Fencing Out Knowledge: Impacts of the Children's Internet Protection Act 10 Years Later,* Kristin Batch, ALA Office for Information Technology Policy and ALA Office for Intellectual Freedom, 2014, available at www.ala.org/offices/sites/ala.org.offices/files/content/oitp/publications/issuebriefs/cipa_report.pdf.

Questions for Reflection

- A parent asks to see what her child has checked out. The books include a title on alcoholic parents. What do you do?
- When checking out movies, a parent removes one from her twelve-year-old child's stack and says she's not ready to watch it yet. The child comes back later by herself and wants to check out that movie. What do you do?
- You're helping a high school student with a research project on sexually transmitted diseases. Many of the sites he's trying to access are blocked by the library's Internet filter. What are your options?

Access to Library Resources and Services for Minors

An Interpretation of the *Library Bill of Rights*

Formerly titled "Free Access to Libraries for Minors—An Interpretation of the Library Bill of Rights.*" Incorporates content from "Access for Children and Young Adults to Nonprint Materials—An Interpretation of the* Library Bill of Rights.*" Adopted June 30, 1972, by the ALA Council; amended July 1, 1981; July 3, 1991; June 30, 2004; July 2, 2008; and July 1, 2014.*

A historical essay about this statement can be found in the publication, *A History of ALA Policy on Intellectual Freedom: A Supplement to the Intellectual Freedom Manual, Ninth Edition.*

LIBRARY POLICIES AND procedures that effectively deny minors equal and equitable access to all library resources and services available to other users violate the American Library Association's *Library Bill of Rights*. The American Library Association opposes all attempts to restrict access to library services, materials, and facilities based on the age of library users.

Article V of the *Library Bill of Rights* states, "A person's right to use a library should not be denied or abridged because of origin, age, background, or views." The "right to use a library" includes free access to, and unrestricted use of, all the services, materials, and facilitiess the library has to offer. Every restriction on access to, and use of, library resources, based solely on the chronological age, educational level, literacy skills, or legal emancipation of users violates Article V.

Libraries are charged with the mission of providing services and developing resources to meet the diverse information needs and interests of the communities they serve. Services, materials, and facilities that fulfill the needs and interests of library users at different stages in their personal development are a necessary part of library resources. The needs and interests of each library user, and resources appropriate to meet those needs and interests, must be determined on an individual basis. Librarians cannot predict what resources will best fulfill the needs and interests of any individual user based on a single criterion such as chronological age, educational level, literacy skills, or legal emancipation. Equitable access to all library resources and services shall not be abridged through restrictive scheduling or use policies.

Libraries should not limit the selection and development of library resources simply because minors will have access to them. Institutional self-censorship diminishes the credibility of the library in the community and restricts access for all library users.

Children and young adults unquestionably possess First Amendment rights, including the right to receive information through the library in print, sound, images, data, games, software, and other formats.[1] Constitutionally protected speech cannot be suppressed solely to protect children or young adults from ideas or images a legislative body believes to be unsuitable for them.[2] Librarians and library governing bodies should not resort to age restrictions in an effort to avoid actual or anticipated objections because only a court of law can determine whether or not content is constitutionally protected.

The mission, goals, and objectives of libraries cannot authorize librarians or library governing bodies to assume, abrogate, or overrule the rights and responsibilities of parents and guardians. As *Libraries: An American Value* states, "We affirm the responsibility and the right of all parents and guardians to guide their own children's use of the library and its resources and services." Librarians and library governing bodies cannot assume the role of parents or the functions of parental authority in the private relationship between parent and child. Librarians and governing bodies should maintain that only parents and guardians have the right and the responsibility to determine their children's—and only their children's—access to library resources. Parents and guardians who do not want their children to have access to specific library services, materials, or facilities should so advise their children.

Librarians and library governing bodies have a public and professional obligation to ensure that all members of the community they serve have free, equal, and equitable access to the entire range of library resources regardless of content, approach, or format. This principle of library service applies equally to all users, minors as well as adults. Lack of access to information can be harmful to minors. Librarians and library governing bodies must uphold this principle in order to provide adequate and effective service to minors.

NOTES

1. See *Brown v. Entertainment Merchant's Association, et al.* 564 U.S. 08-1448 (2011): a) Video games qualify for First Amendment protection. Like protected books, plays, and movies, they communicate ideas through familiar literary devices and features distinctive to the medium. And "'the basic

principles of freedom of speech . . . do not vary' with a new and different communication medium."

2. See *Erznoznik v. City of Jacksonville,* 422 U.S. 205 (1975): "Speech that is neither obscene as to youths nor subject to some other legitimate proscription cannot be suppressed solely to protect the young from ideas or images that a legislative body thinks unsuitable for them. In most circumstances, the values protected by the First Amendment are no less applicable when government seeks to control the flow of information to minors." See also *Tinker v. Des Moines School Dist.,* 393 U.S.503 (1969); *West Virginia Bd. of Ed. v. Barnette,* 319 U.S. 624 (1943); *AAMA v. Kendrick,* 244 F.3d 572 (7th Cir. 2001).

Access to Resources and Services in the School Library
An Interpretation of the *Library Bill of Rights*

Formerly titled "Access to Resources and Services in the School Library Media Program—An Interpretation of the Library Bill of Rights.*" Adopted July 2, 1986, by the ALA Council; amended January 10, 1990; July 12, 2000; January 19, 2005; July 2, 2008; and July 1, 2014.*

A historical essay about this statement can be found in the publication, *A History of ALA Policy on Intellectual Freedom: A Supplement to the Intellectual Freedom Manual, Ninth Edition.*

THE SCHOOL LIBRARY plays a unique role in promoting, protecting, and educating about intellectual freedom. It serves as a point of voluntary access to information and ideas and as a learning laboratory for students as they acquire critical thinking and problem-solving skills needed in a pluralistic society. Although the educational level and program of the school necessarily shape the resources and services of a school library, the principles of the American Library Association's *Library Bill of Rights* apply equally to all libraries, including school libraries. Under these principles, all students have equitable access to library facilities, resources, and instructional programs.

School librarians assume a leadership role in promoting the principles of intellectual freedom within the school by providing resources and services that create and sustain an atmosphere of free inquiry. School librarians work closely with teachers to integrate instructional activities in classroom units designed to equip students to locate, evaluate, and use a broad range of ideas effectively. Intellectual freedom is fostered by educating students in the use of critical thinking skills to empower them to pursue free inquiry responsibly and independently. Through resources, programming, and educational processes, students and teachers experience the free and robust debate characteristic of a democratic society.

School librarians cooperate with other individuals in building collections of resources that meet the needs as well as the developmental and maturity levels of students. These collections provide resources that support the mission of the school district and are consistent with its philosophy, goals, and objectives. Resources in school library collections are an integral component of the curriculum and represent diverse points of view on both current and historical issues. These resources include materials that support the intellectual growth, personal development, individual interests, and recreational needs of students.

While English is, by history and tradition, the customary language of the United States, the languages in use in any given community may vary. Schools serving communities in which other languages are used make efforts to accommodate the needs of students for whom English is a second language. To support these efforts, and to ensure equitable access to resources and services, the school library provides resources that reflect the linguistic pluralism of the community.

Members of the school community involved in the collection development process employ educational criteria to select resources unfettered by their personal, political, social, or religious views. Students and educators served by the school library have access to resources and services free of constraints resulting from personal, partisan, or doctrinal disapproval. School librarians resist efforts by individuals or groups to define what is appropriate for all students or teachers to read, view, hear, or access regardless of technology, formats or method of delivery.

Major barriers between students and resources include but are not limited: to imposing age, grade-level, or reading-level restrictions on the use of resources; limiting the use of interlibrary loan and access to electronic information; charging fees for information in specific formats; requiring permission from parents or teachers; establishing restricted shelves or closed collections; and labeling. Policies, procedures, and rules related to the use of resources and services support free and open access to information.

It is the responsibility of the governing board to adopt policies that guarantee students access to a broad range of ideas. These include policies on collection development and procedures for the review of resources about which concerns have been raised. Such policies, developed by persons in the school community, provide for a timely and fair hearing and assure that procedures are applied equitably to all expressions of concern. It is the responsibility of school librarians to implement district policies and procedures in the school to ensure equitable access to resources and services for all students.

II.3
Children
& Youth

Minors and Internet Activity

An Interpretation of the *Library Bill of Rights*

Formerly titled "Minors and Internet Interactivity—An Interpretation of the Library Bill of Rights.*" Adopted July 15, 2009, by the ALA Council; amended July 1, 2014.*

A historical essay about this statement can be found in the publication, *A History of ALA Policy on Intellectual Freedom: A Supplement to the Intellectual Freedom Manual, Ninth Edition.*

THE DIGITAL ENVIRONMENT offers opportunities for accessing, creating, and sharing information. The rights of minors to retrieve, interact with, and create information posted on the Internet in schools and libraries are extensions of their First Amendment rights. (See also other interpretations of the American Library Association's *Library Bill of Rights,* including "Access to Digital Information, Services, and Networks" "Access to Library Resources and Services for Minors.")

Academic pursuits of minors can be strengthened with the use of interactive web tools, allowing young people to create documents and share them online; to upload pictures, videos, and graphic material; to revise public documents; and to add tags to online content to classify and organize information. Instances of inappropriate use of such academic tools should be addressed as individual behavior issues, not as justification for restricting or banning access to interactive technology. Schools and libraries should ensure that institutional environments offer opportunities for students to use interactive web tools constructively in their academic pursuits, as the benefits of shared learning are well documented.

Personal interactions of minors can be enhanced by social tools available through the Internet. Social networking websites allow the creation of online communities that feature an open exchange of information in various forms, such as images, videos, blog posts, and discussions about common interests.

Interactive web tools help children and young adults learn about and organize social, civic, and extra-curricular activities. Many interactive sites invite users to establish online identities, share personal information, create web content, and join social networks. Parents and guardians play a critical role in preparing their children for participation in online activity by communicating their personal family values and by monitoring their children's use of the Internet. Parents and guardians are responsible for what their children—and only their children—access on the Internet in libraries.

The use of interactive web tools poses two competing intellectual freedom issues—the protection of minors' privacy and the right of free speech. Some have expressed concerns regarding what they perceive to be an increased vulnerability of young people in the online environment when they use interactive sites to post personally identifiable information. In an effort to protect minors' privacy, adults sometimes restrict access to interactive web environments. Filters, for example, are sometimes used to restrict access by youth to interactive social networking tools, but at the same time deny minors' rights to free expression on the Internet. Prohibiting children and young adults from using social networking sites does not teach safe behavior and leaves youth without the necessary knowledge and skills to protect their privacy or engage in responsible speech. Instead of restricting or denying access to the Internet, librarians and teachers should educate minors to participate responsibly, ethically, and safely.

The First Amendment applies to speech created by minors on interactive sites. Use of these social networking sites in a school or library allows minors to access and create resources that fulfill their interests and needs for information, for social connection with peers, and for participation in a community of learners. Restricting expression and access to interactive web sites because the sites provide tools for sharing information with others violates the tenets of the *Library Bill of Rights*. It is the responsibility of librarians and educators to monitor threats to the intellectual freedom of minors and to advocate for extending access to interactive applications on the Internet.

As defenders of intellectual freedom and the First Amendment, libraries and librarians have a responsibility to offer unrestricted access to Internet interactivity in accordance with local, state, and federal laws and to advocate for greater access where it is abridged. School and library professionals should work closely with young people to help them learn skills and attitudes that will prepare them to be responsible, effective, and productive communicators in a free society.

A DEEPER LOOK

Intellectual Freedom and Young People

Pat Scales

Our Nation's understanding and appreciation of the First Amendment is not passed along genetically. It must be reaffirmed and defended, over and over. Keep fighting and keep winning.

—Paul Steinle

THE YOUTH IN America have First Amendment rights, yet most don't realize that they do. Children shouldn't have to wait until they first study the Constitution in elementary school to learn about the meaning of "free speech." They don't have to be in middle school or high school to grasp how the First Amendment applies to their own lives.

Teaching the principles of "free speech" should begin long before a child starts school, and be reaffirmed every year thereafter. Every time a librarian or teacher listens to a child's opinion, regardless of how simple or complex, they have modeled the basic principles of the First Amendment. A three-year-old in a preschool story time may say that she doesn't like Maurice Sendak's *Where the Wild Things Are* because the monsters are too scary. Other children in the group may embrace the book. It doesn't matter why children accept or reject a book; it only matters that their voices are heard. The same applies to movies they select, and computer games they play. Most children reject what they aren't ready for.

There are many opportunities to teach the First Amendment to adolescents. They have at least a cursory knowledge of the Constitution, and most have learned to recite the Preamble in the same way they deliver a poem by Shel Silverstein, Edgar Allan Poe, or Sylvia Plath. They know that the First Amendment is about "free speech," but few understand how it relates to their lives. Librarians are in the position to help them make that connection. This may happen informally in the library when young users are searching for books, or when they are using the Internet to find information for their own personal interest or a class project. It should include a discussion about "rights and responsibility," and respecting the ideas and beliefs of others.

Justice William J. Brennan Jr., who served on the Supreme Court for thirty-nine years, championed individual rights and authored significant opinions regarding free expression. He thought that the best way to convey the First Amendment to the young was through story. My years as a middle school and high school librarian gave me many chances to help students understand the relationship between free speech, the freedom to read, and the right to acquire and deliver information. Here are three stories from my experience:

Freedom to Read

A seventh-grade girl came into the library during homeroom and asked me for *The Giver* by Lois Lowry. A classmate overheard her request and said, "My mother won't let me read that book because it's offensive to our religious beliefs." I turned to the girl and said, "It's fine if your mother doesn't want you to read the book, and I respect her reasons. But Amy's mother wants her to read it."

Free Speech

An editor of a newsletter in the Midwest wrote that she didn't think that *Shiloh,* the 1992 Newbery Medal winner by Phyllis Reynolds Naylor, is appropriate for children. The publisher sent me a copy of the newsletter, and I turned it over to a sixth-grade language arts class. They wrote letters to the editor, and she printed all of them. She even made a statement that the comments from the sixth graders changed her opinion of the novel.

Rights and Responsibility

A group of residential high school students created a website so that classmates could stay in touch over the summer. It was password-protected, but one girl betrayed the group and printed and distributed a picture of two male classmates with the caption "gay." When the director of security told the students they had to take down the site, they came to my office and asked me to speak in their defense. I did defend their right to create and keep the website, but I also had a discussion with the students about their poor judgment in posting the picture, and the importance of making smart decisions.

The American Library Association believes strongly that young people are entitled to freely access ideas and information, subject only to the limitations imposed by their parents or guardians. The principles outlined in the *Library Bill of Rights* apply to children and young people as well as adults.

The role of the librarian is to guide and advise young people on how to find and use the best available material for their information needs.

Now a great threat to librarians' service to youth is the groups and organizations that have developed websites that offer lists of controversial materials and warn parents that schools and libraries are "corrupting" youth. Other websites use emoticons and graphs to rate the content of books, movies, computer games, television programs, websites, and so on. These sites claim they aren't about censorship, but are simply helping parents make smart choices for their children.

One of these sites gives *Speak,* a novel by Laurie Halse Anderson about date rape, "three bombs for violence" and "two lips for sex." These labels have branded this novel "controversial" and a number of frightened librarians and parents have reacted to the ratings and denied teens access to this powerful book. In a workshop with Laurie Halse Anderson, I learned about a fourteen-year-old girl who read *Speak,* and after she finished the book she gave it to her mother and said, "This is what daddy has been doing to me." The girl could never find the words to tell her mother, and the novel became her voice. Had this girl, and her mother, not had access to this novel, the sexual abuse might have continued. Books and information have the power to change lives. This is the message that young users deserve to hear.

Librarians are trained to help parents, children, and teens make choices that are right for them. No website provides such personal guidance. Most young adults aren't fooled by the motives of those who attempt to deny them access to books and information. They understand that censorship is about misguided cynicism, and that intellectual freedom is about respect of ideas. If American youth are taught that the Constitution is more than a historic document, and if they comprehend how the First Amendment is applicable to their own lives, then they are very likely to become engaged citizens and lifelong "free speech" advocates.

The Law Regarding Minors' First Amendment Rights to Access Information

Theresa Chmara

IT IS WELL established that minors have First Amendment rights and that those rights include the right to receive information. Although school officials retain substantial discretion in designing school curricula, attempts to censor access to materials in the school library will not be permitted without a demonstration that the restricted materials are educationally unsuitable

**What's a
"Public Forum"?**

This essay uses the
term *public forum*.
To learn more about
what that means
and how it applies
to libraries, please
read part I, chapter 4,
"The Right to Receive
Information: Libraries,
the First Amendment,
and the Public Forum
Doctrine." (p.43)

or pervasively vulgar. Censorship in the public library should not be permitted unless the material is found by a court of law to be obscene, child pornography, or, in the case of minors, harmful to minors.

The landmark case of *Tinker v. Des Moines Independent Community School District* established that students do not "shed their constitutional rights to freedom of speech or expression at the schoolhouse gate."[1] In that case, the Supreme Court ordered a public school to allow students to wear black armbands in protest of the Vietnam War, explaining that "in our system, students may not be regarded as closed-circuit recipients of only that which the State chooses to communicate."[2]

More recently, in *American Amusement Machine Association v. Kendrick,* an appellate court considering the constitutionality of an ordinance restricting minors' access to certain video arcade games echoed the Supreme Court's admonition in *Tinker* that minors must have a broad range of information for intellectual growth, holding that "people are unlikely to become well-functioning, independent-minded adults and responsible citizens if they are raised in an intellectual bubble."[3] Building on the recognition that access to information is fundamentally necessary, courts have held that minors' First Amendment liberties include the right to receive information and plainly extend beyond schools.

In *Board of Education v. Pico,* a school board had attempted to remove from a school library controversial titles such as *Slaughterhouse Five* and *Soul on Ice.*[4] The school board's action did not restrict minors' own expression, as the ban on armbands in *Tinker* had, but the Supreme Court rejected the action because the board was restricting what minors could read. The court stated that "the right to receive ideas is a necessary predicate to the recipient's meaningful exercise of his own rights of speech, press, and political freedom"[5] and made clear that "students too are beneficiaries of this principle."[6]

The Supreme Court has limited minors' rights to receive information in two instances in which adults' constitutional rights remain broader. First, the court has given public schools significant latitude to restrict minors' receipt of information if the school's judgment is based objec-

**Minors and
the Internet**

To learn more about
the Children's Internet Protection Act
and Internet filtering,
please read "Internet
Filtering and Intellectual Freedom" in part
II, chapter 2.

tively on the fact that information is "educationally unsuitable" rather than on an official's subjective disagreement with or disapproval of the content of the information. The determination of whether material is "educationally unsuitable" is a fact-based inquiry that will generally require the testimony of educational experts. The *Pico* plurality held unconstitutional the removal of books from school libraries where the removal was based on the ideas the books expressed, but it permitted removal of books if officials were motivated by concerns that the books were "educationally unsuitable" or "pervasively vulgar."[7] The plurality also recognized that schools must have substantial discretion in designing curricula.[8]

The second restriction on minors' rights to receive information allows states to deem certain materials obscene for minors even if the materials are protected for adults. In *Ginsberg v. New York* the court upheld the conviction of a magazine vendor for selling an adult magazine to a sixteen-year-old.[9] The court explained that although the magazine clearly was not obscene for adults, the state had acted within First Amendment bounds in adopting a distinct, broader definition of obscenity for minors. Because obscene speech enjoys no First Amendment protection, under *Ginsberg* states may completely bar minors from receiving material deemed obscene for them but not for adults. Accordingly, most states have enacted "harmful to minors" obscenity statutes. In *FCC v. Pacifica Foundation,* the Supreme Court restricted the broadcast of speech that was merely "indecent," not "obscene as to minors" under *Ginsberg,* largely because children might hear the indecent speech.[10] The court, however, has declined to extend *Pacifica* to other media, including telephone communications[11] and, most notably, the Internet in *Reno v. American Civil Liberties Union.*[12]

Moreover, courts have recognized limits on the *Ginsberg* principle. First, the Supreme Court has made clear that states may not simply ban minors' exposure to a full category of speech, such as nudity, when only a subset of that category can plausibly be deemed obscene for them.[13] Second, courts have held that states must determine *Ginsberg* "obscenity" by reference to the entire population of minors—including the oldest minors. One of the grounds on which the Supreme Court distinguished *Reno* from *Ginsberg* was that the "harmful to minors" statute at issue in *Ginsberg* did not apply to seventeen-year-olds, whereas the Communications Decency Act at issue in *Reno* did.[14] The court went on to stress "that the strength of the government's interest in protecting minors is not equally strong throughout the [age] coverage of this broad statute."[15] Likewise, some lower courts have upheld restrictions on displays of adult magazines only if the restrictions did not prohibit the display of materials that would be appropriate for older minors.[16]

Although minors do not shed their First Amendment rights at the schoolhouse gate, the Supreme Court has held that students' speech rights are not "automatically coextensive with the rights of adults in other settings"[17] and has generally applied those rights "in light of the special characteristics of the school environment."[18] In *Pico,* for example, although the court's plurality opinion prohibited school officials from removing school library books based on the officials' disagreement with the ideas expressed in the books, it noted that removal decisions motivated by concerns that a book was "educationally unsuitable" or "pervasively vulgar" would be constitutional.[19]

Likewise, the court in *Hazelwood School District v. Kuhlmeier* permitted a high school principal to order the removal of certain articles from a school newspaper.[20] The student journalism class that wrote and edited the newspaper had planned to run several controversial stories about student pregnancy and the impact of divorce on the school's students. The principal justified the removal decision on the grounds that the articles were inappropriate for the maturity level of the intended readers, that the privacy interests of the articles' subjects were not adequately protected, and the danger that the controversial views would be attributed to the school.[21] The Supreme Court rejected the students' First Amendment claims, finding that a lower standard of review should apply when there is a danger that student expression will be perceived as "bear[ing] the imprimatur of the school."[22]

Similarly, in *Bethel School District No. 403 v. Fraser,* the court held that a student could be disciplined for having delivered a speech that was sexually explicit, but not legally obscene, at an official school assembly.[23] In upholding the school's disciplinary action, the court found it "perfectly appropriate for the school to disassociate itself to make the point to the pupils that vulgar speech and lewd conduct is wholly inconsistent with the 'fundamental values' of public school education."[24]

In a more recent school discipline case, *Morse v. Frederick,* the Supreme Court reiterated the important right that students have to participate in political speech, while at the same time providing school officials with authority to discipline students who advocate illegal drug use.[25] Joseph Frederick was a high school student in Juneau, Alaska, at the time of the incident. The Olympic torch relay was traveling through Juneau and students were dismissed from school to view the relay. Frederick held up a sign reading "Bong Hits 4 Jesus" across the street from the school during the festivities. The principal of the high school, Deborah Morse, approached him and demanded he put down the banner. When he refused on the basis of his First Amendment rights, Morse crumpled the banner and suspended him from school for ten days.

Frederick filed suit, alleging that the actions of the principal were unconstitutional. The United States Supreme Court held that the principal's actions were constitutional. Specifically, the Supreme Court held that "schools may take steps to safeguard those entrusted to their care from speech that can reasonably be regarded as encouraging illegal drug use" and that "the school officials in this case did not violate the First Amendment by confiscating the pro-drug banner and suspending the student responsible for it."[26]

In concurring in the majority opinion, however, Justices Alito and Kennedy emphasized that they joined in the majority based "on the understanding that (*a*) it goes no further than to hold that a public school may restrict speech that a reasonable observer would interpret as advocating illegal drug use and (*b*) it provides no support for any restriction of speech that can plausibly be interpreted as commenting on any political or social issue, including speech on issues such as 'the wisdom of the war on drugs or of legalizing marijuana for medicinal use.'"[27] Justice Alito emphasized that "the opinion of the Court does not endorse the broad argument advanced by petitioners and the United States that the First Amendment permits public school officials to censor any student speech that interferes with a school's 'educational mission.'"[28]

Hazelwood, Bethel School District, and *Morse* are significant decisions but are of limited application to disputes involving students' speech rights in public school libraries. School officials certainly cannot rely on those decisions to restrict students' speech at will, especially when that speech cannot reasonably be perceived as bearing the imprimatur of the school. Moreover, while courts plainly have given school officials a greater degree of control over decisions related to the school curriculum,[29] these decisions do not directly implicate school libraries, which provide students with both curricular and extracurricular materials.[30]

Numerous lower court decisions have recognized the distinction in *Hazelwood* between curricular and noncurricular speech restrictions. In applying the *Hazelwood* case to other situations, lower courts have applied greater deference to school officials attempting to control curricular speech restrictions. For example, in *Virgil v. School Board of Columbia County,* the court of appeals affirmed a school board's decision to remove selected portions of *The Miller's Tale* and *Lysistrata* from a humanities course curriculum, stating that "in matters pertaining to the curriculum, educators have been accorded greater control over expression than they may enjoy in other spheres of activity."[31] In upholding the removal, the court emphasized that the disputed materials remained in the school library,[32] which, unlike a course curriculum, was a "repository for 'voluntary inquiry.'"[33]

Students' First Amendment rights in the school library context, therefore, are broader than those in a class, a school-sponsored assembly, or other curriculum-based activities. In the context of book removals from libraries, courts must determine whether the removal is based on educational suitability or is an attempt to impose viewpoint or content discrimination. Recent decisions of lower federal courts have echoed the reasoning and the result of *Pico* and further clarified the rights of minors. For example, in *Campbell v. St. Tammany Parish School Board,* the court of appeals confirmed that "the key inquiry in a book removal case is the school officials' substantial motivation in arriving at the removal decision."[34] Considering the plaintiffs' constitutional challenge to a school board's decision to remove a book on voodoo from the town's school libraries, the court held that a determination of the board's motivation could not be made without a trial. The court observed that "in light of the special role of the school library as a place where students may freely and voluntarily explore diverse topics, the school board's non-curricular decision to remove a book well after it had been placed in the public school libraries evokes the question whether that action might not be an unconstitutional attempt to 'strangle the free mind at its source.'"[35]

Similarly, the district court in *Case v. Unified School District No. 233* found a school board's removal of *Annie on My Mind* unconstitutional where a "substantial motivation" behind the library removal was the officials' disagreement with the views expressed in the book.[36] The defendants had claimed that the book was "educationally unsuitable," a removal criterion deemed permissible by the Supreme Court's plurality decision in *Pico.*[37] Nonetheless, the court refused to credit the defendant's assertions, explaining that "there is no basis in the record to believe that these Board members meant by 'educational suitability' anything other than their own disagreement with the ideas expressed in the book."[38]

In a more recent case, *American Civil Liberties Union of Florida v. Miami-Dade School Board,* the Eleventh Circuit upheld the school board's removal of a picture book on Cuba on the ground that the book was factually inaccurate because it failed to provide additional details about the subject matter.[39] The district court had concluded that the removal decision was politically motivated but the appellate court disagreed.[40] School board members defended their removal decision by arguing that the books were offensive to some members of the Cuban community and educationally unsuitable because they are viewpoint-neutral and do not include detailed facts about Cuba's totalitarian dictatorship. The ACLU expert noted, however, that the "alleged omissions are appropriate omissions given the age level and purpose for which the book is intended."[41] The determination of whether a decision to censor materials is based on educational suitability or political motivation will be a fact-based inquiry in every instance. The reach of the Eleventh Circuit's decision in the Miami-Dade case is thus limited to that case alone. The inquiry in a censorship case focuses on "motivation," and each court faced with that inquiry must determine if the particular school board or government entity removed particular books based on their own viewpoints or objective educational concerns. The Eleventh Circuit's conclusion that the Miami-Dade School Board did not engage in politically motivated censorship therefore would not preclude another court from finding in a different situation that removal of the same books in another library was unconstitutional viewpoint discrimination.

The removal of books from open shelves, rather than an outright removal from the library, also raises First Amendment concerns with respect to the rights of minors. In *Counts v. Cedarville School District,* a federal district court in Arkansas addressed a dispute over whether books from the *Harry Potter* series should be removed from a school library. A parent of two children in the Cedarville School District filed a complaint arguing that *Harry Potter and the Sorcerer's Stone* should be removed from the library. Following procedures for resolving challenges to library materials, the book was reviewed by the library committee. That committee of fifteen reviewers concluded unanimously that the book should remain in the library. The Cedarville School Board then ignored that decision and ordered that all of the books in the *Harry Potter* series be removed from the library shelves and held in the offices of the librarian, available only to children with parental permission to read the books.[42]

Parents in the school district sued the school board, alleging that their child's rights were violated by the removal of the book from the open shelves of the library. The district court agreed. The court held that the minor's rights were violated even by the removal of the books from the open shelves because the books were "stigmatized."[43] The court held, moreover, that having to request the books from a librarian placed a burden on the minor's exercise of her First Amendment rights. The court also held that it was irrelevant that the minor plaintiff had the books at home, had parental permission, or otherwise had access to the books because the books' removal from the open shelves of her school library violated her rights—absent a showing that the books were educationally unsuitable or pervasively vulgar. Finally, the court held that the school board did not allege a sufficient justification for the removal of the books in that there was no evidence to support the claim that the books would promote disobedience, disrespect for authority, or disruption in the school.

Overall, courts carefully scrutinize any decision to remove a book from a school library, imposing stricter constitutional standards than those applicable to curricular decisions, over which school officials have greater, though not absolute, control. Certainly, the case law forbids any removal action motivated by the school officials' disagreement with the views or ideas expressed in the book. Even purportedly viewpoint-neutral justifications—

such as "educational suitability"—likely will be subjected to skeptical, exacting judicial review and will require testimony from educational experts to support the removal on that basis.

In the context of a public library, which generally is considered to be a limited or designated public forum, government officials must meet an even more exacting standard to support removal of materials. Unless the material has been found by a court to be obscenity, child pornography, or material deemed "harmful to minors," any content-based decision to remove material from the public library will be deemed unconstitutional unless the government can demonstrate that the removal meets the standard of strict scrutiny. Strict scrutiny requires evidence that the restriction is necessary to achieve a compelling government interest and is narrowly tailored to achieve that interest.[44]

NOTES

1. *Tinker v. Des Moines Independent Community School District,* 393 U.S. 503, 506 (1969).

2. *Id.* at 511.

3. *American Amusement Machine Association v. Kendrick,* 244 F.3d 572, 577 (7th Cir. 2001).

4. *Board of Education v. Pico,* 457 U.S. 853 (1982) (plurality opinion).

5. *Id.* at 867.

6. *Id.* at 868. Other cases in which the Supreme Court emphasized minors' right to receive information include *Erznoznik v. City of Jacksonville,* 422 U.S. 205, 213-14 (1975) (holding that "speech . . . cannot be suppressed solely to protect the young from ideas or images that a legislative body thinks unsuitable for them") and *Bolger v. Youngs Drug Products Corp.,* 463 U.S. 60, 75 n. 30 (1983) (criticizing a federal ban on mailing unsolicited contraceptive advertisements because it ignored adolescents' "pressing need for information about contraception").

7. *Pico,* 457 U.S. at 871.

8. *Id.* at 864.

9. *Ginsberg v. New York,* 390 U.S. 629 (1968).

10. *FCC v. Pacifica Foundation,* 438 U.S. 726, 749-50 (1978).

11. *Sable Communications of California v. FCC,* 492 U.S. 115, 127-28 (1989).

12. *Reno v. ACLU,* 524 U.S. 844, 864-65 (1997).

13. *Erznoznik,* 422 U.S. at 212-14 (1975).

14. See *Reno,* 524 U.S. at 864-65.

15. *Id.* at 878.

16. *American Booksellers Association v. Webb,* 919 F.2d 1493, 1504-05 (11th Cir. 1990); *American Booksellers Association v. Virginia,* 882 F.2d 125, 127 (4th Cir. 1989).

17. *Bethel School District No. 403 v. Fraser*, 478 U.S. 675, 682 (1986).

18. *Pico*, 457 U.S. at 868 (quoting *Tinker*, 393 U.S. at 506).

19. *Id.* at 871.

20. *Hazelwood School District v. Kuhlmeier*, 484 U.S. 267 (1988).

21. *Id.* at 274.

22. *Id.* at 271, 273 (holding that curriculum decisions are permissible if they are "reasonably related to legitimate pedagogical concerns").

23. *Bethel School District*, 478 U.S. at 685–86.

24. *Id.*

25. *Morse v. Frederick*, 551 U.S. 393 (2007).

26. *Id.*

27. *Id.*

28. *Id.*

29. See, *e.g.*, *Pico*, 457 U.S. at 864.

30. See id. at 860.

31. *Virgil v. School Board of Columbia County*, 862 F.2d 1517, 1520 (11th Cir. 1989).

32. *Id.* at 1523, n. 8.

33. *Id.* at 1525 (quoting *Pico*, 457 U.S. at 869); *but see Pratt v. Independent School District No. 831*, 670 F.2d 771, 779 (8th Cir. 1982) (refusing to allow a school board to strike a short story, "The Lottery," from the school curriculum merely because the story remained available in the school library).

34. *Campbell v. St. Tammany Parish School Board*, 64 F.3d 184, 190 (5th Cir. 1995).

35. *Id.*

36. *Case v. Unified School District No. 233*, 908 F. Supp. 864 (D. Kan. 1995).

37. *Pico*, 457 U.S. at 871.

38. *Case*, 908 F. Supp. at 875.

39. *American Civil Liberties Union of Florida v. Miami-Dade School Board*, 557 F.3d 1177 (11th Cir. 2009), *cert. denied*, 130 S.Ct. 659 (2009).

40. *American Civil Liberties Union of Florida v. Miami-Dade School Board*, 439 F. Supp. 2d 1242 (S.D. Fla. 2006).

41. *Id.*

42. *Counts v. Cedarville School District*, 295 F. Supp. 2d 996, 1000–01 (W.D. Ark. 2003).

43. *Id.* at 999.

44. *Perry Education Association v. Perry Local Educators' Association*, 460 U.S. 37, 45 (1983).

Collection Development and Management

ISSUE AT A GLANCE

Key Concepts

- Library collections should represent the diversity of people and ideas in society. In selecting resources, librarians should strive for a diversity of viewpoints (including those that are controversial), formats, languages, and publishers.
- A balanced collection reflects a diversity of materials and resources, not an equality in numbers.
- The presence of books, digital content, and other resources in the library does not indicate endorsement of their contents by the library.
- Collection development and the selection of materials and resources should be done according to professional standards and the library's collection development policy.
- Procedures and guidelines for weeding should be included in the collection development policy to avoid the process being used as a means of censorship.
- Viewpoint-neutral directional aids help users locate materials, but labels and rating systems that attempt to prejudice users are inappropriate and can be a censor's tool.

What Does the Law Say?

- The ratings affixed to movies, video games, and music recordings are *not* law. They are voluntary rating systems designed and assigned by private organizations as an informative advisory. Courts have invalidated laws and ordinances that enforce ratings systems as a means to deny minors access to resources on the grounds that such restrictions violate minors' First Amendment rights.

Creating Policy for Your Library

- Consider formally adopting the *Library Bill of Rights* (see part I, chapter 2) as policy for your library. It contains statements about the importance and value of diversity in library collections.
- Be sure you have a collection development policy, including online resources and websites, and that you follow it (see part I, chapter 3).

Especially for Academic Libraries

- Guard against using the excuse of "unscholarly" to avoid the purchase of controversial content. Academic libraries often include holdings that are considered "unscholarly," "pseudoscience," or offensive to groups (for example, Holocaust denial literature) for the purpose of studying the controversy or for the historical record.
- See "Intellectual Freedom Principles for Academic Libraries" in part II, chapter 1.

Especially for Public Libraries

- The library collection should reflect the interests of the entire community, not just the majority.

Especially for School Libraries

- A school library must serve the entire student body, supporting not only the formal curriculum, but students' personal research and recreational reading needs, as well.
- Providing a broad range of materials on controversial issues helps students develop analytical skills and learn to make informed decisions based on information from multiple points of view.

- Reading-level stickers are prejudicial and should not be used to limit students' use of resources.

To Learn More

- Visit the ALA "Intellectual Freedom" website (www.ala.org/advocacy/intfreedom) for links to information about collection development and rating systems.
- See "Religion in American Libraries: Questions and Answers," available at www.ala.org/advocacy/intfreedom.

Questions for Reflection

- What's the difference between selection and censorship?
- A prominent local politician offers to donate a selection of religiously themed materials to your library. What's your response?
- When should materials be weeded from collections?

OFFICIAL ALA POLICY STATEMENTS

Diversity in Collection Development
An Interpretation of the *Library Bill of Rights*

Adopted July 14, 1982, by the ALA Council; amended January 10, 1990; July 2, 2008; and July 1, 2014.

COLLECTION DEVELOPMENT SHOULD reflect the philosophy inherent in Article II of the American Library Association's *Library Bill of Rights:* "Libraries should provide materials and information presenting all points of view on current and historical issues. Materials should not be proscribed or removed because of partisan or doctrinal disapproval."

A historical essay about this statement can be found in the publication, *A History of ALA Policy on Intellectual Freedom: A Supplement to the Intellectual Freedom Manual, Ninth Edition.*

Library collections must represent the diversity of people and ideas in our society. There are many complex facets to any issue, and many contexts in which issues may be expressed, discussed, or interpreted. Librarians have an obligation to select and support access to content on all subjects that meet, as closely as possible, the needs, interests, and abilities of all persons in the community the library serves.

Librarians have a professional responsibility to be inclusive in collection development and in the provision of interlibrary loan. Access to all content legally obtainable should be assured to the user, and policies should not unjustly exclude content even if they are offensive to the librarian or the user. This includes content that reflect [*sic*] a diversity of issues, whether they be, for example, political, economic, religious, social, ethnic, or sexual. A balanced collection reflects a diversity of content, not an equality of numbers.

Collection development responsibilities include selecting content in different formats produced by independent, small and local producers as well as information resources from major producers and distributors. Content should represent the languages commonly used in the library's service community and should include formats that meet the needs of users with disabilities. Collection development and the selection of content should be done according to professional standards and established selection and review procedures. Failure to select resources merely because they may be potentially controversial is censorship, as is withdrawing resources for the same reason.

Over time, individuals, groups, and entities have sought to limit the diversity of library collections. They cite a variety of reasons that include prejudicial language and ideas, political content, economic theory, social philosophies, religious beliefs, sexual content and expression, and other potentially controversial topics. Librarians have a professional responsibility to be fair, just, and equitable and to give all library users equal protection in guarding against violation of the library patron's right to read, view, or listen to content protected by the First Amendment, no matter what the viewpoint of the author, creator, or selector. Librarians have an obligation to protect library collections from removal of content based on personal bias or prejudice.

Intellectual freedom, the essence of equitable library services, provides for free access to all expressions of ideas through which any and all sides of a question, cause, or movement may be explored. Librarians must not permit their personal beliefs to influence collection development decisions.

Evaluating Library Collections
An Interpretation of the *Library Bill of Rights*

Adopted February 2, 1973, by the ALA Council;
amended July 1, 1981; and June 2, 2008.

A historical essay about this statement can be found in the publication, *A History of ALA Policy on Intellectual Freedom: A Supplement to the Intellectual Freedom Manual, Ninth Edition.*

THE CONTINUOUS REVIEW of library materials is necessary as a means of maintaining an active library collection of current interest to users. In the process, materials may be added and physically deteriorated or obsolete materials may be replaced or removed in accordance with the collection maintenance policy of a given library and the needs of the community it serves. Continued evaluation is closely related to the goals and responsibilities of each library and is a valuable tool of collection development. This procedure is not to be used as a convenient means to remove materials that might be viewed as controversial or objectionable. Such abuse of the evaluation function violates the principles of intellectual freedom and is in opposition to the Preamble and Articles I and II of the *Library Bill of Rights,* which state:

> The American Library Association affirms that all libraries are forums for information and ideas, and that the following basic policies should guide their services.

> I.   Books and other library resources should be provided for the interest, information, and enlightenment of all people of the community the library serves. Materials should not be excluded because of the origin, background, or views of those contributing to their creation.

> II. Libraries should provide materials and information presenting all points of view on current and historical issues. Materials should not be proscribed or removed because of partisan or doctrinal disapproval.

The American Library Association opposes internal censorship and strongly urges that libraries adopt guidelines setting forth the positive purposes and principles of evaluation of materials in library collections.

II 4
Collections

Labeling and Rating Systems

An Interpretation of the *Library Bill of Rights*

Adopted July 13, 1951, by the ALA Council; amended June 25, 1971; July 1, 1981; June 26, 1990; January 19, 2005; July 15, 2009; and July 1, 2014.

> A historical essay about this statement can be found in the publication, *A History of ALA Policy on Intellectual Freedom: A Supplement to the Intellectual Freedom Manual, Ninth Edition.*

LIBRARIES DO NOT advocate the ideas found in their collections or in resources accessible through the library. The presence of books and other resources in a library does not indicate endorsement of their contents by the library. Likewise, providing access to digital information does not indicate endorsement or approval of that information by the library. Labeling and rating systems present distinct challenges to these intellectual freedom principles.

Many organizations use or devise rating systems as a means of advising either their members or the general public regarding the organizations' opinions of the contents and suitability or appropriate age for use of certain books, films, recordings, websites, games, or other materials. The adoption, enforcement, or endorsement of any of these rating systems by a library violates the American Library Association's *Library Bill of Rights* and may be unconstitutional. If enforcement of labeling or rating systems is mandated by law, the library should seek legal advice regarding the law's applicability to library operations.

Viewpoint-neutral directional labels are a convenience designed to save time. These are different in intent from attempts to prejudice or discourage users or restrict their access to resources. Labeling as an attempt to prejudice attitudes is a censor's tool. The American Library Association opposes labeling as a means of predisposing people's attitudes toward library resources.

Prejudicial labels are designed to restrict access, based on a value judgment that the content, language, or themes of the resource, or the background or views of the creator(s) of the resource, render it inappropriate or offensive for all or certain groups of users. The prejudicial label is used to warn, discourage, or prohibit users or certain groups of users from accessing the resource. Such labels sometimes are used to place materials in restricted locations where access depends on staff intervention.

Viewpoint-neutral directional aids facilitate access by making it easier for users to locate resources. Users may choose to consult or ignore the directional aids at their own discretion.

Directional aids can have the effect of prejudicial labels when their implementation becomes proscriptive rather than descriptive. When directional aids are used to forbid access or to suggest moral or doctrinal endorsement, the effect is the same as prejudicial labeling.

Libraries sometimes acquire resources that include ratings as part of their packaging. Librarians should not endorse the inclusion of such rating systems; however, removing or destroying the ratings—if placed there by, or with permission of, the copyright holder—could constitute expurgation (see "Expurgation of Library Resources: An Interpretation of the *Library Bill of Rights*"). In addition, the inclusion of ratings on bibliographic records in library catalogs is a violation of the *Library Bill of Rights*.

Prejudicial labeling and ratings presuppose the existence of individuals or groups with wisdom to determine by authority what is appropriate or inappropriate for others. They presuppose that individuals must be directed in making up their minds about the ideas they examine. The fact that libraries do not advocate or use proscriptive labels and rating systems does not preclude them from answering questions about them. The American Library Association affirms the rights of individuals to form their own opinions about resources they choose to read or view.

A DEEPER LOOK

The Law Regarding Rating Systems

Deborah Caldwell-Stone

MANY PERSONS BELIEVE that ratings affixed to movies, video games, and music recordings are "law," and that a library breaks the law if it collects or provides access to materials rated "mature," or for use by adult audiences.

This perception is incorrect. The organizations that assign ratings, such as the Motion Picture Association of America (MPAA), the Entertainment Software Ratings Board (ESRB), and the Recording Industry Association of America (RIAA) are not government agencies, nor are their activities sanctioned by local, state, or federal government. All are private trade associations whose members produce and distribute movies, games, and music. Each organization administers its ratings program as a benefit for its members, who want to give parents advance information about the movie, game, or song so the parents can decide whether or not a movie, game, or song is appropriate for their child.

An item's rating is meant to serve only as an informative advisory for parents. A rating such as the MPAA's "R" rating is not, and has never been, a legal determination that a particular motion picture is "obscene," or "obscene as to minors," or "harmful to minors." Only a court of law can make that determination.

Moreover, such ratings systems are strictly voluntary. No law requires a filmmaker, game designer, or musician to submit their work for a rating, and no law requires a theater or retailer to follow the ratings guidelines when selling movie tickets, DVDs, games, or music. Those theater owners and dealers who enforce a ratings system do so voluntarily to provide a service to parents.

Trade associations are not the only private organizations rating media. Nonprofit organizations and websites now exist that purport to rate books, films, video games, television shows, and even computer applications for suitability for children and young adults. These sites, which include Common Sense Media, The Literate Mother, and Compass Book Ratings, appear to provide objective reviews of a book, film, or game by offering greater details about its contents, but ultimately are a kind of rating system that assigns a precise age level to the book, film, or game.[1] Similarly, Lexile scores and Accelerated Reader levels function as a kind of rating that assigns a particular age, grade, or developmental level to a book. Like MPAA ratings for films, these determinations about a book or film's age or developmental appropriateness have no force of law and are not a legal finding that a book or other resource is unsuitable for minors.

Genre Labels and Religious Fiction

Sometimes something as simple as a genre spine label can raise significant constitutional concerns. Such is the case with the genre label that uses a cross to designate Christian fiction.

The use of such labels, especially when other religious fiction is not labeled, can communicate a message of preference for Christianity, which violates the First Amendment's requirement that public libraries and schools maintain neutrality towards religion and show no preference between religion and nonbelief. Moreover, the use of a cross as a genre label or as a means of classifying materials is especially problematic, as federal courts have ruled that crosses are the preeminent symbol of Christianity, so much so that the prominent use or display of a cross by a government agency in any context can violate the principle of separation of church and state embodied in the Establishment Clause of the First Amendment.

The use of labels to identify Christian books raises many issues for libraries striving to provide reference and readers' advisory services in a manner that serves the entire community. When only one type of religious fiction is labeled, only one religion has visibility in the library and persons of other faiths may feel unwelcome and underrepresented. It may also be divisive, pitting one view of Christianity, for example, against the views of other Christian denominations. The use of crosses as genre labels may also imply that the book has been vetted or approved by the library based upon its religious content and is "safe for use." Libraries should avoid those practices that imply any endorsement or favoritism towards a particular viewpoint or belief.

For libraries that want to identify religious fiction as a genre, neutral labels such as "inspirational fiction" will avoid any unconstitutional entanglement with religion, especially if the genre classification includes books and materials without a religious viewpoint.

First Amendment concerns arise when the ratings or age levels assigned by a trade association or a nonprofit group or website are used to regulate or restrict minors' access to films, games, and other media. Courts have invalidated laws and ordinances that enforce ratings systems as a means of denying minors access to films, games, and other content, on the grounds that such restrictions violate minors' First Amendment rights. Among these cases are *Engdahl v. City of Kenosha,* which invalidated a Kenosha, Wisconsin ordinance that used MPAA ratings to prohibit minors from seeing R-rated films; and *Motion Picture Association of America v. Specter,* which invalidated a Philadelphia criminal ordinance that penalized any theater allowing minors to view films rated "not suitable for children" by the MPAA.[2] Both the Seventh Circuit Court of Appeals in Chicago and the Eighth Circuit Court of Appeals in St. Louis invalidated state and local ordinances that used the ESRB's private ratings system to restrict minors' access to video games.[3] In 2011, the Supreme Court held that a California statute barring minors from purchasing violent games violated minors' First Amendment rights, holding that "even where the protection of children is the object, the constitutional limits on governmental action apply."[4]

Given these legal authorities, librarians should not adopt policies that use private content ratings systems to restrict library users' access to library materials, regardless of the user's age. Instead, they should adopt and promote policies and practices that provide library users and parents with information to guide their choices and their children's choices and provide programming that equips young people with critical viewing and thinking skills that will enable them to make good judgments about the films, music, and games they view and use.

NOTES

1. For additional discussion about the inappropriate use of these organizations' ratings to restrict young people's reading choices, see Pat Scales, "Weighing In: Three Bombs, Two Lips, and a Martini Glass," *Booklist,* August, 2010; and Brian Kenney, "Fear Factor: Kids' Lit Style," *School Library Journal,* July 1, 2010. See also "Intellectual Freedom and Young People," part II, chapter 3.

2. *Engdahl v. City of Kenosha,* 317 F. Supp. 1133 (E.D. Wis. 1970); and *Motion Picture Association of America v. Specter,* 315 F. Supp. 824 (E.D. Pa. 1970).

3. See, for example, *American Amusement Mach. Association v. Kendrick,* 244 F.3d 954 (7th Cir. 2001); and *Interactive Digital Software Association v. St. Louis County,* 329 F.3d 954 (8th Cir. 2003).

4. *Brown v. Entertainment Merchants Association,* 131 S. Ct. 2729 (2011).

Copyright

II.5
Copyright

ISSUE AT A GLANCE

Key Concepts

- Copyright law is essential to the operation of libraries. It promotes learning and the dissemination of information by giving authors and others economic incentive to create new works that, along with works in the public domain, make up library collections.
- Increasingly, libraries acquire copyrighted works by license instead of outright purchase. In these cases, librarians should negotiate for the same rights provided to libraries and their users by copyright law, such as lending through interlibrary loan.
- Library workers should be aware of the concept of "fair use," which employs four factors (the purpose of the use, the nature of the work, the amount used, and the effect on the market) to guide decision making about the use of copyrighted materials. Most copyright questions can be addressed only by evaluating the case at hand in light of the fair use factors.
- Library workers should educate library users about copyright law, including its exceptions and limitations. They should be familiar with the special rights accorded to libraries under copyright law as well as the limitations on those rights.

What Does the Law Say?

- The Copyright Act of 1976 is the basis for U.S. copyright law. Codified in Title 17 of the U.S. Code, it has been modified through subsequent acts such as the Digital Millennium Copyright Act and Copyright Term Extension Act. All of these laws have implications for libraries in both the analog and digital environment. Because the law can be ambiguous and does not explicitly define all of the copyright issues that libraries and their users face, interpretation is required.
- Copyright includes exceptions and limitations that allow libraries and their users to interact with and use copyrighted materials in non-infringing ways.
- "First sale" is an exception to a copyright holder's right to control distribution of copyrighted material once it has been legally sold. It allows libraries to lend materials without having to compensate the rights holders beyond the initial purchase.

Creating Policy for Your Library

- Consider adopting the *Code of Ethics of the American Library Association* (see part I, chapter 2) as policy for your library. It contains statements related to intellectual property, of which copyright is part.
- Because the law is interpreted, when drafting copyright policies and procedures regarding operations such as interlibrary loan and preservation, it is wise to seek advice from legal counsel and other librarians with copyright expertise who can provide model policies.

Especially for Academic Libraries

- The widespread adoption of learning management systems has made it easier for faculty to post and share copyrighted material in the digital environment. Consider hosting regular workshops on using the library's online reserves system and educating faculty about the policies and procedures at your institution.
- Consult the Association of Research Libraries' "Code of Best Practices in Fair Use" for guidance on a range of copyright-related issues in academic libraries (www.arl.org/focus-areas/copyright-ip/fair-use/code-of-best-practices).

Especially for Public Libraries

- While library workers may be knowledgeable about what's allowable with copyrighted material in print, the variety and complexity of licenses for digital resources make it difficult to have standard policies and procedures. Make sure the staff is aware of restrictions and permissions for both licensed and purchased resources.

Especially for School Libraries

- The creativecommons.org website offers a search tool you can use to help students and teachers find creative works that require no permission or license fees to be used and adapted in projects.

To Learn More

- Visit the ALA "Copyright" website at www.ala.org/advocacy/copyright.
- Consult with the copyright specialist at the ALA Washington Office (800) 941-8478, who can direct you to additional educational tools.

Questions for Reflection

- A library user asks for assistance with copying a music CD from the library's collection to her personal device. What's your response?
- Many libraries have posted signs warning against violation of copyright at photocopiers. Should there also be signs on computers regarding copyrighted digital content?
- When teachers want to distribute multiple copies of articles or short excerpts from text to students for educational purposes, what would you advise?
- A faculty member wants to show a DVD in the class. Is this a problem? What if the faculty member wants to stream the DVD instead?

II.5
Copyright

Copyright

An Interpretation of the *Code of Ethics*

Adopted June 30, 2014, by the ALA Council.

ARTICLE IV OF the *Code of Ethics of the American Library Association* states that librarians "respect intellectual property rights and advocate balance between the interests of information users and rights holders." Copyright[1] is the aspect of intellectual property most pertinent for libraries. Copyright, as established by the U.S. Constitution and the Copyright Act, is

> A historical essay about this statement can be found in the publication, *A History of ALA Policy on Intellectual Freedom: A Supplement to the Intellectual Freedom Manual, Ninth Edition.*

a system of rights granted by the law combined with limitations on those rights.

A shared purpose of copyright and libraries is to benefit the public through the creation and dissemination of information and creative works. In pursuit of this goal, copyright law should balance the public's need to access and use informative and creative works and the interests of rights holders. Libraries have both the opportunity and the obligation to work towards that balance when they engage in activities such as acquiring information resources for their communities, curating and preserving cultural heritage, establishing services and programs to enhance access to information, and lending books or other resources.

Article 1, Section 8 of the U.S. Constitution empowers Congress to pass laws "To promote the Progress of Science and useful Arts, by securing for limited Times to Authors and Inventors the exclusive Right to their respective Writings and Discoveries." Copyright law incentivizes creation of writings, art, music, and other works by granting creators the right to control and profit from some uses of their work, while limiting those rights to ensure balance with others' rights and interests.

Copyright law provides a copyright holder the rights to make copies of the work, create derivatives, distribute the work to the public, and perform or display the work in public. Copyright law provides the public the right to make fair use of the copyrighted work, to use noncopyrightable aspects of the work, to sell or transfer a copy of the work (the "first sale doctrine"), and ultimately to have full use of the work when the copyright term expires. Copyright law also provides numerous specific exceptions for libraries, archives, and nonprofit educational institutions. Depending on the nature of the institution, these exceptions may include the ability to make copies for users, preserve and replace copies of works, and perform or display works in the course of teaching.

Libraries and their parent institutions have a responsibility to promote and maintain policies and procedures that are consistent with their ethical obligations, their institutional missions, and the law, including copyright law. Such policies and procedures should respect both the rights of copyright holders and the rights of users of copyrighted works.

Librarians are sources of copyright information for their user communities. Consequently, librarians should remain informed about copyright developments, particularly those that can limit or restrict the rights of users or libraries. Librarians should develop a solid understanding of the purpose of the law and knowledge of the details of the law relevant to the activities of the library, the ability to critically analyze circumstances relying on fair use or other limits to the rights of copyright holders, and the confidence to implement the law using good judgment.[2] Librarians and library staff should be educated to recognize and observe copyright and its limits, to understand and act on their rights and those of their users, and to be ready to inform or properly refer users with questions pertaining to copyright.

Librarians have a proud history of advocating for the public interest. Copyright law should not expand the rights of copyright holders without sufficiently considering or benefitting the public interest. When the balance between rights holders and information users needs to be restored, librarians should engage with rights holders and legislators and advocate on behalf of their users and user rights.

NOTES

1. According to the U.S. Copyright Office, copyright is "a form of protection provided by the laws of the United States for 'original works of authorship,' including literary, dramatic, musical, architectural, cartographic, choreographic, pantomimic, pictorial, graphic, sculptural, and audiovisual creations." Source: www.copyright.gov/help/faq/definitions.html.

2. For more information about copyright law and related issues, see the publications of the OITP (Office for Information Technology Policy) Advisory Copyright Education Subcommittee.

The Law Regarding Copyright

Carrie Russell

The Difference between Intellectual Freedom and Intellectual Property

Intellectual freedom and intellectual property are two distinct concepts that influence one another. Democracy is dependent on both.

Intellectual property is a mechanism that addresses how information and knowledge are generated and distributed. It is a concept embodied in a set of laws—including copyright, patent law, trademark law, and trade secrets law—that protects original, creative expression and invention. The "property" that is protected is the intellectual thought and creativity that leads to art, literature, design, innovation, or invention. Copyright is the form of intellectual property that most impacts libraries. In general, U.S. copyright law provides an author or rights holder with a statutory monopoly, which is the exclusive right to monetize or otherwise benefit from the intellectual thought or creativity.

Intellectual freedom, on the other hand, is a set of principles—some guaranteed by the U.S. Constitution or considered fundamental human rights—that protects freedom of expression. Intellectual freedom, a hallmark of the library profession, includes the right to hold opinions, speak freely, read information, and listen without intrusion.

Copyright Law and Library Operations

Many common library operations have copyright implications. You should be mindful of potential copyright concerns and consider consulting with your library's legal counsel or the library's copyright specialist regarding functions including:

- Interlibrary loan
- Course reserves
- Digitization of documents and other materials
- Posting of faculty articles in institutional repositories
- Film exhibitions
- Streaming media

What Are Trade Secrets, Trademarks, and Patents?

Trade secrets, trademarks, and patents are other intellectual property laws used to protect original works. Patents protect inventions and unique ways of doing things, such as how to build a particular type of doorknob. Trademarks are used to ensure the singular "identity" of a product so rights holders can ensure that customers will not confuse it with a similar but competing product. Both slogans and logos are trademarks. Trade secrets are the unique "know-how" required to create a product, such as the secret recipe of a popular soft drink. Some creative processes, logos, or expressions can be protected by more than one intellectual property right. Mickey Mouse is the perennial example.

The Constitutional Basis of Copyright

The Constitution provides that Congress "promote the Progress of Science and useful Arts, by securing for limited Times to Authors and Inventors exclusive right to their Respective Writing and Discoveries."[1] Copyright gives creators the exclusive right to sell or vend their works, providing financial reward and incentive to continue creative endeavor and experimentation. The development of a copyright law has a prominent place in Article I of the Constitution and reflects the founders' commitment to the enrichment of the public through learning and creative advancement, and to an extent, the pledge for equality. A successful democracy is dependent on equal access to information to enhance the development of the "well-informed citizenry."

Current Copyright Law and Libraries

The Copyright Act of 1976 is the current copyright law. It has been amended over time—by extending the copyright term, for example, or by adopting the Digital Millennium Copyright Act of 1998. The 1976 law was discussed and debated by Congress for nearly twenty years before enactment.

At its drafting, Congress acknowledged that libraries and archives have a privileged status with certain benefits under the law. As sites of learning, libraries and archives required specific exceptions to copyright to effectively operate on behalf of the public. Because of their elevated status, libraries can copy, preserve, and archive information without prior authorization from the rights holders. In addition, libraries have protection from liability, the right to circumvent technology if the library makes a good faith determination that such circumvention is necessary to acquire a copy of a work, the right to make transfers of analog works to digital formats (under certain conditions), and more. Furthermore, the 1976 Act codified "fair use" in Section 107, basing its construction around a history of court case rulings that some unauthorized uses of exclusive rights are "fair," and not infringing.

The Fair Use Exception

Fair use is a flexible exception to the restrictions of copyright law. It is not a bright-line rule; rather, it is applied on a case-by-case basis by evaluating "four factors of fair use":

(1) The purpose and character of the use, including whether such use is of a commercial nature or is for nonprofit educational purposes
(2) The nature of the copyrighted work
(3) The amount and substantiality of the portion used in relation to the copyrighted work as a whole
(4) The effect of the use upon the potential market for or value of the copyrighted work[2]

Fair use is the most important exception in the law because it can be considered in situations that will never be addressed or anticipated in the law. Libraries rely on fair use for numerous activities including preserving media, digitizing specific collections, and making accessible copies for people with disabilities. Fair use is not a rare occurrence. People often use fair use in small ways throughout each day without realizing it, particularly in learning or creative environments.

Current Efforts to Change Copyright Law

At the time of publishing the *Intellectual Freedom Manual,* the U.S. House of Representatives' Committee of the Judiciary, Subcommittee on the Courts, Intellectual Property, and the Internet is reviewing copyright law in response to dramatic changes in the ways people create, copy, and distribute information due to technological innovation, networks, and new digital formats. The world is a much different place than it was in 1976, and existing law is out of touch.

While only Congress is responsible for drafting and enacting the copyright law, several government agencies can influence the law, including the United States Patent and Trademark Office (USPTO), the Office of the United

States Trade Representative (USTR), the State Department, the Institute of Museum and Library Services (IMLS), and others. Major multinational corporations, Internet companies, independent filmmakers, photographers, illustrators, and the recording, music, computer, and publishing industries also have an interest in copyright law. Libraries, museums, archives, and their users have a stake, as well. All are participants in the copyright law review process by lobbying, promoting solutions, and "being at the table" as this multi-year effort progresses.

Why Librarians Should Care about Copyright Law

There are many reasons that librarians should be focused on copyright law. Librarians are professionals with the social responsibility to ensure that the public has access to information. We embrace a copyright law that encourages the development of new knowledge and creativity that enhances our lives and informs us. Yet, First Amendment rights and freedom of inquiry and expression can be thwarted by copyright. Because rights holders have a statutory monopoly giving them exclusive control over several rights, they also have the power to withhold knowledge and control speech. Many librarians are concerned that information has been "locked up" through the expansion of copyright, increases in the duration of copyright protection, elimination of formalities, aspects of the Digital Millennium Copyright Act, licensing, and more. Perhaps most importantly, copyright has become central to international trade agreements where enforcement of copyright, limitations on fair use, and other agreements benefit the U.S. economy. Unfortunately, this view commonly neglects the public interest aspect of the law.

How the Expansion of Copyright Law Has Affected Access to and Use of Information

Over the last century, copyright has grown from the one exclusive right to sell original, creative works to five exclusive rights (six, when you include digital audio transmission of sound recordings). By giving creators additional exclusive rights, such as the right to publicly display and perform copyrighted works and the right to create new works based on the original, the copyright monopoly has become more than just a vending right, and can create barriers to information access, use, and free expression by other people. When rights holders have the exclusive right to create derivative works, it is an infringement for another person to write a short story based on the original work. Instead, permission must be sought from the copyright holder who can deny the request. If a filmmaker wants to include a short piece of someone else's footage to enhance her documentary, she must seek permission and will likely be required to pay a royalty fee. Critical thought and opinion that make use of copyrighted works can be removed from digital networks at the request of a rights holder, often with limited recourse.

Extending the duration of copyright term to life of the author plus seventy years has delayed the movement of creative works to the public domain where they become freely available for anyone to use. In addition, copyright law no longer requires creators of works to formally register the work, renew their copyright, or assign the copyright symbol to a work. This means that a work is automatically covered by copyright at the point it is created and fixed in a tangible medium. Therefore, one must assume that any work created after 1923 is protected by copyright. Because formal registration and renewal of the copyright are no longer required, it can be difficult to find rights holders because there is no record of whom to contact to ask permission. If a person cannot locate a rights holder for permission, he or she is likely to forgo use of the work.

All of these developments have contributed to the "orphan works" problem, leaving many creative works in libraries, archives, and personal collections languishing instead of being accessible for search and use. The public does not know that these works even exist, which certainly conflicts with the goal of promoting "science and useful arts."

The Digital Millennium Copyright Act also expanded the copyright law by making it unlawful to circumvent digital protection mechanisms that block access to a work. But sometimes locks must be broken in order to make things work. A person with visual disabilities must circumvent e-readers in order to turn on the text-to-speech function. An instructor must break the content-scrambling code of a DVD in order to show a short clip in the classroom. A cell phone must be unlocked for it to function with a different telecommunications provider.

Licensing can be exceedingly problematic because the rights holder can require users to sign contracts that eliminate rights typically enjoyed under copyright law. Many contracts, especially "click on" agreements, cannot be negotiated and often are enforced through the use of digital technologies. Licensing is not new and has always been a part of the copyright law. No doubt, licenses were problematic in the past, but licenses in the digital environment, enforced by technology and without negotiation, are vehicles for new business models, where what used to be allowed is now forbidden. For example, library lending of an e-book can be restricted by contract, with the technological means to enforce that contract. And when e-books, music, and media are available only in digital form, one can no longer rely on analog alternatives governed by copyright because they do not exist.

The digital environment, in combination with licensing, also gives rights holders the opportunity to create additional rights, or divvy up existing rights into smaller pieces. They can demand payment for digital public performances (streaming), the right to transfer journal articles (interlibrary loan), or the right to load content to an iPad. All of these activities are lawful under the copyright law. In today's digital environment and with widespread use of licensing, users have fewer rights than they did in the past.

Creative Commons

Unless one knows otherwise, all works not yet in the public domain are protected by copyright. This massive amount of creative expression may require prior permission from or compensation to the rights holder in order to "use" the work. A "permissions culture" is prevalent and slows down or prevents the ability to continue creative endeavors by locking up access and use of protected works. It impedes the spontaneous flow of inquiry, innovation, and learning, ultimately limiting the creation of new works and new knowledge that benefits the public. Creative Commons was organized to address this problem.

Creative Commons (www.creativecommons.org) is a nonprofit organization founded in 2001 by Lawrence Lessig, Eric Eldred, and other advocates in response to copyright expansion, including the extension of the copyright term. A Creative Commons license allows the creator or rights holder of a work to voluntarily "give up" some or all of the exclusive rights provided by copyright law so that his work may be more freely used. The author or rights holder can create and assign a Creative Commons license to her works, thereby legally "announcing" that she is not claiming all of the exclusive rights or other conditions of copyright available to her. For example, one might assign a license that releases users from the burden of asking permission when the use is for nonprofit, educational purposes. In another license, the rights holder may claim all rights of copyright, but for a shorter term of copyright—perhaps fourteen years, the original term of copyright—instead of life of the author plus seventy years.

When applying a Creative Commons license, a symbol indicating the license terms for the work can be posted on the work, similar to placing a copyright notice on a work. The licenses are publicly available on the Web, making it easy for users to find the rights holder and seek permission when required. In addition, when these works are available in digital formats in a

Creative Commons or other database, a user can search for works that can be used. For example, the Creative Commons website provides troves of photographs and recorded music, some in the public domain or at least with limited copyright restrictions.

Creative Commons and other more open options, such as open-source software and open-educational texts are ways to work around the broad expansion of the copyright law. These options are valued because they not only make works more freely available but also put the authors or rights holders in "the driver's seat," letting them decide how their creative works can be used.

Conclusion

A brief review of just some of the copyright inequities should give librarians who care about intellectual freedom a reason to care about copyright, as well. Librarians should monitor the current copyright review process. Given the power of lobbying forces, libraries face an uphill battle maintaining the user exceptions currently in place. Proposals for extended licensing systems will distort and diminish fair use and other user rights. In a legal system where innovation, creativity, and the free flow of information wanes, so too will intellectual freedom.

NOTES

1. U.S. Constitution, Article 1, clause 7.
2. U.S. Code, Title 17, §107.

Meeting Rooms, Exhibit Spaces, and Programs

ISSUE AT A GLANCE

Key Concepts

- Libraries may create exhibits or hold programs to provide library users with additional opportunities for information, education, and recreation.
- Just as libraries do not necessarily endorse the viewpoints of those whose work is represented in the collections, they also do not necessarily endorse the viewpoints expressed in public meetings, exhibits, or programs in the library.
- If the library makes meeting rooms and/or exhibit spaces available to the public, it must do so on an equitable basis, regardless of the beliefs or affiliations of individuals or groups requesting their use.
- A library may limit the use of its meeting rooms and/or exhibit spaces to strictly "library-related" activities.

What Does the Law Say?

- Libraries are not required to make meeting rooms and/or exhibit spaces available for public use, but if they do, restrictions on their use must be viewpoint-neutral and content-neutral and pertain only to the time, place, and manner of use.

Creating Policy for Your Library

- Consider formally adopting the *Library Bill of Rights* (see part I, chapter 2) as policy for your library. It contains a statement about providing meeting rooms and exhibit spaces on an equitable basis.
- If you offer meeting rooms for use by the public, be sure you have a policy governing their use. The policy may define restrictions based on time, place, and manner of use, but such restrictions should *not* pertain to the content of the meeting or to the viewpoints and affiliations of the sponsors (see part I, chapter 3).
- If you make exhibit spaces available for use by community groups, be sure you have a policy assuring that the space is provided on an equitable basis. The policy may include rules regarding the time, place, and manner of use, as long as the rules are viewpoint-neutral and are applied in the same manner to all groups (see part I, chapter 3).

Especially for Academic Libraries

- See "Intellectual Freedom Principles for Academic Libraries" in part II, chapter 1.

To Learn More

- Visit the ALA "Intellectual Freedom" website (www.ala.org/advocacy/intfreedom).
- See "Religion in American Libraries: Questions and Answers," available at www.ala.org/advocacy/intfreedom.

Questions for Reflection

- A church group asks to reserve your meeting room for a program on the biblical path to prosperity. What do you do?
- A grant-funded program promoting understanding of a non-Christian religion is the subject of complaints, and the complainant asks for the library to sponsor a Christian-themed program to balance the offerings. What's your response?
- A local women's group sponsors an exhibit related to the anniversary of the *Roe v. Wade* court decision. How do you respond to complaints from a member of the library board?

Advocating for Intellectual Freedom
An Interpretation of the *Library Bill of Rights*

Formerly titled "Importance of Education to Intellectual Freedom—An Interpretation of the Library Bill of Rights." *Adopted July 15, 2009, by the ALA Council; amended July 1, 2014.*

> A historical essay about this statement can be found in the publication, *A History of ALA Policy on Intellectual Freedom: A Supplement to the Intellectual Freedom Manual, Ninth Edition.*

EDUCATING THE AMERICAN public, including library staff, on the value of intellectual freedom is fundamental to the mission of libraries of all types. Intellectual freedom is a universal human right that involves both physical and intellectual access to information and ideas. Libraries provide physical access through facilities, resources, and services and foster awareness of intellectual freedom rights within the context of educational programs and instruction in essential information skills.

The universal freedom to express information and ideas is stated in the Universal Declaration of Human Rights, Article 19:

> Everyone has the right to freedom of opinion and expression; this right includes freedom to hold opinions without interference and to seek, receive, and impart information and ideas through any media and regardless of frontiers.

The importance of education to the development of intellectual freedom is expressed in the Universal Declaration of Human Rights, Article 26:

(1) Everyone has the right to education. Education shall be free, at least in the elementary and fundamental stages. . . .

(2) Education shall be directed to the full development of the human personality and to the strengthening of respect for human rights and fundamental freedoms. It shall promote understanding, tolerance and friendship among all nations, racial, or religious groups, and shall further the activities of the United Nations for the maintenance of peace.

In addition, Article I of the American Library Association's *Library Bill of Rights* "affirms that all libraries are forums for information and ideas." Physical access to information is listed as the first principle:

> Books and other library resources should be provided for the interest, information, and enlightenment of all people of the community the library serves. Materials should not be excluded because of the origin, background, or views of those contributing to their creation.

Article II of the *Library Bill of Rights* emphasizes the importance of fostering intellectual access to information by providing materials that allow users to evaluate content and context and find information representing multiple points of view:

> Libraries should provide materials and information presenting all points of view on current and historical issues. Materials should not be proscribed or removed because of partisan or doctrinal disapproval.

Libraries of all types foster education by promoting the free expression and interchange of ideas, leading to empowered lifelong learners. Libraries use resources, programming, and services to strengthen intellectual and physical access to information and thus build a foundation of intellectual freedom: developing collections (both real and virtual) with multiple perspectives and individual needs of users in mind; providing programming and instructional services framed around equitable access to information and ideas; and teaching of information skills and intellectual freedom rights integrated appropriately throughout the spectrum of library programming.

Through educational programming and instruction in information skills, libraries empower individuals to explore ideas, access and evaluate information, draw meaning from information presented in a variety of formats, develop valid conclusions, and express new ideas. Such education facilitates intellectual access to information and offers a path to a robust appreciation of intellectual freedom rights.

Exhibit Spaces and Bulletin Boards
An Interpretation of the *Library Bill of Rights*

Adopted July 2, 1991, by the ALA Council; amended June 30, 2004; and July 1, 2014.

A historical essay about this statement can be found in the publication, *A History of ALA Policy on Intellectual Freedom: A Supplement to the Intellectual Freedom Manual, Ninth Edition.*

LIBRARIES OFTEN PROVIDE exhibit spaces and bulletin boards in physical and/or electronic formats. The uses made of these spaces should conform to the American Library Association's *Library Bill of Rights:* Article I states, "Materials should not be excluded because of the origin, background, or views of those contributing to their creation." Article II states, "Materials should not be proscribed or removed because of partisan or doctrinal disapproval." Article VI maintains that exhibit space should be made available "on an equitable basis, regardless of the beliefs or affiliations of individuals or groups requesting their use."

In developing library exhibits, staff members should endeavor to present a broad spectrum of opinion and a variety of viewpoints. Libraries should not shrink from developing exhibits because of controversial content or because of the beliefs or affiliations of those whose work is represented. Just as libraries do not endorse the viewpoints of those whose work is represented in their collections, libraries also do not endorse the beliefs or viewpoints of topics that may be the subject of library exhibits.

Exhibit areas often are made available for use by community groups. Libraries should formulate a written policy for the use of these exhibit areas to assure that space is provided on an equitable basis to all groups that request it. Written policies for exhibit space use should be stated in inclusive rather than exclusive terms. For example, a policy that the library's exhibit space is open "to organizations engaged in educational, cultural, intellectual, or charitable activities" is an inclusive statement of the limited uses of the exhibit space. This defined limitation would permit religious groups to use the exhibit space because they engage in intellectual activities, but would exclude most commercial uses of the exhibit space.

A publicly supported library may designate use of exhibit space for strictly library-related activities, provided that this limitation is viewpoint neutral and clearly defined.

Libraries may include in this policy rules regarding the time, place, and manner of use of the exhibit space, so long as the rules are content neutral and are applied in the same manner to all groups wishing to use the space.

A library may wish to limit access to exhibit space to groups within the community served by the library. This practice is acceptable provided that the same rules and regulations apply to everyone, and that exclusion is not made on the basis of the doctrinal, religious, or political beliefs of the potential users.

The library should not censor or remove an exhibit because some members of the community may disagree with its content. Those who object to the content of any exhibit held at the library should be able to submit their complaint and/or their own exhibit proposal to be judged according to the policies established by the library.

Libraries may wish to post a permanent notice near the exhibit area stating that the library does not advocate or endorse the viewpoints of exhibits or exhibitors.

Libraries that make bulletin boards available to public groups for posting notices of public interest should develop criteria for the use of these spaces based on the same considerations as those outlined above. Libraries may wish to develop criteria regarding the size of material to be displayed, the length of time materials may remain on the bulletin board, the frequency with which material may be posted for the same group, and the geographic area from which notices will be accepted.

Library-Initiated Programs as a Resource
An Interpretation of the *Library Bill of Rights*

Adopted January 27, 1982, by the ALA Council; amended June 26, 1990; and July 12, 2000.

LIBRARY-INITIATED PROGRAMS SUPPORT the mission of the library by providing users with additional opportunities for information, education, and recreation. Article I of the *Library Bill of Rights* states: "Books and other library resources should be provided for the interest, information, and enlightenment of all people of the community the library serves."

A historical essay about this statement can be found in the publication, *A History of ALA Policy on Intellectual Freedom: A Supplement to the Intellectual Freedom Manual, Ninth Edition.*

Library-initiated programs take advantage of library staff expertise, collections, services and facilities to increase access to information and information resources. Library-initiated programs introduce users and potential users to the resources of the library and to the library's primary function as a facilitator of information access. The library may participate in cooperative or joint programs with other agencies, organizations, institutions, or individuals as part of its own effort to address information needs and to facilitate information access in the community the library serves.

Library-initiated programs on site and in other locations include, but are not limited to, speeches, community forums, discussion groups, demonstrations, displays, and live or media presentations.

Libraries serving multilingual or multicultural communities should make efforts to accommodate the information needs of those for whom English is a second language. Library-initiated programs that cross language and cultural barriers introduce otherwise underserved populations to the resources of the library and provide access to information.

Library-initiated programs "should not be proscribed or removed (or canceled) because of partisan or doctrinal disapproval" of the contents of the program or the views expressed by the participants, as stated in Article II of the *Library Bill of Rights*. Library sponsorship of a program does not constitute an endorsement of the content of the program or the views expressed by the participants, any more than the purchase of material for the library collection constitutes an endorsement of the contents of the material or the views of its creator.

Library-initiated programs are a library resource, and, as such, are developed in accordance with written guidelines, as approved and adopted by the library's policy-making body. These guidelines should include an endorsement of the *Library Bill of Rights* and set forth the library's commitment to free and open access to information and ideas for all users.

Library staff select topics, speakers and resource materials for library-initiated programs based on the interests and information needs of the community. Topics, speakers and resource materials are not excluded from library-initiated programs because of possible controversy. Concerns, questions or complaints about library-initiated programs are handled according to the same written policy and procedures that govern reconsiderations of other library resources.

Library-initiated programs are offered free of charge and are open to all. Article V of the *Library Bill of Rights* states: "A person's right to use a library should not be denied or abridged because of origin, age, background, or views."

The "right to use a library" encompasses all the resources the library offers, including the right to attend library-initiated programs. Libraries do not deny or abridge access to library resources, including library-initiated programs, based on an individual's economic background or ability to pay.

II.6
Meeting
Rooms,
Spaces, and
Programs

Meeting Rooms

An Interpretation of the *Library Bill of Rights*

Adopted July 2, 1991, by the ALA Council.

MANY LIBRARIES PROVIDE meeting rooms for individuals and groups as part of a program of service. Article VI of the *Library Bill of Rights* states that such facilities should be made available to the public served by the given library "on an equitable basis, regardless of the beliefs or affiliations of individuals or groups requesting their use."

> A historical essay about this statement can be found in the publication, *A History of ALA Policy on Intellectual Freedom: A Supplement to the Intellectual Freedom Manual, Ninth Edition.*

Libraries maintaining meeting room facilities should develop and publish policy statements governing use. These statements can properly define time, place, or manner of use; such qualifications should not pertain to the content of a meeting or to the beliefs or affiliations of the sponsors. These statements should be made available in any commonly used language within the community served.

If meeting rooms in libraries supported by public funds are made available to the general public for non-library sponsored events, the library may not exclude any group based on the subject matter to be discussed or based on the ideas that the group advocates. For example, if a library allows charities and sports clubs to discuss their activities in library meeting rooms, then the library should not exclude partisan political or religious groups from discussing their activities in the same facilities. If a library opens its meeting rooms to a wide variety of civic organizations, then the library may not deny access to a religious organization. Libraries may wish to post a permanent notice near the meeting room stating that the library does not advocate or endorse the viewpoints of meetings or meeting room users. Written policies for meeting room use should be stated in inclusive rather than exclusive terms. For example, a policy that the library's facilities are open "to organizations engaged in educational, cultural, intellectual, or charitable activities" is an inclusive statement of the limited uses to which the facilities may be put. This defined limitation would permit religious groups to use the facilities because they engage in intellectual activities, but would exclude most commercial uses of the facility.

A publicly supported library may limit use of its meeting rooms to strictly "library-related" activities, provided that the limitation is clearly circumscribed and is viewpoint neutral.

Written policies may include limitations on frequency of use, and whether or not meetings held in library meeting rooms must be open to the public. If state and local laws permit private as well as public sessions of meetings in libraries, libraries may choose to offer both options. The same standard should be applicable to all.

If meetings are open to the public, libraries should include in their meeting room policy statement a section that addresses admission fees. If admission fees are permitted, libraries shall seek to make it possible that these fees do not limit access to individuals who may be unable to pay, but who wish to attend the meeting. Article V of the *Library Bill of Rights* states that "a person's right to use a library should not be denied or abridged because of origin, age, background, or views." It is inconsistent with Article V to restrict indirectly access to library meeting rooms based on an individual's or group's ability to pay for that access.

A DEEPER LOOK

The Law Regarding Access to Meeting Rooms and Exhibit Spaces

Theresa Chmara

THE USE OF meeting rooms and exhibit spaces raises an array of issues for public libraries, public schools, and public universities. As an initial matter, courts have held unequivocally that governments need not make their meeting room facilities or exhibit spaces available to the public.[1] In *Lehman v. City of Shaker Heights*, the Supreme Court concluded that the denial of access to advertising space on a city's rapid transit vehicles to a political candidate did not violate the First Amendment.[2] The court held that "no First Amendment forum is here to be found," because the city did not intend to open the forum and had restricted it to commercial advertising.[3] The court held that "were we to hold to the contrary, display cases in public hospitals, libraries, office buildings, military compounds, and other public facilities immediately would become Hyde

What's a "Public Forum"?

This essay uses the term *public forum*. To learn more about what that means and how it applies to libraries, please read part I, chapter 4, "The Right to Receive Information: Libraries, the First Amendment, and the Public Forum Doctrine."

Parks open to every would-be pamphleteer and politician" and "this the Constitution does not require."[4]

Once a meeting room or exhibit space is open to the public, however, restrictions on use will be upheld only if the state has a compelling interest and the restrictions are narrowly tailored to achieve that interest. As part of that analysis, the court will evaluate whether the restriction is objective and narrowly defined. Thus, "courts have been reluctant to accept policies based on subjective or overly general criteria."[5] If the library opens its space to the public for the display of visual art, the same principles would apply.

Once a facility or exhibit space is made available for public use, then the exclusion of an entire category of speech on the basis of its content cannot be justified under the First Amendment. Courts have, for example, rejected the theory that public entities must exclude religious groups from facilities on the ground that permitting access to religious groups violates the Establishment Clause of the First Amendment. The mere fact that a group is religious is insufficient to exclude the group and constitutes exclusion on the basis of content. In *Lamb's Chapel v. Center Moriches Union Free School District*, a church group was denied access to a school facility on the ground that it was planning to show a film with a religious theme.[6] The court concluded the exclusion was unconstitutional because "the challenged governmental action has a secular purpose, does not have the principal or primary effect of advancing or inhibiting religion, and does not foster an excessive entanglement with religion."[7]

An open question remains as to whether a government entity may permit religious groups to use a facility but deny access to groups intending to conduct a religious service. In *Good News Club v. Milford Central School*, the court held that it was unconstitutional to exclude a private children's Christian organization from a school facility and reiterated that excluding a group from a limited public forum on the basis that it is a religious organization constitutes viewpoint discrimination.[8] The court alluded to, but failed to resolve, whether there is a distinction between a religious group's use of a facility to hold a meeting and a religious group's use of a facility to hold a religious service.[9] There has been disagreement on this issue among the lower courts.

In *Faith Center Evangelistic Ministries v. Glover*, a religious organization was banned from using a library meeting room on the ground that it was conducting a "religious service." The federal district court held that the restriction on access for "religious services" was unconstitutional on the following grounds: (1) religious worship constitutes protected speech, (2) religious worship cannot be distinguished from other religious speech, (3) exclusion of religious worship constitutes viewpoint discrimination, and (4) the Establishment Clause does not justify the exclusion of a religious group.

The Ninth Circuit (appellate court), with one judge dissenting, reversed the district court's finding of unconstitutionality. The court held that the library is a limited public forum (which the court described as a subset of the designated public forum) and that "the county's decision to exclude Faith Center's religious worship services from the meeting room is reasonable in light of the library policy so that the Antioch forum is not transformed into an occasional house of worship."[10]

The court held that Faith Center Church could not be prohibited from engaging in the following activities in the library meeting room: workshops on how to communicate with God, Bible discussions, teaching the Bible, praying, singing, sharing testimonies, and discussing political or social issues. The court held, however, that Faith Center Church could be excluded because its flyers described the use of the library meeting room as a "religious service." The majority conceded that it would be "challenging" for the county or even the courts to draw a line between religious speech that is permissible (praying, Bible study, religious singing) and "religious worship," but, relying on Faith Center Church's own description of its meeting as a forum for "praise and worship," concluded that "the County may not be able to identify whether Faith Center has engaged in pure religious worship, but Faith Center can and did."[11]

The appellate court remanded the matter to the lower court for a determination of whether the Establishment Clause required the library to exclude the religious group. On remand, the district court concluded that the library policy violates the Establishment Clause of the First Amendment because it requires an excessive government entanglement with religion when the library engages in a determination of whether a particular event in its meeting room constitutes a religious service.[12] In July 2009, the library removed its restriction on the use of meeting rooms for religious services.

By contrast, in *Citizens for Community Values, Inc. v. Upper Arlington Public Library Board of Trustees,* a federal district court held that a library policy that excluded "religious services" was unconstitutional. The court held that the library meeting room was a limited public forum and that "its practice of severing out and excluding activities it concludes are 'inherent elements of a religious service,' constitutes unlawful viewpoint discrimination, and consequently violates Plaintiff's First Amendment free speech rights."[13]

There is no question, however, that a library may impose restrictions on the use of its facilities, provided that the restrictions are content-neutral and pertain to time, place, and manner. For example, in *Concerned Women for America, Inc. v. Lafayette County,* the court held unconstitutional a public library's refusal of access to an auditorium by a prayer group, holding that "there is no evidence that CWA's meeting would disrupt or interfere with the general use of the library" and that "should the contrary prove to be true, library officials may respond by imposing reasonable time, place or manner restrictions on access to the auditorium, provided any regulations are justified without reference to the content of the regulated speech."[14]

In order to advance their avowed mission of serving the community, many public libraries prefer to open their facilities for use by non-library groups but are interested in preventing the use of public facilities for business ventures. While that would appear to be consistent with the mission of public libraries, drafters of library policies must be cautious to use narrow, precise definitions in drafting such restrictions. For example, in *Board of Trustees of State University of New York v. Fox,* a university regulation that prohibited the use of dormitories for a "commercial purpose" was challenged.[15] While remanding the case for further proceedings, the Supreme Court cautioned that "government restrictions upon commercial speech may be no more broad than is necessary to serve its substantial interests"[16] and that restrictions must not "burden substantially more speech than is necessary to further the government's legitimate interests."[17]

In recent years, public libraries have sought to offer meeting rooms or exhibit spaces to the public but also to craft restrictions to exclude groups that might cause a controversy or whose use would result in public disapproval. Courts unequivocally have rejected such attempts. The Supreme Court has held that "avoidance of controversy is not a valid ground for restricting speech in a public forum" but that "the First Amendment does not forbid a viewpoint-neutral exclusion of speakers who would disrupt a non-public forum and hinder its effectiveness for its intended purpose."[18]

NOTES

1. *Lamb's Chapel v. Center Moriches Union Free School District,* 508 U.S. 384 (1993).

2. *Lehman v. City of Shaker Heights,* 418 U.S. 298 (1974).

3. *Id.* at 304.

4. *Id.;* see also *Widmar v. Vincent,* 454 U.S. 263, 267–68 (1981) (holding that "the Constitution forbids a State to enforce certain exclusions from a forum generally open to the public, even if it was not required to create the forum in the first place").

5. *Hopper v. City of Pasco,* 241 F.3d 1067, 1077 (9th Cir.), *cert. denied,* 534 U.S. 951 (2001); see also *DeBoer v. Village of Oak Park,* 267 F.3d 558, 573 (7th Cir. 2001) (holding that "any regulations governing a speaker's access to a forum must contain 'narrow, objective, and definite standards' to guide a govern-

mental authority, so that such regulations do not operate as a prior restraint that may result in censorship").

6. *Lamb's Chapel v. Center Moriches Union Free School District*, 508 U.S. 384 (1993).

7. *Id.* at 395.

8. *Good News Club v. Milford Central School*, 533 U.S. 98, 120 (2001).

9. *Id.* at 133-34 (Stevens, J., dissenting).

10. *Faith Center Evangelistic Ministries v. Glover*, 480 F.3d 891 (9th Cir. 2007).

11. *Id.*

12. *Faith Center Church Evangelistic Ministries v. Glover*, Case No. C 04-03111 (N.D. Cal. 6/19/09) (relying on *Lemon v. Kurtzman*, 403 U.S. 602, 612-13 (1971)).

13. *Citizens for Community Values, Inc. v. Upper Arlington Library Board of Trustees*, Case No. C-2-08-223 (S.D. Ohio 8/14/08).

14. *Concerned Women for America, Inc. v. Lafayette County*, 883 F.2d 32, 35 (5th Cir. 1989).

15. *Board of Trustees of State University of New York v. Fox*, 492 U.S. 469 (1989).

16. *Id.* at 476.

17. *Id.* at 478 (quoting *Ward v. Rock against Racism*, 491 U.S. 781 [1989]).

18. *Cornelius v. NAACP Legal Defense & Ed. Fund, Inc.*, 473 U.S. 788, 811 (1985); see also *Pfeifer v. City of West Allis*, 91 F. Supp. 2d 1253, 1267 (E.D. Wis. 2000) (holding that "the avoidance of controversy is not a valid ground for restricting speech in a public forum"); *Hopper*, 241 F.3d at 1079 (holding that "[a] ban on 'controversial art' may all too easily lend itself to viewpoint discrimination, a practice forbidden even in limited public fora"); *Planned Parenthood/Chicago Area v. Chicago Transit Authority*, 767 F.2d 1225, 1230 (7th Cir. 1985) ("question[ing] whether a regulation of speech that has as its touchstone a government official's subjective view that the speech is 'controversial' could ever pass constitutional muster").

II.6
Meeting
Rooms,
Spaces, and
Programs

Privacy and Confidentiality

ISSUE AT A GLANCE

Key Concepts

- Privacy is essential to free inquiry because it enables library users to select, access, and use information without fear of embarrassment, judgment, surveillance, punishment, or ostracism.
- Libraries should minimize the collection of personally identifiable user information, store it locally and securely, and be sure that library practices do not divulge user information or put it on public view (e.g., self-service hold shelves that reveal a user's identity).
- Libraries should not share personally identifiable user information with third parties (including vendors, "Friends of the Library" groups, and law enforcement) *except* with the permission of the user or in response to a search warrant or other court order.

What Does the Law Say?

- The courts have upheld the right to privacy based on the Bill of Rights of the U.S. Constitution (First and Fourth Amendments), and numerous decisions in case law have defined and extended rights to privacy. Also, many states provide guarantees of privacy in their constitutions and statutes.
- All states and the District of Columbia have either laws or attorney general opinions protecting the confidentiality of library records

(including the records of children and youth in many cases). Check to see if your state law applies to your library.

- The right of parents or guardians to access their minor children's public library records varies from state to state. Consult the law in your state. Parents' and guardians' access to their minor children's school library records is also governed by the Family Educational Rights and Privacy Act.

Creating Policy for Your Library

- Consider formally adopting *Libraries: An American Value* and the *Code of Ethics of the American Library Association* (see part I, chapter 2) as policy for your library. They contain statements about protecting library users' privacy and confidentiality.
- Be sure you have a privacy policy that outlines the way your library (1) limits the collection of personally identifiable information, (2) deletes information when no longer needed, (3) avoids placing personal information on public view, and (4) responds to third-party requests for user information (see part I, chapter 3).

Especially for Academic Libraries

- Many faculty members mistakenly assume they have the right to monitor student coursework and are puzzled when the library refuses to tell them what their students are reading.
- It's helpful to educate colleagues in the campus IT department about librarians' ethical obligation to promote access and protect privacy. The IT community often operates under a different set of professional values that may lean more toward the protection of campus electronic resources.
- Special collections libraries often keep circulation records long-term to deter theft. (Often serial thieves visit a series of special collections libraries, and circulation records can help trace these thefts.) Such records should be kept in a secured place and consulted only when necessary to trace a missing item. Special collections librarians who are well acquainted with their users' research interests should keep this information confidential unless the user gives explicit permission for the librarian to share it with others who are working on a similar topic and might want to exchange ideas.

- See "Intellectual Freedom Principles for Academic Libraries" in part II, chapter 1.

Especially for School Libraries

- Creating a privacy policy that defines who may access minors' library records and the conditions under which this may occur provides some protection for students' privacy.
- Teachers often want to know what their students are reading or what resources they are using, but it is never appropriate for the school librarian to share this information. The teacher should ask the student directly.
- Reading-level labels on books may compromise the privacy of students and expose them to teasing and judgment by peers who are at different levels.

To Learn More

- Visit the ALA "Intellectual Freedom" website (www.ala.org/advocacy/intfreedom) for links to information about privacy, including "Questions and Answers on Privacy and Confidentiality."
- Consult the ALA "Privacy Tool Kit" (www.ala.org/advocacy/privacy confidentiality/toolkitsprivacy/privacy) for information about privacy audits, policy writing, sample policies, and more.
- Visit the "Choose Privacy Week" website (chooseprivacyweek.org).
- See also part II, chapter 8, "Visits and Requests from Law Enforcement" and "The Universal Right to Free Expression" in part II, chapter 1.
- See also "State Privacy Laws Regarding Library Records" (www.ala .org/advocacy/privacyconfidentiality/privacy/stateprivacy).

Questions for Reflection

- Your library wants to offer self-service holds. What's the best procedure for identifying patrons' holds without compromising their identity?
- A patron asks to see what her thirteen-year-old daughter has checked out. One of the books is about alcoholic parents. What do you do? What if it was a book about witchcraft?

II.7
Privacy

- Your meeting rooms have a schedule that's posted on the door. What information should you post? How long do you keep the reservation information, and why?

OFFICIAL ALA POLICY STATEMENTS

Privacy

An Interpretation of the *Library Bill of Rights*

Adopted June 19, 2002, by the ALA Council; amended July 1, 2014.

> A historical essay about this statement can be found in the publication, *A History of ALA Policy on Intellectual Freedom: A Supplement to the Intellectual Freedom Manual, Ninth Edition.*

Introduction

PRIVACY IS ESSENTIAL to the exercise of free speech, free thought, and free association. The courts have established a First Amendment right to receive information in a publicly funded library.[1] Further, the courts have upheld the right to privacy based on the Bill of Rights of the U.S. Constitution.[2] Many states provide guarantees of privacy in their constitutions and statute law.[3] Numerous decisions in case law have defined and extended rights to privacy.[4]

In a library (physical or virtual), the right to privacy is the right to open inquiry without having the subject of one's interest examined or scrutinized by others. Confidentiality exists when a library is in possession of personally identifiable information about users and keeps that information private on their behalf.[5] Confidentiality extends to "information sought or received and resources consulted, borrowed, acquired or transmitted" (ALA *Code of Ethics*), including, but not limited to: database search records, reference questions and interviews, circulation records, interlibrary loan records, information about materials downloaded or placed on "hold" or "reserve," and other personally identifiable information about uses of library materials, programs, facilities, or services.

Protecting user privacy and confidentiality has long been an integral part of the mission of libraries. The ALA has affirmed a right to privacy since 1939.[6] Existing ALA policies affirm that confidentiality is crucial to freedom of inquiry.[7] Rights to privacy and confidentiality also are implicit in the *Library Bill of Rights*[8] guarantee of free access to library resources for all users.

Rights of Library Users

The *Library Bill of Rights* affirms the ethical imperative to provide unrestricted access to information and to guard against impediments to open inquiry. Article IV states: "Libraries should cooperate with all persons and groups concerned with resisting abridgement of free expression and free access to ideas." When users recognize or fear that their privacy or confidentiality is compromised, true freedom of inquiry no longer exists.

In all areas of librarianship, best practice leaves the user in control of as many choices as possible. These include decisions about the selection of, access to, and use of information. Lack of privacy and confidentiality has a chilling effect on users' choices. All users have a right to be free from any unreasonable intrusion into or surveillance of their lawful library use.

Users have the right to be informed what policies and procedures govern the amount and retention of personally identifiable information, why that information is necessary for the library, and what the user can do to maintain his or her privacy. Library users expect and in many places have a legal right to have their information protected and kept private and confidential by anyone with direct or indirect access to that information. In addition, Article V of the *Library Bill of Rights* states: "A person's right to use a library should not be denied or abridged because of origin, age, background, or views." This article precludes the use of profiling as a basis for any breach of privacy rights. Users have the right to use a library without any abridgement of privacy that may result from equating the subject of their inquiry with behavior.[9]

Responsibilities in Libraries

The library profession has a long-standing commitment to an ethic of facilitating, not monitoring, access to information. This commitment is implemented locally through the, [sic] adoption of and adherence to library privacy policies that are consistent with applicable federal, state, and local law.

Everyone (paid or unpaid) who provides governance, administration, or service in libraries has a responsibility to maintain an environment respectful and protective of the privacy of all users. Users have the responsibility to respect each others' privacy.

For administrative purposes, librarians may establish appropriate time, place, and manner restrictions on the use of library resources.[10] In keeping with this principle, the collection of personally identifiable information should only be a matter of routine or policy when necessary for the fulfillment of the mission of the library. Regardless of the technology used, everyone who collects or accesses personally identifiable information in any format has a legal and ethical obligation to protect confidentiality.

Libraries should not share personally identifiable user information with third parties or with vendors that provide resources and library services unless the library has obtained the permission of the user or has entered into a legal agreement with the vendor. Such agreements should stipulate that the library retains control of the information, that the information is confidential, and that it may not be used or shared except with the permission of the library.

Law enforcement agencies and officers may occasionally believe that library records contain information that would be helpful to the investigation of criminal activity. The American judicial system provides a mechanism for seeking release of such confidential records: a court order issued following a showing of good cause based on specific facts by a court of competent jurisdiction. Libraries should make such records available only in response to properly executed orders.

Conclusion

The American Library Association affirms that rights of privacy are necessary for intellectual freedom and are fundamental to the ethics and practice of librarianship.

NOTES

1. Court opinions establishing a right to receive information in a public library include *Board of Education. v. Pico*, 457 U.S. 853 (1982); *Kreimer v. Bureau of Police for the Town of Morristown*, 958 F.2d 1242 (3d Cir. 1992); and *Reno v. American Civil Liberties Union*, 117 S.Ct. 2329, 138 L.Ed.2d 874 (1997).

2. See in particular the Fourth Amendment's guarantee of "the right of the people to be secure in their persons, houses, papers, and effects, against unreasonable searches and seizures," the Fifth Amendment's guarantee against self-incrimination, and the Ninth Amendment's guarantee that "the enumeration in the Constitution, of certain rights, shall not be construed to deny or disparage others retained by the people." This right is explicit in Article Twelve of the *Universal Declaration of Human Rights*: "No one shall

be subjected to arbitrary interference with his privacy, family, home or correspondence, nor to attacks upon his honour and reputation. Everyone has the right to the protection of the law against such interference or attacks." See www.un.org/Overview/rights.html. This right has further been explicitly codified as Article Seventeen of the *International Covenant on Civil and Political Rights*, a legally binding international human rights agreement ratified by the United States on June 8, 1992. See www.unhchr.ch/html/menu3/b/a_ccpr.htm.

3. Ten state constitutions guarantee a right of privacy or bar unreasonable intrusions into citizens' privacy. Forty-eight states protect the confidentiality of library users' records by law, and the attorneys general in the remaining two states have issued opinions recognizing the privacy of users' library records.

4. Cases recognizing a right to privacy include *NAACP v. Alabama,* 357 U.S. 449 (1958); *Griswold v. Connecticut,* 381 U.S. 479 (1965); *Katz v. United States,* 389 U.S. 347 (1967); and *Stanley v. Georgia,* 394 U.S. 557 (1969). Congress recognized the right to privacy in the Privacy Act of 1974 and Amendments (5 USC Sec. 552a), which addresses the potential for government's violation of privacy through its collection of personal information. The Privacy Act's "Congressional Findings and Statement of Purpose" states in part: "the right to privacy is a personal and fundamental right protected by the Constitution of the United States." See http://caselaw.lp.findlaw.com/scripts/ts_search.pl?title=5&sec=552a.

5. The phrase "personally identifiable information" was established in ALA policy in 1991. See "Policy Concerning Confidentiality of Personally Identifiable Information about Library Users." Personally identifiable information can include many types of library records, including: information that the library requires an individual to provide in order to be eligible to use library services or borrow materials, information that identifies an individual as having requested or obtained specific materials or materials on a particular subject, and information that is provided by an individual to assist a library staff member to answer a specific question or provide information on a particular subject. Personally identifiable information does not include information that does not identify any individual and that is retained only for the purpose of studying or evaluating the use of a library and its materials and services. Personally identifiable information does include any data that can link choices of taste, interest, or research with a specific individual.

6. Article XI of the *Code of Ethics for Librarians* (1939) asserted that "it is the librarian's obligation to treat as confidential any private information obtained through contact with library patrons." See *Code of Ethics for Librarians* (1939). Article III of the current *Code* (2008) states: "We protect each library user's right to privacy and confidentiality with respect to infor-

mation sought or received and resources consulted, borrowed, acquired, or transmitted."

7. See these ALA policies and documents: "Access to Library Resources and Services for Minors"; *Freedom to Read; Libraries: An American Value*; "Library Principles for a Networked World"; "Policy Concerning Confidentiality of Personally Identifiable Information about Library Users"; "Policy on Confidentiality of Library Records"; "Suggested Procedures for Implementing Policy on the Confidentiality of Library Records."

8. Adopted June 18, 1948; amended February 2, 1961, and January 23, 1980; inclusion of "age" reaffirmed January 23, 1996, by the ALA Council.

9. Existing ALA policy asserts, in part, that "The government's interest in library use reflects a dangerous and fallacious equation of what a person reads with what that person believes or how that person is likely to behave. Such a presumption can and does threaten the freedom of access to information." "Policy Concerning Confidentiality of Personally Identifiable Information about Library Users."

10. See: "Guidelines for the Development and Implementation of Policies, Regulations and Procedures Affecting Access to Library Materials, Services and Facilities."

Resolution on the Retention of Library Usage Records

Adopted June 28, 2006 by the ALA Council.

WHEREAS, "Protecting user privacy and confidentiality is necessary for intellectual freedom and fundamental to the ethics and practice of librarianship" (ALA Policy Manual, 53.1.16; "Privacy: An Interpretation of the *Library Bill of Rights*"); and

A historical essay about this statement can be found in the publication, *A History of ALA Policy on Intellectual Freedom: A Supplement to the Intellectual Freedom Manual, Ninth Edition.*

WHEREAS, Library usage records containing personally identifiable information (PII) are maintained for the sole purpose of effectively managing library resources; and

WHEREAS, The confidentiality of library usage records is protected by law in all fifty states and in the District of Columbia; and

WHEREAS, "The government's interest in library use represents a dangerous and fallacious equation of what a person reads with what that person believes or how that person is likely to behave" (ALA Policy Manual, 52.4.2; "Confidentiality of Personally Identifiable Information About Library Users"); and

WHEREAS, The American Library Association strongly recommends the adoption of policies recognizing "circulation records and other records identifying the names of library users to be confidential" (ALA Policy Manual, 52.4; "Confidentiality of Library Records"); now, therefore, be it

RESOLVED, That the American Library Association urges all libraries to:

- Limit the degree to which personally identifiable information is collected, monitored, disclosed, and distributed; and
- Avoid creating unnecessary records; and
- Limit access to personally identifiable information to staff performing authorized functions; and
- Dispose of library usage records containing personally identifiable information unless they are needed for the efficient and lawful operation of the library, including, but not limited to data-related logs, digital records, vendor-collected data, and system backups; and
- Ensure that the library work with its organization's information technology unit to ensure that library usage records processed or held by the IT unit are treated in accordance with library records policies; and
- Ensure that those records that must be retained are secure; and
- Avoid library practices and procedures that place personally identifiable information on public view; and
- Assure that vendor agreements guarantee library control of all data and records; and
- Conduct an annual privacy audit to ensure that information-processing procedures meet privacy requirements by examining how information about library users and employees is collected, stored, shared, used, and destroyed; and, be it further

RESOLVED, That the American Library Association urges all libraries to adopt or update a privacy policy protecting users' personally identifiable information, communicating to library users how their information is used, and explaining the limited circumstances under which personally identifiable information could be disclosed; and, be it further

RESOLVED, That the American Library Association urges members of the library community to advocate that records retention laws and regulations limit retention of library usage records containing personally identifiable information to the time needed for efficient operation of the library.

Note: A new numbering system for the ALA Policy Manual was developed after the adoption of this resolution.

ALA Policy Manual 53.1.16, "Privacy: An Interpretation of the *Library Bill of Rights*" is now Policy Manual B.2.1.16.

ALA Policy Manual, 52.4.2, "Confidentiality of Personally Identifiable Information about Library Users" is now Policy Manual B.8.5.2.

ALA Policy Manual, 52.4, "Confidentiality of Library Records" is now Policy Manual B.8.5.

A DEEPER LOOK

RFID in Libraries—Privacy and Confidentiality Guidelines

Adopted June 27, 2006, by the ALA Intellectual Freedom Committee.

A historical essay about this statement can be found in the publication, *A History of ALA Policy on Intellectual Freedom: A Supplement to the Intellectual Freedom Manual, Ninth Edition.*

RADIO FREQUENCY IDENTIFICATION (RFID) technology collects, uses, stores, and broadcasts data. Components of RFID systems include tags, tag readers, computer hardware (such as servers and security gates), and RFID-specific software (such as RFID system administration programs, inventory software, etc.).

RFID technology can enable efficient and ergonomic inventory, security, and circulation operations in libraries. Like other technologies that enable self-checkout of library materials, RFID can enhance individual privacy by allowing users to check out materials without relying on library staff.

Because RFID tags may be read by unauthorized individuals using tag readers, there are concerns that the improper implementation of RFID technology will compromise users' privacy in the library.[1] Researchers have identified serious general concerns about the privacy implications of RFID use, and particular privacy concerns about RFID use in libraries.[2] Libraries implementing RFID should use and configure the technology to maintain the privacy of library users.

The Council of the American Library Association adopted the "Resolution on Radio Frequency Identification (RFID) Technology and Privacy Principles" and requested the development of guidelines for the implementation of RFID technology in libraries.

Basic Privacy and Confidentiality Principles

Protecting user privacy and confidentiality has long been an integral part of the intellectual freedom mission of libraries.[3] The right to free inquiry as assured by the First Amendment depends upon the ability to read and access information free from scrutiny by the government or other third parties. In their provision of services to library users, librarians have an ethical obligation, expressed in the ALA *Code of Ethics,* to preserve users' right to privacy and to prevent any unauthorized use of personally identifiable information. As always, librarians should follow these principles when adopting any new technology.

Policy Guidelines

When selecting and implementing RFID technology, librarians should:

- Use the RFID selection and procurement process as an opportunity to educate library users about RFID technology and its current and future use in the library and society as a whole. A transparent selection process allows a library to publicize its reasons for wanting to implement an RFID system while listening to its users and giving them a larger voice in the public debate over RFID technology.
- Consider selecting an "opt-in" system that allows library users who wish to use or carry an RFID-enabled borrower card to do so while allowing others to choose an alternative method to borrow materials. Because all members who share integrated library systems may not wish to implement an RFID system, this option also may be necessary for library consortia.
- Review and update appropriate privacy policies and procedures to continue protecting users' privacy, in accordance with Article III of

II.7
Privacy

the ALA *Code of Ethics* and "Privacy: An Interpretation of the *Library Bill of Rights.*"

• Ensure that institutional privacy policies and practices addressing notice, access, use, disclosure, retention, enforcement, security, and disposal of records are reflected in the configuration of the RFID system. As with any new application of technology, librarians should ensure that RFID policies and procedures explain and clarify how RFID affects users' privacy. The ALA "Privacy Tool Kit" can assist libraries in drafting appropriate policies.[4]

• Delete personally identifiable information (PII) collected by RFID systems, just as libraries take reasonable steps to remove PII from aggregated, summary data.

• Notify the public about the library's use of RFID technology. Disclose any changes in the library's privacy policies that result from the adoption of an RFID system. Notices can be posted inside the library and in the library's print and online publications.

• Assure that all library staff continue to receive training on privacy issues, especially regarding those issues that arise due to the implementation and use of RFID technology.

• Be prepared to answer users' questions about the impact of RFID technology on their privacy. Either staff at all levels should be trained to address users' concerns, or one person should be designated to address them.

Best Practices

As with any new application of technology, librarians should strive to develop best practices to protect user privacy and confidentiality. With respect to RFID technology, librarians should:

• Continue their longstanding commitment to securing bibliographic and patron databases from unauthorized access and use.

• Use the most secure connection possible for all communications with the integrated library systems (ILS) to prevent unauthorized monitoring and access to personally identifiable information.

• Protect the data on RFID tags by the most secure means available, including encryption.

• Limit the bibliographic information stored on a tag to a unique identifier for the item (e.g., bar code number, record number, etc.). Use the security bit on the tag if it is applicable to your implementation.

- Block the public from searching the catalog by whatever unique identifier is used on RFID tags to avoid linking a specific item to information about its content.
- Train staff not to release information about an item's unique identifier in response to blind or casual inquiries.
- Store no personally identifiable information on any RFID tag. Limit the information stored on RFID-enabled borrower cards to a unique identifier.
- Label all RFID tag readers clearly so users know they are in use.
- Keep informed about changes in RFID technology, and review policies and procedures in light of new information.

Talking to Vendors about RFID

When dealing with vendors, librarians should:

- Assure that vendor agreements guarantee library control of all data and records and stipulate how the system will secure all information.
- Investigate closely vendors' assurances of library users' privacy.
- Evaluate vendor agreements in relationship with all library privacy policies and local, state, and federal laws.
- Influence the development of RFID technology by issuing Requests for Proposals requiring the use of security technology that preserves privacy and prevents monitoring.

II.7
Privacy

NOTES

1. Lori Bowen Ayre, "Wireless Tracking in the Library: Benefits, Threats, and Responsibilities," in *RFID: Applications, Security, and Privacy*, ed. Simson Garfinkel and Beth Rosenberg (Upper Saddle River, NJ: Addison-Wesley, 2006).

2. David Molnar and David Wagner, "Privacy and Security in Library RFID: Issues, Practices, and Architectures," CCS'04, October 25-29, 2004, Washington, DC, www.cs.berkeley.edu/~daw/papers/librfid-ccs04.pdf.

3. "Privacy Tool Kit," www.ala.org/advocacy/privacyconfidentiality/toolkits privacy/privacy.

4. Ibid.

The Law Regarding Privacy and Confidentiality in Libraries

Deborah Caldwell-Stone

PRIVACY LAW IN the United States is a complex subject that encompasses hundreds of laws, regulations, court decisions, and constitutional provisions that address a wide range of topics, including harms to reputation, health information, financial information, school records, employment records, business and consumer data, government access to private records, government search and seizure, electronic surveillance, and national security.[1] Many, if not most of these laws can affect or regulate the operation of the library in a myriad of ways.

The particular concern for the librarian and trustee seeking to promote and protect intellectual freedom in the library is the laws, regulations, and court decisions that protect intellectual privacy—the ability to read, consider, and develop ideas and beliefs free from any surveillance or unwanted interference by the government or others.[2]

Defining Privacy and Confidentiality in Libraries

The ability to keep one's reading habits private is the bedrock foundation for the unrestricted right to read and receive ideas. The freedom to read and receive information cannot survive in an environment where one's reading is monitored and made known to the government or to the public. Only when an individual is assured that his choice of reading material does not subject him to criticism, reprisals, or punishment can the individual fully enjoy his freedom to explore ideas, weigh arguments, and decide for himself what he believes.

A lack of privacy in what one reads and views in the library can have a significant chilling effect upon library users' willingness to exercise their First Amendment right to read. Librarians recognize that if library users are to be truly free to make individual choices about what they read and view, they must have a reasonable expectation that their library use will be kept confidential. For this reason, librarians have a long history of advocating for—and protecting—the confidentiality of library records and the privacy of library use.

"Privacy: An Interpretation of the *Library Bill of Rights*" (part II, chapter 7) defines the right to privacy in a library as "the right to engage in open

Implementing a New Library Service or Technology? Don't Forget about Privacy

The law in most states requires libraries to protect the privacy of library users, and many research studies show that people continue to care about privacy. When you implement a new service or technology, be sure you're not divulging user information to a third party. If you are, you owe it to your users to inform them and give them an alternative that protects their privacy.

Here are a few examples to consider:

- Chat, text, or e-mail reference services that route user questions through a third party

- E-book packages that require users to identify themselves to a vendor or publisher

- Integrated library systems that store user data in the cloud or on a third-party server

- Self-service "hold" shelves that reveal the identities and/or reading interests of users

- Subscription databases and online catalogs that do not allow anonymous searching and require users to sign in or create "profiles"

- Unencrypted e-mail notices that reveal the titles of items due, overdue, or recalled

- Social media or integrated library systems that invite users to save and share reading histories, search histories, or reviews with the users' names or unique identifiers

inquiry without having the subject of one's interest examined or scrutinized by others," and states that "users have the right to use a library without any abridgement of privacy that may result from equating the subject of their inquiry with behavior."[3] Confidentiality exists when a library is in possession of personally identifiable information about library users and keeps that information private on their behalf.[4]

The First Amendment and the Right to Privacy

The right to privacy in what one reads or views in the library, and the associated right to have the records of those activities kept confidential, is founded upon the First Amendment and its protection of the right to read and receive information anonymously.

The principle that a right to privacy or anonymity is necessary for the free exercise of First Amendment rights can be traced to the Supreme Court's recognition that the Bill of Rights protects not only the enumerated rights, but also the conditions that assure the uninhibited exercise of those rights. In *Griswold v. Connecticut,* the Supreme Court held that the Constitution provides for, and protects, additional, or peripheral, rights that are found in the "penumbras" of the specific guarantees contained in the Bill of Rights.[5] Included in these peripheral rights is a right to privacy that originates in "zones of privacy" associated with the First Amendment, the Fourth Amendment, the Fifth Amendment's guarantee against self-incrimination, the Ninth Amendment, and the Fourteenth Amendment's provision for due process.[6] Thus, the First Amendment protects the privacy of a person's reading habits, associations, and communications as a peripheral right necessary to give full meaning to the First Amendment's enumerated rights of speech, press, belief, and assembly.

Protecting the right to speak anonymously or read anonymously helps to assure that no one is discouraged from considering or receiving controversial ideas. As the Supreme Court explained in *McIntyre v. Ohio Elections Commission,* "anonymity is a shield from the tyranny of the majority. It thus exemplifies the purpose behind the Bill of Rights and of the First Amendment in particular: to protect unpopular individuals from retaliation—and their ideas from suppression—at the hand of an intolerant society."[7]

Two decisions by the Supreme Court provide direct support for the right to read and receive information and ideas, and a right to privacy or anonymity to protect that right. In *Lamont v. Postmaster General,* the Supreme Court struck down a law requiring individuals to identify themselves to the Post Office in order to receive publications that were allegedly communist propaganda.[8] The court's opinion relied upon the law's "chilling effect"—the law's potential to deter individuals from exercising their right to obtain and read controversial materials—as the grounds for overturning the law as an abridgment of the First Amendment right to receive information without identifying oneself.

A later Supreme Court decision, *Stanley v. Georgia,* famously defended "the right to be free from state inquiry into the contents of [one's] library," when it overturned the conviction of an individual convicted of possessing (for personal use only) materials deemed obscene by the state of Georgia.[9] The Supreme Court rejected the state's argument that mere possession of disfavored materials justified the state's invading the individual's home and privacy. It held that the right to receive information and ideas, regardless of their social worth, is "fundamental to our free society" as is "the right to be free from unwanted governmental intrusions into one's privacy." The court explained:

If the First Amendment means anything, it means that a State has no business telling a man, sitting alone in his own house, what books he may read or what films he may watch. Our whole constitutional heritage rebels at the thought of giving government the power to control men's minds.[10]

Subsequent court decisions in state and federal courts explicitly recognize that the First Amendment protects the right to read and receive ideas anonymously, free from any government inquiry or interference that might chill the exercise of that right. In particular, demands by law enforcement or the government to examine records held by a bookstore or library in order to determine what books a person has read (or what websites the person has visited) are viewed by courts as government action that can encroach upon the individual's First Amendment rights. Thus, when Monica Lewinsky and two bookstores challenged a subpoena that would have required the bookstores to turn over records of Lewinsky's book purchases to a federal grand jury, the court ruled that the government would need to demonstrate a compelling need for the information sought and show a sufficient connection between the information sought and the grand jury investigation before the court would enforce the subpoena.[11]

The Fourth Amendment and the Right to Privacy

Modern Fourth Amendment law relies on the Supreme Court's opinion in *Katz v. United States*,[12] which overruled the court's 1928 decision in *Olmstead v. United States.* In *Olmstead,* the court held that the Fourth Amendment did not apply to government wiretapping, as the act of wiretapping did not require the government to trespass inside a private home.[13] The court's decision in *Katz,* which addressed the warrantless wiretapping of a call made in a phone booth, rejected the idea that a physical trespass was required to trigger Fourth Amendment protection. Instead, the court held that the Fourth Amendment "protects people, not places" and that what a person "seeks to preserve as private, even in areas accessible to the public, may be constitutionally protected."[14] The test set forth in *Katz* stated that Fourth Amendment protections would apply if a person held an "actual (subjective) expectation of privacy" and the expectation is "one that society is prepared to recognize as 'reasonable.'"[15]

Fourth Amendment protections require law enforcement officials to establish "probable cause" in a court of law in order to obtain a search warrant before conducting any search. "Probable cause" can be established if the officials can show the court evidence supporting a reasonable belief that a crime is about to be committed or that the search will produce evidence of a crime. After the court issues the search warrant, officials may then undertake the search under the parameters authorized by the warrant. This may include a physical search of a home, business, or institution or the compelled production of physical items, papers, information, and electronic data.

Without a reasonable expectation of privacy, the Fourth Amendment does not apply. As the court noted in *Katz*, "What a person knowingly exposes to the public, even in his own home or office, is not a subject of Fourth Amendment protection."[16]

This Fourth Amendment disqualification extends to any personal information or records shared with a business or institution. In *United States v. Miller*, the Supreme Court held that a customer of a bank lacked a reasonable expectation of privacy in his financial records because he had voluntarily shared his financial information with the bank.[17] A later case, *Smith v. Maryland*, similarly held that the Fourth Amendment does not apply to phone numbers dialed on a private line, since a phone company's customers know they have to convey those numbers to the company and cannot expect that those numbers will remain secret.[18]

The rule derived from these cases is known as the "third-party doctrine," and it holds that a person has no reasonable expectation of privacy in records and information shared with and held by a third party. Based on this doctrine, courts have held that Fourth Amendment protections do not apply when the government seeks records or information about a person that is held by a third party.

Library circulation records and users' personal information held by the library appear to fall squarely into this Fourth Amendment exception. The absence of Fourth Amendment protection does not mean that library records are unprotected, however. Other provisions of the Constitution, including the First Amendment, protect personal privacy from invasions by the government. Several state constitutions explicitly recognize a right to privacy and provide additional and greater privacy protections to their residents. Most importantly, state legislatures and Congress can and do pass laws creating extensive statutory privacy protections that shield private information and records from unreasonable and unauthorized disclosure. For example, in response to the Supreme Court's *U.S. v. Miller* decision removing Fourth Amendment protections from bank records, Congress passed the Right to Financial Privacy Act of 1978, which requires government officials to use a search warrant or subpoena to obtain financial records.[19]

An array of state and federal statutes provides some level of protection to library circulation records, student records, and library users' confidential information. In addition, libraries can look to the First Amendment and the constitutional right to privacy to help safeguard library users' privacy and the confidentiality of library records.

State Constitutions and Laws Protecting the Privacy of Library Users' Records

Eleven state constitutions guarantee a right of privacy or bar unreasonable intrusions into the privacy of individuals.[20] Forty-eight states and the District of Columbia have adopted laws that specifically recognize the confidentiality of library records. Two states, Kentucky and Hawaii, do not have library confidentiality laws; instead, each state's attorney general has issued a binding opinion declaring library records confidential.[21]

The requirements of these laws vary from state to state. At a minimum, each statute declares that library circulation records are confidential records not subject to disclosure under the state's open records law or the Freedom of Information Act. Many states extend additional protection to library records by imposing a duty on the library to protect user records from disclosure, and limiting the circumstances under which a library may release records to third parties or law enforcement officers. For example, many state library confidentiality laws require a court order before a library may disclose records to law enforcement officers. A few state statutes make it a crime to disclose library records in a manner contrary to the law. Three states recently amended their library confidentiality statutes to include privacy protections for digital or online resources or to impose legal duties of confidentiality on third-party vendors that manage, store, or transmit library users' data.[22]

Library confidentiality laws may not apply to every library in a state, or may create exceptions to the law for some library users. For example, some state library confidentiality statutes do not apply to privately funded libraries, K–12 school libraries, or academic libraries. A few state laws contain exceptions that permit parents of minor children to examine their children's library records. Many states, however, choose to protect the confidentiality of all library users' records, without regard to the library user's age or the funding, ownership, or control of the library.

State library confidentiality laws should be recognized and included in library policy whenever they are applicable to the library and its users. For private institutions, library confidentiality laws can serve as public policy exemplars that can provide a rationale and a basis for the institutions' own policies protecting the confidentiality of library records.

II.7 Privacy

These laws provide compelling evidence that the states recognize an individual's right to privacy in records of their library use, and that library users have a reasonable expectation that records of their library use will be kept confidential. Librarians and trustees should consult with local legal counsel to determine their rights and responsibilities under state law.

Federal Privacy Statutes Impacting Library Users' Privacy and Confidentiality

There are numerous federal laws and regulations that can potentially affect the library user's privacy or govern the collection, maintenance, use, and dissemination of the user's data. Laws with particular relevance to libraries and educational institutions providing library services are identified below. Librarians, trustees, school librarians, and academic librarians should consult with their library's or institution's legal counsel to determine their rights and responsibilities under these statutes.

- The *Video Privacy Protection Act* forbids the disclosure of personally identifiable loan or rental records for "prerecorded video cassette tapes or similar audio visual material."[23] Such records may be shared only if the borrower consents to disclosure or if the business or institution making the loan is presented with a court order. The law also imposes requirements on the retention and destruction of records.
- The *Electronic Communications Privacy Act* encompasses three provisions that regulate the disclosure of electronic communications. The *Wiretap Act* prohibits the intentional interception, use, or disclosure of wire and electronic communications unless a statutory exception applies.[24] The *Stored Communications Act* prohibits disclosure of stored communications and records held by communications service providers absent a statutory exception.[25] The *Pen Register Act* regulates the issuance of orders allowing the use of pen registers and trap-and-trace devices that record numbers dialed for outgoing calls or that capture the numbers of incoming calls.[26] It does not authorize the collection of the contents of a communication. Libraries and institutions that provide electronic communications services may be governed by these provisions.
- The *Federal Educational Rights and Privacy Act (FERPA)* controls disclosure of a student's educational records and information.[27] It requires educational institutions to adopt policies that permit a

parent or student to inspect and correct the student's educational records. It also prohibits disclosure of a student's records without the parent's or student's written permission. The Family Policy Compliance Office, a part of the U.S. Department of Education, has issued guidance stating that library circulation records and similar records maintained by a school or university library are "educational records" under FERPA. School and academic librarians should consult with their institution's legal counsel to determine their rights and responsibilities under FERPA.

• The *Child Online Privacy Protection Act (COPPA)* applies to operators of commercial websites and online services directed to children under the age of thirteen that collect, use, or disclose personal information from children, and operators of general-audience websites or online services with actual knowledge that they are collecting, using, or disclosing personal information from children under thirteen.[28] The law requires these sites to obtain verifiable parental consent before collecting personal information online from children under thirteen. NOTE: *In general, noncommercial websites, including websites operated by public libraries, nonprofit organizations, schools and universities, are NOT subject to COPPA.* However, changes to the COPPA rules adopted in December 2012 may affect sites maintained by libraries and institutions that integrate outside services into their sites, such as plug-ins, apps, or advertising networks that collect personal information from site visitors. Such sites must comply with COPPA if the site operator knows that the outside service is collecting information from children under thirteen.

Law-Enforcement and Third-Party Demands for Library Records

The confidentiality of library records is not an absolute privilege. While the law may provide a shield to protect against the unreasonable or unjustified disclosure of a library user's records, it also provides law enforcement agents, prosecutors, and third parties with the means to compel production of those records if the facts and circumstances of a case justify disclosure. (See "The Law Regarding Law Enforcement Requests for Library Records" in part II, chapter 8.)

The possibility that a government agency will collect and use information about what a person reads or views in the library as evidence in a criminal investigation can deter individuals from reading certain books or library resources because they fear exposure, embarrassment, or worse. To assure that such government actions do not unduly chill the exercise of First Amendment rights, the law provides opportunities for court review of subpoenas, court orders, and other judicial process.

Both public and private institutions can ask a court to quash or set aside a subpoena or court order seeking individuals' library records if the institution believes producing the records will chill the exercise of the First Amendment right to read and receive information. While the First Amendment is not an absolute shield, judicial review of subpoenas will help assure that readers' First Amendment privacy rights are not infringed unless the government can demonstrate a compelling need for the information sought and a sufficient connection between the information sought and the investigation.

Courts have established a balancing test to be applied when a threat to a First Amendment right is raised as a basis for quashing a grand jury subpoena or other court order. In such cases, the government must demonstrate a compelling interest or need for the information sought and show a substantial connection between the information sought and the investigation, a very high standard of review.[29] If the government makes this showing, the subpoena or court order will be upheld and the records or information will need to be produced to the government pursuant to the terms of the subpoena or court order. If the government fails to provide sufficient evidence of a compelling interest or need for the information, or a link between the information sought and the investigation, the subpoena or court order will be quashed or set aside by the court.[30]

Libraries and bookstores have successfully challenged subpoenas and search warrants in state and federal courts:

- In Decatur, Texas, a subpoena was directed to the library for the names, addresses, and telephone numbers of every individual who had borrowed books on childbearing in the last nine months as part of a child abandonment investigation.[31] The police had no evidence indicating that the person who abandoned the child might have borrowed library books. The court quashed the subpoena on the grounds that the subpoena unreasonably intruded upon the library users' right to privacy.
- The Supreme Court of Colorado held that law enforcement officials could not justify a request for information about a customer's purchases from the Tattered Cover bookstore.[32] The court based its decision in large part on the free speech and privacy rights assured by the

Colorado State Constitution, demonstrating how state constitutions and state laws can provide heightened protections for the right to read anonymously, without government interference.

· The King County Library System in Washington State challenged a warrantless search by the Kent Police Department, after Kent police officers seized computers from its Kent Regional Branch Library as a part of an investigation concerning child pornography.[33] The reviewing court found that the warrantless search violated the library users' right to privacy and entered a preliminary injunction prohibiting the police department from searching or otherwise tampering with the computers and requiring the police to return the computers to the library. Following the entry of these orders, the city settled the case, paying $30,000 in attorneys' fees to counsel for the prevailing library.

The USA PATRIOT Act and the Rise of the Surveillance State

The Uniting and Strengthening America by Providing Appropriate Tools Required to Intercept and Obstruct Terrorism Act (USA PATRIOT Act) is a singular piece of legislation. Adopted with almost no debate in the wake of the September 2001 attacks on the World Trade Center and Pentagon, the USA PATRIOT Act vastly expanded the authority of federal agencies and the departments that investigate crime, terrorism, and foreign espionage to conduct secret surveillance on ordinary persons, while minimizing any judicial supervision of those surveillance activities. The provisions of the USA PATRIOT Act allow the Federal Bureau of Investigation (FBI), National Security Agency (NSA), and other federal law enforcement agencies to access a wide variety of sensitive information about people, including personally identifiable information, phone and e-mail communications, bank and credit records, and data about one's use of the Internet, without a need to show probable cause or any kind of reasonable suspicion of terrorist or criminal activity.

The provisions of the USA PATRIOT Act that raise the most concern for librarians and library users are certain amendments to the Foreign Intelligence Surveillance Act (FISA), wiretap laws, and to laws authorizing the use of National Security Letters, a form of administrative subpoena.

Section 215 amended the business records provision of FISA.[34] It allows the FBI to obtain a court order that requires the recipient to turn over "any tangible thing" for an investigation into terrorism or espionage. Section 215 orders are issued by the Foreign Intelligence Surveillance Court (FISC), a special court whose proceedings are secret and whose decisions are classified and almost never disclosed to the public. The FISC will issue a Section 215 order if an agent presents "reasonable grounds" to believe that the items sought are "relevant" to an authorized investigation. Because "any tangible thing" is broadly defined to include any object or record, these orders can reach library circulation records, Internet sign-up sheets, computer hard drives, databases, and other media held by a library. The secrecy of the search is assured by an automatic gag order that prohibits the recipient of the Section 215 order from disclosing the existence of the order or the fact that records were turned over to the FBI.

Section 505 of the USA PATRIOT Act expands the FBI's ability to use National Security Letters (NSLs), a form of administrative subpoena that is issued on the agent's authority alone, without any judicial review, even by a secret court.[35] NSLs are issued when an FBI agent seeks user information from the library in its capacity as a wire or electronic communication service provider. Like the amended FISA provisions under Section 215, NSLs are accompanied by an automatic gag order that forbids the recipient from disclosing the existence of the NSL. (See "The Law Regarding Law Enforcement Requests for Library Records" in part II, chapter 8, for information on responding to Section 215 orders and NSLs.)

Congress subsequently reauthorized the USA PATRIOT Act in 2006 and 2011, extending the use of Section 215 through December 31, 2015, and permanently adding Section 505 to U.S. law.[36] Congress also approved separate, additional amendments to the Foreign Intelligence Surveillance Act in 2008 that broadened the government's power to conduct secret warrantless surveillance of foreign nationals' international phone calls, text messages, and e-mail.[37] Provisions of this law, identified as Section 702, allow the government to collect any communications to which U.S. persons may be a party and permit the collection of "incidental" communications that may be inadvertently swept up with the targeted communications.[38]

In June 2013, a series of articles published by the British newspaper *The Guardian* revealed details of a vast U.S. domestic surveillance program conducted by the National Security Agency, confirming librarians' fears that the federal agency would misuse its authority to investigate foreign nationals to spy on U.S. citizens. Relying on documents provided by former NSA contractor Edward Snowden, *The Guardian* reported that the NSA was requiring all four major U.S. telecommunications companies to turn over all phone-call metadata to the NSA on an ongoing daily basis, including the identity of the callers and the time and length of the calls, relying on a Section 215 order issued by the FISC authorizing the surveillance.[39] A second initiative conducted under Section 702 of the FISA Amendments Act collects Americans' international calls, text messages, and e-mail messages that are associated with foreign nationals' communications that are targeted by the NSA for surveillance.[40] Despite public outcry against these surveillance programs, they continue today.

Very nearly from the day the USA PATRIOT Act was signed into law, librarians raised concerns about the scope of surveillance authorized under the provisions of the USA PATRIOT Act. In particular, librarians protested the low or nonexistent legal thresholds for obtaining Section 215 court orders and the lack of judicial review for secret subpoenas that provided federal agents with the authority to obtain records and information about individuals' most sensitive First Amendment activities, seeing an enormous potential for abuse in such broad authority to peer into individuals' lives. Such vast surveillance is certain to chill the exercise of fundamental civil liberties such as the right to read, discuss, and think about controversial subjects or political or social issues.

As a result, the American Library Association continues to support legislation that amends or repeals those portions of the USA PATRIOT Act that pose a threat to library users' civil liberties and right to privacy. ALA has pursued this goal for over a decade, working in partnership with the Campaign for Reader Privacy and other civil liberties organizations.[41]

The secrecy provisions of the USA PATRIOT Act place significant barriers in the way of persons wishing to challenge secret surveillance on constitutional grounds. Such challenges are often dismissed because the courts have ruled that persons or institutions can challenge secret government surveillance only if they can prove that they have been harmed because they have been the target of, or subject to, surveillance.[42] But such information is classified, so potential plaintiffs cannot prove their case.[43]

Despite these challenges, librarians and Internet service providers have filed lawsuits challenging the constitutionality of National Security Letters. Most prominent among these was the 2005 lawsuit filed by Barbara Bailey, Peter Chase, George Christian, and Janet Nocek, four individuals who served on the board of directors of the Library Connection, a consortium providing computer and automation services to twenty-seven Connecticut libraries.[44] The lawsuit argued that the laws authorizing the use of NSLs are unconstitutional because they permit the disclosure of First Amendment–protected information without judicial review and prevent recipients from exercising their First Amendment right to participate in the national discussion and debate concerning the USA PATRIOT Act.[45] After months of litigation, the government finally gave up its battle to maintain the gag order and eventually withdrew its demand for the Library Connection's records, preserving the confidentiality of the affected library users.[46]

The litigation concluded with an opinion from the Second Circuit Court of Appeals that found parts of the NSL gag-order provision unconstitutional.[47] The court of appeals issued an order to remedy the law's deficiencies, establishing new standards of review and ordering the FBI to adopt procedures ensuring that NSL recipients are notified of their right to have a federal court review the grounds for issuing the gag order.[48]

Changes in the law and the methods used to conduct surveillance under the USA PATRIOT Act mean that librarians will rarely need to address an NSL or Section 215 order or to consider whether to challenge such an order as the Connecticut librarians did. But in the ongoing debate over surveillance and national security, librarians are uniquely positioned to identify privacy with fundamental democratic values by highlighting how privacy is necessary for the uninhibited exercise of our fundamental First Amendment freedoms. Advocacy, education, and modeling best practices for preserving and defending users' privacy and confidentiality rights will help ensure a future in which library users will be able to pursue any inquiry or read any book without fear of judgment or punishment. For ideas on how to become a library privacy advocate, visit the Choose Privacy Week site at www.choose privacyweek.org.

The Future of Privacy and Confidentiality in Libraries

While the growth of government surveillance unquestionably poses a threat to library users' privacy, the greater challenge to the librarian's ability to protect library users' privacy in the future may arise from librarians' own embrace of the technologies of "big data."

Digitized content, networked services, and sophisticated platforms and databases can provide greater access to information and enhance the library user's experience by providing innovative tools and personalized features for reading and research. At the same time, these new technologies can facilitate and create opportunities for governments, corporations, and individuals to monitor library users' reading and research habits by requiring the tracking, collection, and aggregation of user data in order to provide enhanced services or operational efficiencies.[49]

Self-serve hold systems provide an example of how the use of library user data to provide efficient library service can threaten user privacy. Increasingly, a growing number of libraries are implementing self-service hold systems that reveal the user's identity by attaching the user's name to the book and placing it on a shelf that is browsable by the public. Such systems plainly violate the library's ethical obligation to keep library users' identities and reading habits confidential and frequently violate state library confidentiality laws that forbid disclosure of any information that links the use of a library resource to a particular user.

Self-serve hold systems that disclose library users' identities pose a particular threat to user privacy: they undermine one of the fundamental grounds for extending heightened legal and procedural protection to library users' records and information. Recall that in the United States, an individual's right to privacy under the law—and the right to keep particular kinds of sensitive information private—relies on whether or not the individual has a "reasonable expectation of privacy" in the information that the law is prepared to recognize. If there is no actual expectation that the information will remain private, or if the expectation is unreasonable, the courts are unlikely to protect the privacy of that information.

When libraries place on public display information that associates the library user with the books or library resources she is reading, there is little or no basis for arguing that records of a user's reading history are entitled to heightened legal and procedural protections that shield them from government search and seizure. Nor are there grounds to argue that the library is entitled to keep that information confidential on behalf of the user. In short, public display of a library user's personally identifiable information with the books he reads erodes the legal expectation of privacy in what one reads in the library.[50]

The ability to preserve user privacy is also challenged by the fact that the content, services, platforms, and technologies that enhance library services are provided, operated, and maintained by commercial vendors. Often, commercial vendors do not share librarians' ethical commitment to preserving user privacy and frequently are not bound by state laws mandating that library users' data be kept confidential.[51] Absent such limits, vendors are free to use and share library user data that comes into their control.

Restoring legal protections for library users' data acquired and stored by vendors can be accomplished by one of two methods. The first is a private solution: requiring the vendor to enter into a contract for services whose terms assure that the vendor will protect the confidentiality of users' data with the same care exercised by the library. Suggested terms would acknowledge that the library owns library user data no matter where it is stored or how it moves through networks and require the vendor to adopt privacy policies that conform to the library's own privacy policies and applicable state library confidentiality laws.

The second method is a public policy solution: amending or adopting library confidentiality laws so that the terms apply equally to any entity, public or private, that manages, stores, or uses library user data to provide content and library services. Two states, California and Missouri, have chosen this path, amending their existing library confidentiality statutes to require third-party vendors and service providers who transmit, use, or store library users' data to keep that data confidential and protect it from disclosure to law enforcement or third parties unless the vendor is served with a court order.[52]

As libraries move to adopt digital content and new technologies, librarians need to assure that the use of library users' data for these services does not weaken privacy protections for library users' data or blur the line between public and confidential records. This will require a firm commitment to the profession's obligation to protect the confidentiality of library users' information and the will to advocate for greater legal protections for library users' data that ensure reader privacy and protect against censorship.

NOTES

1. Daniel Solove and Paul Schwartz, *Privacy Law Fundamentals* (International Association of Privacy Professionals, 2011).

2. Neil M. Richards, "Intellectual Privacy," *Texas Law Review* 87 (2008): 389.

3. "Privacy: An Interpretation of the *Library Bill of Rights*" (see part II, chapter 7).

4. *Id.*

5. *Griswold v. Connecticut*, 381 U.S. 479, 484 (1965).

6. *Id.*

7. *McIntyre v. Ohio Elections Commission*, 514 U.S. 334, 357 (1995) (citations omitted).

8. *Lamont v. Postmaster General*, 381 U.S. 301, 307 (1965).

9. *Stanley v. Georgia*, 394 U.S. 557, 564 (1969).

10. Id., 565.

11. *In re Grand Jury Subpoena to Kramerbooks & Afterwords, Inc.*, 26 Med. L. Rptr. 1599 (D.D.C. 1998).

12. *Katz v. United States,* 389 U.S. 347 (1967).

13. *Olmstead v. United States,* 277 U.S. 438, 464 (1928).

14. *Katz,* 389 U.S. at 351–52.

15. *Id.*

16. *Id.*

17. *United States v. Miller,* 425 U.S. 435 (1976).

18. *Smith v. Maryland,* 442 U.S. 735 (1979).

19. Right to Financial Privacy Act, Pub. L. No. 95-630 (1978), codified at 12 U.S.C. 3406.

20. States whose constitutions include guarantees of privacy or provisions protecting against unreasonable intrusions into privacy include Alaska, Arizona, California, Colorado, Florida, Hawaii, Illinois, Louisiana, Montana, South Carolina, and Washington. See Timothy O. Lenz, "'Privacy Talk' about Privacy in the State Courts," *Albany Law Review* 60 (1997): 1613, 1631.

21. For a state-by-state compilation of library confidentiality statutes and opinions, see "State Privacy Laws Regarding Library Records," online at www.ala.org/advocacy/privacyconfidentiality/privacy/stateprivacy.

22. Ariz. Rev. Stat. § 41-151.22 (2013), Cal. Gov. Code §6267 (2012); and Mo. Rev. Statutes §182.815 (2014).

23. 18 U.S.C. §2710.

24. 18 U.S.C. § 2511.

25. 18 U.S.C. §§ 2701.

26. 18 U.S.C. §§ 3121.

27. 20 U.S.C. § 1232g, 34 C.F.R. Part 99.

28. 15 U.S. Code § 6501.

29. *In re Grand Jury Subpoena to Kramerbooks and Afterwords, Inc.,* 26 Med. L. Rptr. 1599 (D.D.C. 1998).

30. *Tattered Cover, Inc. v. City of Thornton,* 44 P.3d 1044 (Colo. 2002).

31. *Decatur Public Library v. District Attorney of Wise County,* No. 90-05-192, 271st Judicial Court (Texas, 1990).

32. *Tattered Cover, Inc.* at 44 P.3d 1059.

33. *King County Library System v. City of Kent and City of Kent Police Department,* Case No. 02-2-17484-1 (W.D. Wash. 2002). Slip opinion on file with the Office for Intellectual Freedom.

34. 18 U.S.C. § 1861.

35. 18 U.S.C. § 2709.

36. P.L. 109-178, USA PATRIOT Act Additional Reauthorizing Amendments Act (2006) and P.L. 112-14, Patriot Sunsets Extension Act (2011).

37. P.L. 110-261, FISA Amendment Acts of 2008.

38. 50 U.S.C. §1881(a)—(c).

39. Glen Greenwald, "NSA Collecting Phone Records of Millions of Verizon Customers Daily," *The Guardian,* June 5, 2013.

40. Barton Gellman and Laura Poitras, "U.S., British Intelligence Mining Data from Nine U.S. Internet Companies in Broad Secret Program," *The Washington Post,* June 7, 2013.

41. See, e.g., Campaign for Reader Privacy, www.readerprivacy.org.

42. *Clapper v. Amnesty Intern. USA,* 133 S. Ct. 1138 (2013).

43. Neil Richards, "The Dangers of Surveillance," *Harvard Law Review* 126 (2013): 1944-45.

44. Eric Lichtblau, "F.B.I., Using Patriot Act, Demands Library's Records," *New York Times,* August 26, 2005, www.nytimes.com/2005/08/26/politics/26patriot.html.

45. *Doe v. Gonzales,* Complaint (2005), at https://www.aclu.org/national-security/aclu-v-gonzales-redacted-complaint.

46. Anahad O'Connor, "Librarians Win as U.S. Relents on Secrecy Law," *New York Times,* April 13, 2006, http://query.nytimes.com/gst/abstract.html?res=980CEED81F30F930A25757C0A9609C8B63.

47. *Doe, Inc. v. Mukasey,* 549 F.3d 861 (2d Cir. 2008).

48. *Id.,* 883–84.

49. Michael Zimmer, "Patron Privacy in the '2.0' Era: Avoiding the Faustian Bargain of Library 2.0," *Journal of Information Ethics* 22, no. 1 (2013): 44–59.

50. The issues raised by self-serve hold systems displaying library users' personally identifiable information spurred the ALA Council to adopt the "Resolution to Protect Library User Confidentiality in Self-Service Hold Practices" in June 2011. The resolution strongly urged libraries to protect library users' privacy by adopting practices and procedures that conceal the library user's identity when identifying materials being held for the library user.

51. Trina J. Magi, "A Content Analysis of Library Vendor Privacy Policies: Do They Meet Our Standards?" *College & Research Libraries* 71, no. 3 (2010): 254–72.

52. Cal. Gov. Code §6267 (2012); and Mo. Rev. Statutes §182.815 (2014).

Visits and Requests from Law Enforcement

ISSUE AT A GLANCE

Key Concepts

- Libraries should not share personally identifiable user information with law enforcement *except* with the permission of the user or in response to some form of judicial process (subpoena, search warrant, or other court order).
- Most law enforcement officers understand that the library has a right to consult with counsel before responding to requests for user information.
- The library can extend cooperation to law enforcement by identifying relevant records or computers and preserving those records or computers until a court order is served on the library.
- Libraries have no affirmative duty to collect or retain information about library users on behalf of law enforcement. However, when

Need to Talk to an Attorney?

If your library has received a subpoena, search warrant, or other demand for records and you do not have access to an attorney, you may call the ALA Office for Intellectual Freedom at (800) 545-2433, ext. 4223, to request a referral to legal counsel.

If an agent for the Federal Bureau of Investigation presents an order and informs you that the order is issued as part of a terrorism or espionage investigation (FISA court order or National Security Letter), it is likely subject to a "nondisclosure order" or "gag order." In this case, you should *not* disclose the existence of the order. Simply say, "I need to speak to an attorney."

library personnel believe that a crime has been committed in the library, the library should contact the police and then use reasonable efforts to preserve any direct evidence of that crime. The library should turn over the evidence to police in accordance with the law, which may require the police to obtain a court order before viewing or copying relevant library records.

What Does the Law Say?

- All states and the District of Columbia have either laws or attorney general opinions protecting the confidentiality of library records. Check to see if your state law applies to your library.
- Neither federal agents nor police officers are legally authorized to demand library records without first providing some form of judicial process (subpoena, search warrant, or other legally enforceable court order) to the library holding the records.
- Requiring a court order is neither unusual nor burdensome. Law enforcement officers have access to judges even after normal business hours. If law enforcement officers believe there is an imminent threat to someone's life or public safety, that there is inadequate time to obtain a warrant, and that they have probable cause for seizure of records, they may simply take custody of the records over the library's objection and will bear any legal risks associated with the decision to proceed without a warrant.
- It may be a violation of state law to voluntarily disclose surveillance camera images to law enforcement, even if the images do not reveal any person's use of specific library materials or resources. Check your state law and consult legal counsel.

Creating Policy for Your Library

- Consider formally adopting *Libraries: An American Value* and the *Code of Ethics of the American Library Association* (see part I, chapter 2) as policy for your library. They contain statements about protecting library users' privacy and confidentiality.
- All libraries, public or private, should have written procedures for handling requests from law enforcement, including subpoenas, search warrants, National Security Letters, and orders issued pursu-

ant to the Foreign Intelligence Surveillance Act and the Electronic Communications Privacy Act.

- Be sure you have a privacy policy that outlines the way your library (1) limits the collection of personally identifiable information, (2) deletes information when no longer needed, (3) avoids placing personal information on public view, and (4) responds to third-party requests for user information.

Especially for Academic Libraries

- The Family Education Rights and Privacy Act may also govern how requests for student records from law enforcement must be managed. Consult with your institution's legal counsel about the necessary policies and procedures.

Especially for School Libraries

- The Family Education Rights and Privacy Act may also govern how requests for student records from law enforcement must be managed. Consult with your institution's legal counsel about the necessary policies and procedures.

To Learn More

- Visit the ALA "Intellectual Freedom" website (www.ala.org/advocacy/intfreedom) for links to information about privacy, including "Questions and Answers on Privacy and Confidentiality."
- Consult the ALA "Privacy Tool Kit" (www.ala.org/advocacy/privacy confidentiality/toolkitsprivacy/privacy) for information about privacy audits, policy writing, sample policies, and more.
- See also part II, chapter 7, "Privacy and Confidentiality" and "The Universal Right to Free Expression" in part II, chapter 1.

Questions for Reflection

- A police officer approaches the desk and says he's looking for a missing child. He wants to review library activity records to see if the child had been in the library that day. What do you do?

- The sheriff asks to install monitoring software on the library's network to look for attempts to access child pornography sites. She promises that all other Internet usage will be ignored. What's your response?
- During rounds, you notice that a library user is looking at a website that appears to feature young children in sexual situations. What do you do?

OFFICIAL ALA POLICY STATEMENT

Policy on Governmental Intimidation

Adopted February 2, 1973, by the ALA Council; amended July 1, 1981; and June 30, 2004.

> A historical essay about this statement can be found in the publication, *A History of ALA Policy on Intellectual Freedom: A Supplement to the Intellectual Freedom Manual, Ninth Edition.*

THE AMERICAN LIBRARY Association opposes any use of governmental prerogatives that leads to the intimidation of individuals or groups and discourages them from exercising the right of free expression as guaranteed by the First Amendment to the U.S. Constitution. ALA encourages resistance to such abuse of governmental power and supports those against whom such governmental power has been employed.

How to Respond to Law Enforcement Requests for Library Records and User Information: Suggested Guidelines

Before Any Visit

- Designate the person or persons who will be responsible for handling law-enforcement requests. In most circumstances, it should be the library director, and, if available, the library's legal counsel. Prepare a list of these persons, along with contact information including home or cell phone numbers for use if they are not present in the library.

- Review the library's confidentiality policy and state confidentiality law with library counsel. Communicate those policies and the requirements of the law to both staff and volunteer workers in the library.

- Train all library workers, *including volunteers,* on the library's procedure for handling law-enforcement requests. They should understand that it is lawful to refer the agent or officer to an administrator in charge of the library, and that they generally do not need to respond immediately to any request.

- A court order may require the removal of a computer workstation or other computer storage device from the library. Have plans in place to address service interruptions and any necessary backups for equipment and software.

These suggested guidelines will help you prepare for and respond to requests from law enforcement while upholding First and Fourth Amendment freedoms, professional ethics, and state law. State and local jurisdictions may have different laws applicable to privacy, confidentiality, and library records. Review these guidelines with your legal counsel and modify them as appropriate for your library. These guidelines are *not* intended as legal advice. If legal advice or expert assistance is required, the services of a competent legal professional should be sought.

II.8
Requests
from Law
Enforcement

During a Visit

PROCEDURES FOR LIBRARY STAFF

If a law enforcement officer requests library records or information about a library user or staff member:

1. Ask for the officer's identification.
2. Inform the officer that the library director or legal counsel is the individual authorized to respond to requests for records and information, and that library policy requires you to refer the officer to the specified person under your policy.
3. Refer the officer to the library director, legal counsel or to a designated alternate authorized by the library director to respond to requests for records and information. (A list of library employees authorized to respond to records and information requests in the absence of the library director should be available to staff.)

What if it's an emergency?

In some cases, especially those involving missing persons, law enforcement may ask you to voluntarily provide records immediately and give you the impression that it's not possible to obtain a court order.

It is important to remember that requiring a court order is neither unusual nor burdensome. Law enforcement officers have access to judges even after normal business hours. You can extend cooperation by preserving the desired records (or by keeping a computer turned on and making sure no one uses it) while the officer seeks a court order.

There is a limited legal exception to the warrant requirement when "exigent circumstances" exist. If members of law enforcement believe an emergency truly exists, that there is inadequate time to obtain a warrant, and that they have probable cause for seizure of records, they may simply take custody of the records over the library's objection. In this case, you should not interfere, but you should also indicate that you are not granting permission. This is necessary so that the law enforcement officials and *not* the library will bear responsibility and any legal risks associated with the decision to proceed without a warrant.

A number of states make provision for exigent circumstances in the state's library confidentiality statute. If so, precisely follow the law's requirements. For example, one state requires any law enforcement officer asking for library records under exigent circumstances to provide a written affidavit to the library affirming that such circumstances exist. Legal counsel should assist the library in interpreting state and local laws on exigent circumstances for inclusion in the policy on release of records and information.

If a law enforcement officer requests library records or information about a library user or staff member and neither the library director, legal counsel, nor a designated alternate is present in the library:

1. Ask for the officer's identification. Record the information that appears on the identity card.
2. Inform the officer that the library director or legal counsel is the individual authorized to respond to requests for records and information, and that library policy requires you to refer the officer to the specified individual.
3. Attempt to reach the library director, a designated alternate, or the library's legal counsel using the phone contact list.
4. If you cannot reach the library director, legal counsel, or a designated alternate, utilize the procedures outlined below for use by the library director or a designated alternate. Provide a written report describing the officer's inquiry to the library director at the earliest opportunity.

PROCEDURES FOR THE LIBRARY DIRECTOR OR A DESIGNATED ALTERNATE:

In all cases:

1. Ask for the officer's identification. Record the information that appears on the identity card. If possible, verify the information with the local FBI office or the police department.
2. Ask a colleague to be present during the interview with the officer. One person should take notes that may be useful if a record of the encounter is needed in the future.

Requests for *voluntary assistance* or *warrantless searches* (the officer does *not* present a subpoena or court order):

1. Explain the library's privacy policy, informing the officer that library records and information about library users and library staff are not made available to law enforcement agencies unless a proper court order in good form has been presented to the library.
2. Without a court order, neither the FBI nor local law enforcement has authority to compel cooperation with an investigation or require answers to questions, other than the name and address of the person speaking to the agent or officer. If the officer persists, explain that, as good citizens and in conformity with professional ethics,

First Amendment freedoms, and state law, the library staff will not respond to informal requests for confidential information in the absence of a court order.

3. If the officer claims that an emergency or other circumstance requires the library to turn over records or provide information without a court order, call the library's legal counsel and ask for assistance. (See also the note associated with this article: "What if it's an emergency?")

4. If the officer employs force to take possession of library records or other library property, do not obstruct the search in any way. Keep a written record describing the incident. Ask any witnesses to the incident to prepare a written record of the interaction between the officer and library employees or volunteers.

5. Provide all notes and records to the library's legal counsel. If a library worker or volunteer is required to respond to a voluntary request or a warrantless search in the absence of the library director or a designated alternate, all materials should be turned over to the library director.

If the law enforcement officer presents a subpoena or similar request for records:

1. Accept the subpoena. Inform the officer that the library's legal counsel responds to subpoenas on behalf of the library. A subpoena does not require an immediate response from the library.

2. Turn the subpoena over to the library's legal counsel. If a library worker or volunteer accepts service of the subpoena in the absence of the library director or a designated alternate, the subpoena should be turned over to the library director for coordination with legal counsel.

3. The library director will work with the library's legal counsel to respond appropriately to the subpoena. Examine the subpoena for any legal defect, including the manner in which it was served on the library, the breadth of its request, its form, or an insufficient showing of good cause made to a court. If a defect exists, legal counsel will advise on the best method to resist the subpoena.

4. Through legal counsel, insist that any defect be cured before records are released and that the subpoena is strictly limited to require release of specifically identified records or documents. If there does not appear to be good cause for the subpoena, or if it seems too broad or intrusive, ask your attorney to file a motion with the issuing court to quash the subpoena in its entirety. Require that the agent, officer,

or party requesting the information submit a new subpoena in good form and without defects.

5. If you decide to comply with the subpoena after consulting with legal counsel, review the information that may be produced in response to the subpoena before releasing the information. Follow the subpoena strictly and do not provide any information that is not specifically requested in it.

6. If disclosure is required, ask the court to enter a protective order (drafted by the library's counsel) keeping the information confidential and limiting its use to the particular case. Ask that access be restricted to those persons working directly on the case.

If the law enforcement officer presents a *search warrant:*

1. Immediately ask the library's legal counsel to provide advice and assistance.

2. Unlike a subpoena, a search warrant may be executed immediately. Ask to have library counsel present before the search begins in order to allow library counsel an opportunity to examine the warrant and to ensure that the search conforms to the terms of the warrant.

3. If the officer refuses to delay the search, read the warrant and any attached documentation. Verify that it is signed by a judge; is issued by a local, state, or federal court in your state or county; and is current and has not expired. If you have questions about the validity of the warrant, call the issuing court to verify the validity of the warrant or order.

4. Identify the items or records specified in the warrant. If the officer will not wait for legal counsel to arrive, you may assist the officer in locating the items or records identified in the search warrant in order to prevent review of other users' records or items not named in the warrant.

5. Do not agree to any additional searches, or volunteer information about the items or records in the warrant. Do not sign any documents on behalf of the library without the advice of the library's legal counsel.

6. Record and keep an inventory of the records or items seized from the library. Ask if it is possible to provide copies to the officers or to make copies for the library's own records.

7. Do not obstruct the search in any way.

8. If the law enforcement officials are unwilling to cooperate with you, simply step aside and do not interfere with the officer. Continue

your attempts to notify legal counsel, and make every effort to keep a written record of the incident. Ask any witnesses to keep a written record of the interaction between law enforcement officials and library employees and volunteers.

9. Request that the officer sign an inventory receipt for the materials with a specific list of all materials seized.

10. Provide all notes and records to the library's legal counsel. If a library worker or volunteer is required to respond to a search warrant in the absence of the library director or a designated alternate, all materials should be turned over to the library director for coordination with legal counsel.

If an agent for the Federal Bureau of Investigation presents an order and informs you that the order is issued as part of a terrorism or espionage investigation and is subject to a "nondisclosure order" or "gag order" (FISA court orders or National Security Letters):

1. Call the library's legal counsel and ask for assistance.

2. Read the order and any attached documentation. If it provides a period of time to respond to the order, respond to the order in the same manner as a subpoena. Except for legal counsel, do not inform other library staff or any other person about the order until authorized to do so by the library's legal counsel.

3. If the order requires the immediate surrender of records or other items, respond to the order in the same manner as a search warrant. Ask the agent if he will delay the search until the library's legal counsel arrives.

4. If required to turn over records or other items at once, do not notify any library staff except for legal counsel and those staff members necessary for the production of the requested records or other items. (For example, it may be necessary to ask a member of the information technology staff to assist with the production of electronic or computer records.) Instruct all staff members who assist in responding to the order that, with the exception of legal counsel, they cannot inform other library staff or any other person about the order unless authorized to do so by the library's legal counsel.

5. If a library worker or volunteer is required to respond to an order issued under the USA PATRIOT Act in the absence of the library director or a designated alternate, she should inform the library director as the custodian of records. It is not unlawful for library staff or volunteers to refer the agent to the library director or his designated alternate; however, except for legal counsel, the staff member

or volunteer should not inform anyone else about the order unless authorized to do so by the library's legal counsel.

The Law Regarding Law Enforcement Requests for Library Records

Deborah Caldwell-Stone

FROM TIME TO time, law enforcement officers may visit the library and ask librarians or library workers to turn over records or data concerning a library user's reading habits or use of the Internet. In most circumstances, however, the law does not permit either federal agents or local law enforcement officers to compel production of an individual's library records or confidential information without first providing the library with some form of *judicial process*—a subpoena, a search warrant, or other legally enforceable court order.

The requirement that a law enforcement officer obtain a subpoena, search warrant, or court order to obtain library records is grounded in the shared consensus that any attempt by the government to compel disclosure of a person's reading habits is a form of government action that can encroach upon the individual's First Amendment rights. Forty-eight states and the District of Columbia have adopted library confidentiality laws reflecting this consensus.[1] These laws generally exempt library records from disclosure under Freedom of Information laws and frequently require law enforcement officers to obtain a court order before a library can disclose records to them.[2]

Fundamental Principles for Responding to a Request from Law Enforcement

1. Always ask for identification.

2. Refer the officer to the library director or the library's legal counsel or other staff person responsible for responding to requests for records or information.

3. Do not disclose any library record or information about a library user without first obtaining permission from the director, the library's legal counsel, or the director's designated substitute.

4. Know how to respond in emergency circumstances, such as when the director or legal counsel cannot be reached or is otherwise unavailable, or when law enforcement officers insist on taking records or other items without a proper order.

5. Understand the steps for responding to particular requests for library records or information.

Courts have quashed or dismissed subpoenas and search warrants when circumstances demonstrate that law enforcement efforts to obtain information about a person's reading habits will harm fundamental First Amendment liberties. The Colorado Supreme Court quashed a search warrant served on the Tattered Cover bookstore, holding that the need to protect the reader's right to read anonymously required the government to demonstrate a compelling need for those records before they could obtain a warrant.[3] Similarly, when a district attorney investigating a child abandonment case sought to obtain the names and phone numbers of every person who had borrowed books on childbirth from the local library, the court quashed the subpoena as an overbroad fishing expedition that threatened to violate library users' privacy rights and chill their exercise of First Amendment freedoms.[4]

Occasionally a law enforcement officer will ask the library to disregard the law and library policy and turn over records without a court order because he believes it is inconvenient or burdensome to get a court order. But requiring a court order is neither unusual nor burdensome. Law enforcement officers have access to judges even after normal business hours, and most courts move quickly to issue such orders when circumstances require it. Any response by the library to a request for library users' records must conform to the laws governing disclosure of library records.

In very rare circumstances, a law enforcement officer will inform the library that there is an emergency that justifies the seizure of records without a warrant. This is the doctrine of "exigent circumstances," which can justify an officer's seizure of evidence without a warrant if the officer reasonably believes that circumstances render it impossible to obtain a warrant and the seizure is necessary to prevent physical harm to a person or prevent the destruction of evidence. In such cases, the officer may simply take custody of the records over the library's objection, and will bear any legal risks associated with the decision to proceed without a warrant. Either the library or the library user can challenge a warrantless search and seizure after the fact, and if the court determines that the facts of the case do not justify the warrantless seizure, it can set aside the search, quash any future search warrants, and enjoin any examination or use of the items or records seized in the search. This was the result when a Washington state police department seized computers from the local public library without a warrant; the court agreed with the library that there were insufficient grounds for the warrantless search and that the search invaded the privacy of library users.[5]

Librarians and library staff should be able to identify the various types of judicial process and know how to respond to particular court orders and requests for library users' information. The list below provides basic information about the various types of judicial process. Please consult with the library's legal counsel for a full understanding of the applicable law.

- A *subpoena* is issued by a grand jury or a court and is usually signed by the prosecuting attorney or judge. The subpoena will identify the records that are sought for the investigation and instruct the library or librarian to produce those records at a certain date, time, and place. If a library is served with a subpoena, it should be carefully examined by the library's legal counsel to assure that the subpoena was issued correctly and contains all required signatures, information, and notices. If the library or the library's legal counsel believes that the subpoena is unjustified for any reason, or believe that compliance with the subpoena will chill the exercise of First Amendment rights in the library, the library's attorney can file a motion to quash the subpoena before a court with jurisdiction over the investigation.

- A *search warrant* is a type of court order that authorizes a law enforcement officer to immediately search for and seize any item, record, or property identified in the body of the court order. It must be signed by a judge after a hearing to determine if "probable cause" exists— that is, good cause exists to believe the search will produce evidence of a crime that is the subject of an ongoing investigation. The law enforcement officer may serve the search warrant on the library at any time, and the library will be required to immediately provide the officer with the records or items identified in the search warrant or permit the officer to search for them.

- *FISA orders* are court orders authorized by the Foreign Intelligence Surveillance Act (FISA), as amended by Section 215 of the USA PATRIOT Act. FISA orders are issued by the Foreign Intelligence Surveillance Court (FISC) and authorize FBI agents to seize "any tangible thing," including documents, records, computer disks, and any other physical object, as long as the FBI agent alleges that the item is relevant to an ongoing investigation into terrorism or foreign espionage. A party served with a FISA order is subject to an automatic nondisclosure order, or "gag order," that forbids recipients of a FISA order from disclosing that they have received the order, or that records have been turned over to the FBI. The gag order does not remove the library's right to consult with legal counsel about the order or to inform the library director or other library staff needed to produce the records.

- *National Security Letters* are specialized administrative subpoenas that are issued by the FBI pursuant to Section 505 of the USA PATRIOT Act. NSLs are used to obtain electronic communication records that may be held by a library providing Internet services. Like recipients of FISA orders, NSL recipients are subject to a nondisclosure order, or "gag order," forbidding any recipient from disclosing

II.8
Requests
from Law
Enforcement

the existence of the NSL or the fact that records were turned over to the FBI. Again, the gag order does not remove the library's right to consult with an attorney or to inform the library director or other library staff needed to produce the records.

Note that only FBI agents are permitted to serve and use the FISA orders and National Security Letters described above, and any agent using those provisions will always have legal documents issued by a federal court or the FBI. Neither state nor local police officers can use these provisions of the USA PATRIOT Act to obtain records.

All libraries, whether public or private, should have written policies and procedures for handling subpoenas, search warrants, and other types of court orders like FISA orders and NSLs. Such written policies assure that every request for records is handled in accordance with the law, professional ethics, and institutional policy.

In addition, academic libraries and school libraries should be aware that even if a state's library confidentiality statute does not require law enforcement officers to obtain a court order to examine a student's library records, the Family Educational Rights and Privacy Act may forbid the disclosure of a student's records unless the student provides written consent or the officer presents the school with a court order.[6]

NOTES

1. Two states, Kentucky and Hawaii, have binding opinions from their attorneys general recognizing the confidentiality of library records.

2. The requirements of these laws vary from state to state. Readers should consult their state's library confidentiality statute to determine the privacy protections extended to library records.

3. *Tattered Cover, Inc. v. City of Thornton*, 44 P.3d 1044 (Colo. 2002).

4. *Decatur Public Library v. District Att'y of Wise County*, No. 90-05-192, 271st Judicial Court (Texas, 1990).

5. *King County Library System v. City of Kent and City of Kent Police Department* (W.D. Wash. 2002).

6. Family Educational Rights and Privacy Act, 20 U.S.C. 1232g.

Workplace Speech

Key Concepts

- As institutions that welcome and promote freedom of expression, libraries should encourage discussion among library workers and administrators of nonconfidential professional and policy matters.

What Does the Law Say?

- Because the relationship between employee and employer is a contractual one, employee speech is governed by the employment contract. The freedom of expression guaranteed by the First Amendment traditionally has not been thought to apply to employee speech in the workplace.
- The doctrine of "employment at will" (applicable in most states) means that employees may resign at any time and employers may dismiss employees at any time unless the dismissal is for prohibited reasons (e.g., racial or age discrimination).
- Federal and state statutes may protect employees from retaliation for "whistle-blowing," or disclosing certain employer misconduct.
- The speech activities of public employees may enjoy limited protection under the First Amendment if they address a matter of public concern and do not impair discipline or harmony in the workplace or

215

interfere with the employer's ability to provide public services. Note, however, that the Supreme Court has ruled that public employees who make statements pursuant to their official duties are not speaking as citizens for First Amendment purposes and may be disciplined by their employer for that speech.

Creating Policy for Your Library

- Consider formally adopting ALA Policy B.9.21 on "Workplace Speech" to help promote free speech in the workplace (www.ala.org/aboutala/governance/policymanual).
- Consider formally adopting the *Code of Ethics of the American Library Association* (see part I, chapter 2) as policy for your library. It contains statements about treating coworkers with respect and fairness.

Especially for Academic Libraries

- Consider formally adopting the American Association of University Professors' *1940 Statement of Principles on Academic Freedom and Tenure* (www.aaup.org/report/1940-statement-principles-academic-freedom-and-tenure). It examines the question of an employee's right to speak as a citizen while balancing the responsibilities of representing an academic institution.

Especially for School Libraries

- Consult with your union to ensure that whistle-blowing and reporting wrongdoing are covered by your collective bargaining agreement. Also, consult the National Education Association's resources on free speech for teachers (www.nea.org/home/20713.htm).

To Learn More

- Questions about speech in the workplace may be directed to the Committee on Professional Ethics, c/o the Office for Intellectual Freedom, ALA, 50 E. Huron St., Chicago, IL 60611.
- Visit the ALA "Professional Ethics" website (www.ala.org/advocacy/proethics).
- See "Questions and Answers on Ethics and Social Media" and "Questions and Answers on Conflicts of Interest," available at www.ala.org/advocacy/proethics.
- See "Religion in American Libraries: Questions and Answers," available at www.ala.org/advocacy/intfreedom.
- Visit the websites of the National Whistleblowers' Center (www.whistleblowers.org) and the Whistleblowers Protection Program (www.whistleblowers.gov).

Questions for Reflection

- Should libraries allow their employees to speak freely about all library-related matters, or should some aspects of library operations be out of bounds for public discussion? If so, what aspects and why?
- What are effective methods for addressing concerns in the workplace?

II.9
Workplace
Speech

Resolution on Workplace Speech

Adopted June 26, 2005, by the ALA Council.

A historical essay about this statement can be found in the publication, *A History of ALA Policy on Intellectual Freedom: A Supplement to the Intellectual Freedom Manual, Ninth Edition.*

WHEREAS, The American Library Association is firmly committed to freedom of expression (policy 53.1.12); and

WHEREAS, The library is an institution that welcomes and promotes the expression of all points of view; and

WHEREAS, Library staff are uniquely positioned to provide guidance on library policy issues that is informed by their experience and education; now, therefore, be it

RESOLVED, That ALA Council amends policy 54 (Library Personnel Practices) by adding:

54.21 Workplace Speech

Libraries should encourage discussion among library workers, including library administrators, of non-confidential professional and policy matters about the operation of the library and matters of public concern within the framework of applicable laws.

Note: A new numbering system for the ALA Policy Manual was developed after the adoption of this resolution.

ALA Policy 53.1.12 is now Policy B.2.1.12.

ALA Policy 54 is now Policy B.9.

ALA Policy 54.21 is now Policy B.9.21.

Questions and Answers on Speech in the Workplace

An Explanatory Statement of the ALA *Code of Ethics*

Adopted July 2001 by the ALA Committee on Professional Ethics; amended January 2004; June 26, 2006; January 24, 2007; and July 1, 2013.

Since libraries have a special responsibility to protect intellectual freedom and freedom of expression, do libraries have a special responsibility to be workplaces that tolerate employee expression more than other professional settings?

Yes. Libraries play a special role in ensuring the free flow of information in a democratic society. Librarians and library workers are often called on to fight censorship and resist efforts to restrict individuals from receiving information and expressing ideas. If librarians and library workers are denied the ability to speak on work related matters, what does this say about our own commitment to free speech? We need to demonstrate our commitment to free speech by encouraging it in the workplace. Libraries are encouraged to adopt ALA policy B.9.21 on "Workplace Speech." This does not provide full legal protection for employees but does help promote free speech in the workplace.

Is there an ethical obligation to raise questions and initiate change about policies I believe to be detrimental to the public interest or to the profession?

The first tenet of the *Code of Ethics of the American Library Association* begins "we provide the highest level of service to all library users. . . ." Examples of possible conflicts between your vision of highest level of service and your employer's could include: you are an academic librarian who disagrees with your university's lack of privacy policy for electronic resources; you are a children's librarian who disagrees with your library's policy of fines for children; you are a library director and your trustees disagree with your stance on filtering. In these and other situations, you should and probably will feel an ethical obligation as a professional to speak out and make your library values known. You will have to use your professional judgment as to when and how to do so, and you must be prepared to accept the consequences.

Does the First Amendment apply to workplace speech?

Through the *Library Bill of Rights* and its interpretations, the American Library Association supports freedom of expression and the First Amendment in the strongest possible terms. The freedom of expression guaranteed by the First Amendment, however, has traditionally not been thought to apply to employee speech in the workplace. The doctrine of "employment at will" (applicable in most states) has meant that just as employees may resign at any time, so too may employers dismiss employees at any time unless the dismissal is for prohibited reasons (e.g. racial or age discrimination). Some employers may believe that if employees were given full rights to free speech on work related issues, loyalty and discipline would be weakened and the coordination needed for the effective and efficient functioning of bureaucracies would dissolve.

Does this mean I have no free speech rights as an employee?

Because the First Amendment only protects individuals against government infringements upon free speech rights, First Amendment protections for speech activities in the workplace are generally not available to employees of private companies or institutions. As one court explained, "the First Amendment free speech provision fails to establish public policy against terminations by private employers for speech-related activities because this provision applies only to government actions and expresses no public policy regarding terminations by private employers." *Grinzi v. San Diego Hospice Corp.,* 120 Cal. App. 4th 72, 79 (2004); see also *George v. Pacific-CSC Work Furlough,* 91 F.3d 1227 (1996).

If you are a government employee, your speech activities in the workplace may enjoy limited protection under the First Amendment. In *Pickering v. Board of Ed.,* 391 U.S. 563 (1968), the Supreme Court crafted a balancing test intended to protect the constitutional rights of an employee speaking as a citizen on matters of public concern while preserving the government employer's interest in ensuring that its employees do not undermine its operations or interfere with accomplishment of its objectives. In brief, if your speech addresses a matter of public concern, and it does not interfere with your employer's ability to provide public services or impair discipline or harmony in the workplace, the courts may side with you. Note, however, that the courts often give great deference to an employer's conclusion that an employee's speech has been disruptive or damaging.

In 2006, the Supreme Court clarified its decision in *Pickering*. In *Garcetti v. Ceballos*, 547 U.S. 410 (2006), the Supreme Court held that public employees who make statements pursuant to their official duties are not speaking as citizens for First Amendment purposes and may be disciplined by their employer for that speech.

What about whistle blowing?

According to *Black's Law Dictionary*, whistle blowing refers to an employee who reports illegal or wrongful activities of an employer or fellow employees. There are federal and state statutes to protect employees from retaliation for disclosing certain kinds of employer misconduct, like fraud, abuse, waste, or the violation of a law, rule, or regulation. Legal counsel can advise you if these statutes apply to your situation.

What about questions of library policy? Do I have free speech rights to speak on internal library matters?

Since the relationship between employee and employer is a contractual one, employee speech is governed by the employment contract, not the First Amendment. The speech environment in a library as a workplace may vary according to the organizational hierarchy and an employee's place in it, the organizational culture, and the personalities that make up that culture. If you are a member of a union, check your union contract to see if it offers any protection. If you are a librarian who has tenure or an arrangement similar to tenure, check your tenure or reappointment documents.

What are some issues to consider when speaking out on a library policy matter?

Try to know all the facts on the issue and attempt to understand it from your employer's point of view. Is the issue important enough to you to risk retribution? Assess your place in the hierarchy and know your workplace culture: you may have more job security than you think. If you are in a union you may be protected by your union contract. A tenured librarian may have more freedom to speak out than a new librarian. Library directors may be expected to make their views known to their trustees. Your boss may be more receptive to criticism at certain times than others. Some bosses may be open to disagreement in private but not in staff meetings. Some may prefer a verbal conversation to a written memo. Consult with your colleagues. Do your colleagues agree with you or are you alone? Can you build support among your colleagues for your position? Can you get others to raise the issue for you or can you do so anonymously? Will it be possible to work from within for change? If your convictions are strong enough, are you willing to resign? You will have to exercise your own professional judgment in assessing your workplace environment.

As a library administrator should I solicit the opinions of my staff on policy and procedural matters?

Article V of the *Code of Ethics* states, "we treat co-workers and other colleagues with respect, fairness and good faith, and advocate conditions of employment that safeguard the rights and welfare of all employees of our institutions." Article VIII states, "we strive for excellence in the profession by . . . encouraging the professional development of co-workers. . . ." Library professionals in leadership positions should encourage discussion on policy and procedural matters and adopt ALA Policy B.9.21 on "Workplace Speech."

If I speak out in the workplace on a matter of professional policy, and my employer retaliates against me, will the ALA support me?

The ALA does not provide mediation, financial aid, or legal aid in response to workplace disputes (please see the "Questions and Answers on the Enforcement of the *Code of Ethics of the American Library Association*" [available on the ALA website] for a history of past efforts related to mediation). Your employer has an array of sanctions that may or may not be imposed on you, including but not limited to: reassignment, passing you up for promotion, passing you up for raises, denying you tenure, passing you up for the best assignments, and ultimately dismissal. If you decide to speak out on a matter involving professional policy, it will be a matter between you and your employer. The ALA does administer the LeRoy C. Merritt Humanitarian

Fund, which has provided financial assistance for librarians who have been discriminated against or denied employment rights because of their defense of intellectual freedom including freedom of speech. More information on the fund can be found at www.merrittfund.org. Some state library associations offer professional liability insurance for members that can help with reimbursement of legal fees related to termination. Check with your state association to see if this is available to you.

Can I be disciplined for workplace-related comments on Facebook and Twitter?

In a number of recent decisions, the National Labor Relations Board has ruled that employers cannot discipline employees for certain work-related conversations conducted on social media, such as Facebook and Twitter. In each case, the NLRB found that employees' posted comments about their workplace were "protected concerted activity" under the National Labor Relations Act because the employees were engaged in conversations discussing the terms and conditions of their employment. Such protections are limited, however, and do not extend to posts or conversations that are unrelated to workplace conditions.

Where can I find more information?

Questions about "Speech in the Workplace" can be directed to the Committee on Professional Ethics c/o the ALA Office of Intellectual Freedom by phone at (312) 280-4223 or by e-mail at oif@ala.org.

Please note that these answers are not a legal opinion nor should they be regarded as legal advice. Please consult legal counsel for legal advice regarding your particular situation.

II.9
Workplace
Speech

PART III

Advocacy and Assistance

Communicating about Intellectual Freedom

*Parts of this chapter are based on the work
of Larra Clark and Macey Morales.*

FEW INSTITUTIONS ENJOY the credibility and goodwill that libraries have. Communicating openly, honestly, and with full understanding of the social, legal, and professional issues involved is the best way to promote intellectual freedom and uphold the image of the library and librarians. The following tips will help you prepare a public and media relations program, deal with crises and controversies that may arise, and more effectively lobby your elected officials.

Identifying the Audience

Who needs to hear the intellectual freedom message? Consider the following:

- Library users
- Library staff
- Library trustees
- Library foundations and "Friends of the Library" groups
- Parents
- Teachers and professors
- Government leaders
- Religious leaders
- Reporters and journalists

It's wise to identify potential supporters of censorship and learn about their primary concerns so you can develop effective messages and engage in meaningful dialogue. The more librarians and their supporters understand

III.
Advocacy
and
Assistance

the feelings and beliefs of those who do not share their views, the easier it will be to relate to them as individuals with serious concerns.

Also, identify and get acquainted with potential allies who can help you speak out in support of intellectual freedom. Potential allies include lawyers, journalists, educators, authors, civil-liberties advocates, and other professional organizations and advocacy groups.

Creating the Message

- *Define a clear and consistent message.*
- *Use simple language that is easily understood.* Adapt it for various audiences. For example, the phrase "intellectual freedom" may resonate with some audiences, but talking about the "freedom to read, hear, or receive information" may be more appropriate for others.
- *Develop a message sheet.* Include the key message, supporting points, facts, examples, and sample questions and answers.
- *Share the message sheet.* Provide copies to your designated spokespeople and to library staff, volunteers, trustees, and advocates.
- *Avoid language that is negative or judgmental.* Address with respect those who express concerns or raise challenges and acknowledge concerns as genuine.

Delivering the Message

Consider the following channels for communicating about intellectual freedom:

- Library website
- Library newsletter
- Library annual report
- Banners and signs
- Flyers and bookmarks
- Library programs and workshops on topics such as guiding your child on the Internet, helping your child select good books, why privacy is important, and the history and future of the First Amendment
- Special events and exhibits such as Banned Books Week, National Library Week, and Choose Privacy Week
- The mass media—newspapers, radio, television, and Internet media (submit news releases, invite the media to library events, write op-eds and letters to the editor, and offer to be a local expert available to comment on intellectual freedom issues)

- Community newsletters
- Blogs and social media
- Speaking engagements at other organizations (contact groups you'd like to target and offer interesting speakers and programs)

Choosing and Preparing Spokespeople

- *Choose knowledgeable, skilled spokespeople.* Intellectual freedom is a complex and sometimes sensitive issue.
- *The library director or board president is usually the official spokesperson.* Heads of departments also may be called on in their areas of expertise.
- *Refer all questions to the official spokesperson.* Be sure that all library staff, trustees, volunteers, and members of your "Friends of the Library" groups know the procedures for referring questions from the media and public.
- *Prepare your speakers for high-pressure situations.* Role-play questions and answers or get professional media training.
- *Organize a network of local advocates.* Ask them to speak out on intellectual freedom issues.

Working with the Media

- *Establish relationships with key members of the media.* Develop a reputation for honest and open communication. A crisis is not the time to build good media relations.
- *Be wary.* Although journalists, in general, understand First Amendment issues, their support should never be assumed.
- *Have a clear message and well-prepared spokespeople.* Regardless of their sympathies, reporters are paid to ask tough questions.
- *Do your homework.* Read, listen, and watch news coverage to get a feel for how issues are covered. Keep in mind that hosts of talk shows may not be trained journalists. Rather, they may be advocates of a particular point of view whose goal may be to boost ratings by fanning the flames of controversy. Be sure to research the nature of a program (or publication) before seeking or accepting an interview.
- *Provide supporting documents.* Share fact sheets and the library's intellectual freedom policies.

- *Treat reporters honestly and respectfully.* When contacted by someone from the media, gather as much information as you can about what he needs and his deadline. Get back to him as quickly as possible, but always make time to prepare an answer. Taking ten minutes to review a message sheet can make a critical difference in how well you communicate.
- *Avoid the infamous words "No comment."* If you truly cannot comment, give a brief explanation: "I'm sorry I can't answer that question. I'll let you know as soon as I can." Or, "I'm sorry I can't answer that. Our board is still discussing the issue."
- *Use the "bridging" technique.* Rather than dodging questions, answer questions simply and honestly, and then quickly move back to your key message. Every question is an opportunity to restate your case and educate.

Dealing with Controversy and Negative Publicity

- *Prepare, but don't overreact.* If, for example, a local television station runs a "Sex at the Library" story about pornography on the Internet, prepare a statement but don't release it until you gauge reaction to the story.
- *Be strategic in your use of the media.* A letter to the editor or an op-ed piece clarifying the library's position can be helpful, especially if it is to correct a misrepresentation of fact. Engaging in a long, defensive battle of letters is neither productive nor a good use of advocates' energy.
- *Anticipate difficult questions and develop answers ahead of time.* Ask your friends and colleagues to help you practice your answers and bridging to your key message (as described in the section above). Practice answering easy questions, too, so you will not be caught off guard.
- *Listen.* Do not judge. Try to identify and address the real concern or issue being addressed.
- *Acknowledge.* Pause to show that you have given the question serious consideration. Frame your answer with a positive response. For example, "I respect your views, but let me give you another perspective," or "We share your concern for children. Our approach is . . ."
- *Be factual.* It is better to say, "I don't know" than to provide inaccurate information. If faced with a claim or information with which you are not familiar, simply say, "I hadn't heard that. I'll have to check," or "What I do know is . . ."

- *Do not repeat loaded or negative words.* If asked, "Why do librarians let children look at smut and porn?" do not repeat the words "smut" and "porn" in your answer.
- *Keep your answers to the point.* Do not volunteer more information than is asked. Remaining silent, as well as asking the same question in different ways, are well-known techniques used by reporters in the hope that their subjects will stray off message.
- *Be truthful.* Speak from your own experience: "In our library the policy is . . ." or "My experience is . . ."
- *Do not assume anything you say is off the record.* It can and may be repeated.
- *Maintain an open, calm, and friendly attitude and posture.* Avoid crossed arms, tapping feet, and other body language that conveys stress. Appearing defensive, angry, or out of control undermines credibility.
- *Stick to the high road.* Do not criticize or get personal with an opponent. Stay focused on the key message.

Lobbying

Robert P. Doyle

When intellectual freedom issues arise in public policy debates, library advocates need to reach out to their local public officials and persuade them to protect our rights. These tips are designed to work at the local, state, or federal level. Share them with your staff, trustees, "Friends of the Library" groups, and supporters.

- *Get to know your public officials before you need their help.* If they already know and trust your opinions, you will be far more successful in getting them to understand your point of view. Education is a big part of the process.
- *Do your homework.* If you are addressing a specific issue, look to the American Library Association (www.ala.org/offices/oif or www.ala .org/offices/wo) or your state library association for background and how best to frame the message. Even if your message is a general one, such as advocating for freedom of information, these are both good resources to help prepare yourself for the visit or conversation.
- *Whomever you need to contact, try to do it in person if at all possible.* A face-to-face meeting is better than a phone call, a phone call is better than an e-mail message, and an e-mail message is better than no contact at all. Try not to leave a voice-mail message. Instead, tell the

person answering the phone that you'll call back later. Talking to staff is the first step in building a relationship.

- *Shrink the message.* Share the most important facts and the few best arguments. Keep your talking points short and focused. If you're writing an e-mail message, use bullet points and stick to only one main idea.
- *Make it personal.* Explain how the issue impacts you and your institution . . . and the elected official's constituents. Use examples and quotes if you have them. Bring the issue to life.
- *Make a clear request.* Ask officials specifically to *support* the legislation if it furthers your cause. If you are against the legislation, as in the case of mandatory filters, ask them to *oppose* it. If you have concluded that the legislation is likely to pass and you can't defeat it, you might make a specific request asking them to amend, or change, the legislation.
- *Be polite but direct, and try to get a commitment to support the library position.* Don't push too hard, but if they are clearly on board, you might ask them to speak out publicly or reach out to their colleagues. In some cases, you may be looking for someone to sponsor a particular piece of legislation that you have drafted, but that generally requires a very close working relationship.
- *Mobilize.* Ask your library leaders, staff, "Friends of the Library" groups, library supporters, civic leaders, and others to contact their public officials. Form a coalition of like-minded organizations to support your position.
- *Use the media, new and traditional.* Draw broader attention to the issue and the library perspective using all channels—websites, letters to the editor, blog posts, electronic discussion lists, social media, and so on.
- *Don't forget to follow through.* After the issue is resolved, make sure to thank those who supported the library position. But also keep in touch with those who might have opposed or abstained. You might need their support the next time around.

Where to Get Help and Get Involved

Nanette Perez and Trina Magi

LOOKING FOR INFORMATION, assistance, or ways to help protect intellectual freedom? This chapter describes a host of resources and opportunities in the following areas:

- Challenge Support and Information
- Educational and Public-Awareness Programs
- Publications and Online Resources
- American Library Association Policy-Making and Networking
- State and Federal Legislation—Information and Advocacy
- Legal Defense of Intellectual Freedom and Humanitarian Aid for Librarians
- Building Intellectual Freedom Coalitions
- Intellectual Freedom Awards

The American Library Association's *Office for Intellectual Freedom (OIF)* is the first place to turn for librarians and library governing bodies seeking to preserve and promote intellectual freedom. As the administrative arm of ALA's intellectual freedom groups, the OIF implements ALA policies on intellectual freedom and educates librarians and the public about the importance of intellectual freedom in libraries. The OIF maintains a variety of services, programs, publications, and online resources described below. ALA also maintains collaborative relationships with other entities concerned about intellectual freedom.

The *intellectual freedom committees of state library associations* are also an excellent place to turn. The relationship of the Office for Intellectual Freedom with the state committees is one of mutual cooperation and assistance.

III
Advocacy
and
Assistance

The OIF supports the work at the state level with information, coordination, and ideas. The state committees can be the OIF's eyes and ears at the local level. When incidents or controversies arise, state intellectual freedom committees frequently mobilize support and, in cooperation with ALA, provide embattled librarians with on-the-spot assistance. Visit the OIF website (www.ala.org/offices/oif) for links to information about state groups, activities, laws, and resolutions. Please keep the OIF informed about all state matters affecting intellectual freedom. Send your information to Office for Intellectual Freedom, American Library Association, 50 E. Huron St., Chicago, IL 60611 or to oif@ala.org as soon as possible.

Take Action

Opposing censorship is important work. How can you help protect intellectual freedom?

- Make intellectual freedom a central part of your library's mission.
- Educate others about the importance of intellectual freedom and how the changing environment makes the need for intellectual freedom in libraries even more critical. Local civic groups are always looking for speakers, so volunteer.
- Advocate support for the library's role in preserving intellectual freedom. Talk to local library and school boards, the media, and elected officials.
- Monitor the news and your community for incidents of censorship and report them to the ALA Office for Intellectual Freedom.
- Lend your support to others who face censorship challenges.
- Respond to requests for support from the ALA Office for Intellectual Freedom on controversies in your area.
- Stay up-to-date on legislation and court cases that could affect intellectual freedom in libraries.
- Network with civil liberties groups and other organizations that are dedicated to intellectual freedom principles. Your support for them will mean increased support for libraries.
- Be a leader. Start a local group dedicated to ensuring that intellectual freedom in libraries is preserved. When local libraries are under attack, a well-organized and articulate local group is a great help.
- Get involved professionally. Join ALA's intellectual freedom groups or volunteer to work with intellectual freedom committees at the state and regional levels.
- Join the Freedom to Read Foundation and donate to the Merritt Humanitarian Fund.
- Use social media to inform friends and community members about current intellectual freedom activities and challenges. Write letters to your local press.

Challenge Support and Information

Challenge Support

Office for Intellectual Freedom
www.ala.org/challengereporting
(800) 545-2433, ext. 4223
oif@ala.org

The Office for Intellectual Freedom receives requests for assistance with challenges to library materials or services on a daily basis. OIF staff members provide reviews and information about the author of the challenged material, applicable ALA policies, and advice about the implementation of reconsideration policies, as well as other counseling specific to the situation. If needed, the OIF will provide a written position statement defending the principles of intellectual freedom in materials selection or specific library services. If requested, the OIF will provide contact information for state library staff, state library association intellectual freedom committees, or other persons with the experience and expertise to provide assistance to library staff facing challenges or to offer testimony or support before library boards or other governing bodies.

When a challenge arises, librarians should review the resources available on the OIF website or contact the OIF directly for in-depth assistance. Help is available for ALA members and nonmembers alike.

Challenge Database

Office for Intellectual Freedom
www.ala.org/oif
oif@ala.org

In 1990 the Office for Intellectual Freedom established a database to record and report statistics on challenges to library materials across the country. The database is a useful tool for identifying trends in types of censorship cases and for documenting responses and solutions to these cases. Librarians are encouraged to document and report challenges and their outcome to the OIF. *All identifying information is kept confidential.*

You may submit reports on challenges to library materials or services by phone, fax, e-mail, or online form available at www.ala.org/challengereporting. You may send articles, letters, and other news of challenges occurring in your area to the Office for Intellectual Freedom at 50 E. Huron St., Chicago, IL 60611 or oif@ala.org. You may also respond to ALA's call for information

III
Advocacy
and
Assistance

about challenges at the start of each year. The OIF compiles an annual list of the top ten most frequently challenged books for the immediate past year. The press release announcing this list helps create awareness of Banned Books Week, the annual celebration of the freedom to read.

Educational and Public-Awareness Programs

In addition to the educational programs listed below, the Office for Intellectual Freedom can offer guidance and suggestions on speakers and topics to fit any intellectual freedom program. For more information, contact the OIF directly at oif@ala.org or (800) 545-2433, ext. 4223.

Banned Books Week
Office for Intellectual Freedom
www.ala.org/bbooks
   (use this site to learn more about banned and challenged books)
www.bannedbooksweek.org
   (use this site to publicize or learn about events)
(800) 545-2433, ext. 4223
oif@ala.org

ALA is one of the sponsors of the annual Banned Books Week: Celebrating the Freedom to Read. Observed each year since 1982 during the last week of September, the event reminds Americans not to take their freedom to read for granted. For more information on the history and current celebration of Banned Books Week, or to order promotional materials, visit www.ala.org/bbooks.

Choose Privacy Week
Office for Intellectual Freedom
www.chooseprivacyweek.org
(800) 545-2433, ext. 4223
oif@ala.org

Choose Privacy Week is an Office for Intellectual Freedom initiative that invites library users into a national conversation about privacy rights in a digital age. The campaign gives libraries resources and tools to educate and engage their users, helping citizens think critically and make more informed choices about their privacy. For more information or to order promotional materials, visit www.chooseprivacyweek.org.

Online Learning
Office for Intellectual Freedom
www.ala.org/offices/oif/oifprograms/webinars
(800) 545-2433, ext. 4223
oif@ala.org

The Office for Intellectual Freedom offers free and low-cost webinars on timely intellectual freedom topics such as self-service holds and reader privacy, CIPA and filtering, reporting challenges, and intellectual freedom across the globe. Webinars are recorded, and webcasts are available free on the OIF website at www.ala.org/offices/oif/oifprograms/webinars.

ALA Conference Programs
Intellectual Freedom Committee
www.ala.org/groups/committees/ala/ala-if
Committee on Professional Ethics
www.ala.org/groups/committees/ala/ala-profethic

During ALA conferences the Intellectual Freedom Committee sponsors issues briefing sessions that educate attendees about current topics in intellectual freedom, as well as an IF 101 course to help acclimate new members of ALA to intellectual freedom. In addition, the IFC cosponsors at least two programs at each ALA Annual Conference, one with the ALA Committee on Legislation, and another with the Association of American Publishers. The committee also schedules open hearings, as needed, on policies and statements to gather suggestions from ALA members. The ALA Committee on Professional Ethics hosts meetings and programs on intellectual freedom topics, as well.

Publications and Online Resources

ALA Office for Intellectual Freedom Website
www.ala.org/oif

ALA "Intellectual Freedom" Website
www.ala.org/advocacy/intfreedom

These websites are rich resources. They provide information about initiatives and projects, educational programs, and intellectual freedom groups. They also include links to documents, guidelines, publications, and tool kits focusing on issues such as challenges and censorship, privacy, and CIPA.

III. Advocacy and Assistance

IFACTION electronic list

lists.ala.org/sympa

IFACTION is a news-only, no-discussion electronic list on intellectual freedom issues. It alerts subscribers not only to news items of interest, but also to legislation affecting intellectual freedom issues, such as filtering, privacy, online social networks, media concentration, and network neutrality. Anyone interested in intellectual freedom issues is welcome to subscribe, ALA members and nonmembers alike. Go to lists.ala.org/sympa and click "ALA Offices" > "Office for Intellectual Freedom."

IFFORUM electronic list

lists.ala.org/sympa

IFFORUM is a self-subscribing, unmoderated electronic discussion list maintained by the Office for Intellectual Freedom as an avenue of discussion on intellectual freedom topics. Anyone interested in intellectual freedom issues is welcome to subscribe, ALA members and nonmembers alike. Go to lists.ala .org/sympa and click "ALA Offices" > "Office for Intellectual Freedom."

Social Media

The Office for Intellectual Freedom provides news, videos, educational programs, and event coverage through a variety of social media, including:

- OIF blog (www.oif.ala.org/oif)
- Twitter (www.twitter.com/oif)
- Facebook (www.facebook.com/alaoif)
- YouTube (www.youtube.com/oiftube)

Newsletter on Intellectual Freedom

ALA Subscriptions

(800) 545-2433, ext. 4290

One of the most important intellectual freedom publications is the bimonthly *Newsletter on Intellectual Freedom (NIF)*. Unique in its coverage of library court cases, the NIF was initiated in 1952 and has been edited and produced by the Office for Intellectual Freedom staff since 1970. Addressed to both librarians and others concerned about intellectual freedom, the NIF provides a comprehensive, national picture of censorship efforts, court cases, legislation, and current readings on the subject. Through original and reprinted articles, the NIF provides access to various views about intellectual freedom and a means of reporting on the activities of the OIF, Intellectual Freedom Committee, and the Freedom to Read Foundation. Since 2003, the NIF also has been available as an online publication. It is available by subscription from ALA Subscriptions. Additional information about the NIF is found at www.ala.org/offices/oif/oifprograms/ifpubs/nif/newsletter intellectual.

Monographs, Resource Guides, Training Materials, and Manuals
ALA Store
www.alastore.ala.org
(800) 545-2433, ext. 7

In addition to the *Intellectual Freedom Manual,* the Office for Intellectual Freedom publishes *Banned Books* by Robert P. Doyle, and produces the Banned Books Week materials. The OIF also works with ALA Editions to develop publications on intellectual freedom topics. Past titles include *Privacy and Confidentiality Issues: A Guide for Libraries and Their Lawyers,* by Theresa Chmara (2008); *Protecting Intellectual Freedom in Your School Library,* by Pat R. Scales (2009); *Protecting Intellectual Freedom in Your Academic Library,* by Barbara M. Jones (2009); and *Protecting Intellectual Freedom in Your Public Library,* by June Pinnell-Stephens (2012). The OIF also consulted in the publication of *Hit List for Young Adults 2: Frequently Challenged Books.* All of these resources, as well as new ones, are available for purchase at the ALA Store.

American Library Association Policy-Making and Networking

Intellectual Freedom Committee
www.ala.org/groups/committees/ala/ala-if

The Intellectual Freedom Committee (IFC), a standing ALA Council committee, was established to recommend such steps as may be necessary to safeguard the rights of library users, libraries, and librarians in accordance with the First Amendment to the United States Constitution and the *Library Bill of Rights* as adopted by the ALA Council. The committee works closely with the Office for Intellectual Freedom and with other units and officers of the association in matters touching intellectual freedom and censorship. The IFC fulfills its charge by recommending policies concerning intellectual freedom to the ALA Council. The council-approved policy statements (e.g., interpretations of the *Library Bill of Rights*) not only provide librarians with policies to adopt in their own libraries but also establish a professional standard that ALA is committed to defend. The IFC also writes and disseminates guidelines and organizes conference programs to assist librarians in promoting and defending intellectual freedom. IFC documents are available at www.ala.org/groups/committees/ala/ala-if.

Committee members must be members of ALA and are appointed by the ALA president. To volunteer, go to www.ala.org and click "Committees" > "Volunteer Form."

Committee on Professional Ethics
www.ala.org/groups/committees/ala/ala-profethic

The Committee on Professional Ethics (COPE), a standing ALA Council committee, is charged with maintaining, revising, and augmenting the *Code of Ethics of the American Library Association*. The committee accomplishes this by regularly reviewing the code and by developing explanatory interpretations and additional statements. Examples include "Questions and Answers on Speech in the Workplace," "Questions and Answers on Enforcement of the *Code of Ethics*," and "Copyright—An Interpretation of the *Code of Ethics*." COPE meets at ALA conferences and develops educational programs on ethical issues for the library profession. COPE documents are available at www.ala.org/groups/committees/ala/ala-profethic.

Committee members must be members of ALA and are appointed by the ALA president. To volunteer, go to www.ala.org and click "Committees" > "Volunteer Form."

Intellectual Freedom Round Table
www.ala.org/ifrt

ALA Round Tables are membership units that provide an additional avenue for membership discussion, opinion, and response. The Intellectual Freedom Round Table (IFRT), established in 1974, allows ALA members to maintain close contact with ALA's overall intellectual freedom program. The IFRT is a grassroots organization and a good place to enter the ALA intellectual freedom network of interested members. Any ALA member is welcome to join.

The IFRT provides a forum for the discussion of activities, programs, and intellectual freedom problems faced by libraries and librarians; serves as a channel of communication on intellectual freedom matters; promotes a greater opportunity for involvement among the members of the ALA in defense of intellectual freedom; and promotes a greater feeling of responsibility in the implementation of ALA policies on intellectual freedom.

The IFRT also sponsors intellectual freedom programs at ALA conferences and provides an online newsletter for members. The IFRT and individual IFRT members frequently assist the Intellectual Freedom Committee, the Office for Intellectual Freedom, and the Freedom to Read Foundation in joint activities.

The IFRT also administers three awards: the John Phillip Immroth Memorial Award, the Gerald Hodges Intellectual Freedom Chapter Relations Award, and the Eli M. Oboler Memorial Award. These awards are described in the "Intellectual Freedom Awards" section of this chapter.

For information about joining IFRT, please visit the website.

State and Federal Legislation—Information and Advocacy

Legislation that limits intellectual freedom can severely restrict the activities of librarians striving to provide service in accordance with the First Amendment, their state constitutions, and the principles of the *Library Bill of Rights*. When requested, ALA, through the Intellectual Freedom Committee, the Office for Intellectual Freedom, and/or the Freedom to Read Foundation, supplies testimony informing lawmakers of the potential effects of the legislation on the principles of intellectual freedom as applied to library service. Pending legislation in the U.S. Congress is frequently brought to the attention of these groups by the ALA Washington Office. With the assistance of legal counsel, the OIF provides analyses of proposed state or local statutes affecting intellectual freedom brought to its attention.

The OIF works with ALA's Washington Office, the ALA Committee on Legislation, the ALA Intellectual Freedom Committee, and the Freedom to Read Foundation to monitor current federal legislative activities and to develop strategies to defeat legislation aimed at restricting access to information. In addition, the OIF works with the Media Coalition to track state-level legislation related to intellectual freedom.

III. Advocacy and Assistance

Legal Defense of Intellectual Freedom and Humanitarian Aid for Librarians

Freedom to Read Foundation
www.ftrf.org
(312) 280-4226; (800) 545-2433, ext.4223
ftrf@ala.org

The Freedom to Read Foundation (FTRF) was incorporated as a separate organization in 1969 by the ALA to act as its legal defense arm for intellectual freedom in libraries. The purposes of the FTRF are to:

- Promote and protect the freedom of speech and of the press
- Protect the public's right of access to information and materials stored in the nation's libraries
- Safeguard libraries' right to include in their collections and to make available to the public any creative work they may legally acquire
- Support libraries, librarians, authors, publishers, and booksellers in their defense of First Amendment rights by supplying them with legal counsel or the means to secure it

The FTRF's work has been divided into three primary activities: (1) the allocation and disbursement of grants to individuals and groups primarily for the purpose of aiding them in litigation, (2) direct participation in litigation dealing with freedom of speech and of the press, and (3) education about the importance of librarians and the First Amendment to our democratic institutions. The main focus of the Freedom to Read Foundation's litigation program is issues that impact the freedom to read or access to materials or other information in libraries. The foundation also joins other organizations in broader free-speech cases.

Librarians affected by legislation or official actions that adversely affect intellectual freedom; those whose professional positions and personal well-being are endangered because of their defense of intellectual freedom; and library boards, librarians, and library employees threatened with legal action on such grounds should contact the FTRF. In addition, the FTRF provides memoranda to assist librarians in opposing censorship. Although they are general discussions of issues and not opinion letters, these memoranda are posted to the FTRF website to help librarians understand the legal implications of issues affecting libraries and librarians. A time line of FTRF activities also can be found on the FTRF's website, www.ftrf.org.

Anyone may join the Freedom to Read Foundation. In 2015 a regular membership cost $35.

LeRoy C. Merritt Humanitarian Fund
www.ala.org/groups/affiliates/relatedgroups/merrittfund/
  merritthumanitarian
(800) 545-2433, ext. 4223
merritt@ala.org

Librarians requiring immediate financial aid should contact the LeRoy C. Merritt Humanitarian Fund. Established in 1970 as a special trust in memory of Dr. LeRoy C. Merritt, the Merritt Fund is devoted to the support, maintenance, medical care, and welfare of librarians who, in the trustees' opinion, are:

- Denied employment rights or discriminated against on the basis of gender, sexual orientation, race, color, creed, age, disability, or place of national origin
- Denied employment rights because of defense of intellectual freedom; that is, threatened with loss of employment or discharged because of their stand for the cause of intellectual freedom, including promotion of freedom of the press, freedom of speech, and freedom of librarians to select items for their collections from all the world's written and recorded information

The Merritt Fund is supported solely by donations from concerned individuals and groups. For information about making a donation, visit www.ala .org/groups/affiliates/relatedgroups/merrittfund/donations/donations.

Building Intellectual Freedom Coalitions

Both the Intellectual Freedom Committee and the Office for Intellectual Freedom cooperate with national, state, and regional organizations in activities that support free expression. ALA members are encouraged to help build coalitions, as well. Coalitions can be formed around one central issue or several issues. Such groups exist (or could exist) in almost every community. Often, the formal and informal ties ALA members establish with these coalitions enable ALA to cooperate with and assist the groups in effectively opposing censorship.

III.
Advocacy
and
Assistance

To create these ties, libraries, librarians, and state intellectual freedom committees can join or cooperate with booksellers, publishers, artists, teachers, civil libertarians, journalists, authors, musicians, and other groups and individuals with First Amendment concerns in local, state, and regional coalitions in defense of intellectual freedom. It is important to understand that in coalitions, there will be points of contention. The key is to find common ground on which to focus. Do not dismiss potential partners because you don't agree on everything.

An intellectual freedom coalition is useful for a number of purposes, such as supporting intellectual freedom legislation, defeating legislation that would negatively affect libraries, and overturning decisions to remove or restrict access to library resources or services. Most important, by forming coalitions, concerned citizens and organizations can learn who their friends

Intellectual Freedom Organizations

The following organizations often share librarians' concerns about intellectual freedom and can be good sources of information and support:

American Booksellers Association
www.bookweb.org

American Booksellers for Free Expression
www.bookweb.org/abfe

American Civil Liberties Union
www.aclu.org

Association of American Publishers Freedom to Read Committee
www.publishers.org/committees/5

Bill of Rights Defense Committee
www.bordc.org

Center for Democracy and Technology
www.cdt.org

Cooperative Children's Book Center, School of Education, University of Wisconsin-Madison: "What If... Questions and Answers on Intellectual Freedom"
ccbc.education.wisc.edu/freedom/whatif/default.asp

Copyright and Fair Use Center, Stanford University Libraries
fairuse.stanford.edu

Electronic Frontier Foundation
www.eff.org

Electronic Privacy Information Center
www.epic.org

First Amendment Center
www.firstamendmentcenter.org

Freedom to Read Foundation
www.frtf.org

Internet Education Foundation
neted.org

Media Coalition
www.mediacoalition.org

National Coalition against Censorship
www.ncac.org

National Council of Teachers of English, Anti-Censorship Center
www.ncte.org/action/anti-censorship

PEN American Center
www.pen.org

Privacy Rights Clearinghouse
www.privacyrights.org

Student Press Law Center
www.splc.org

are before an intellectual freedom crisis occurs, concentrate limited funds and personnel where they are most needed, and reach broader audiences.

The Office for Intellectual Freedom is available to advise individuals and organizations seeking local or national intellectual freedom coalitions for partnership and collaboration, or to consult on organizing and managing a new coalition. Contact the OIF at (800) 545-2433, ext. 4223, or at oif@ala.org.

Intellectual Freedom Awards

A number of ALA units offer awards related to intellectual freedom, as described below. Please check with the various divisions of ALA to learn about additional awards that may be available.

FREEDOM TO READ FOUNDATION

- *Judith Krug Fund Banned Books Week Event Grants* are given to organizations to help them stage "Read-Outs" (events at which people gather to read from books that have been banned or challenged) or other events during Banned Books Week.
- *Freedom to Read Foundation Roll of Honor* recognizes and honors individuals who have contributed substantially to the FTRF through adherence to its principles and/or substantial monetary support.
- *Gordon M. Conable Conference Scholarship* is an annual scholarship for library school students and new professionals to attend ALA's annual conference. The goal of the scholarship is to advance two principles that Gordon held dear: intellectual freedom and mentoring.

INTELLECTUAL FREEDOM ROUND TABLE

- *John Phillip Immroth Memorial Award,* an annual award that recognizes extraordinary personal courage in the defense of intellectual freedom
- *Gerald Hodges Intellectual Freedom Chapter Relations Award* (formerly the State and Regional Intellectual Freedom Achievement Award), which recognizes an ALA chapter, division, round table, or affiliate organization that has developed a strong multiyear, ongoing program or a single, one-year project that exemplifies support for intellectual freedom, library user confidentiality, or anticensorship efforts
- *Eli M. Oboler Memorial Award,* a biennial award that recognizes the best work in the area of intellectual freedom published in the two calendar years prior to the presentation of the award

III. Advocacy and Assistance

OFFICE FOR INTELLECTUAL FREEDOM AND GOVERNANCE OFFICE

- *Lemony Snicket Prize for Noble Librarians Faced with Adversity,* an annual award established by ALA in partnership with Daniel Handler, a.k.a. Lemony Snicket, to recognize and honor librarians who have faced adversity with integrity and dignity intact

Parts of this chapter are based on the work of Don Wood and Angela Maycock, former program officers of OIF.

GLOSSARY OF TERMS

by Candace Morgan

arbitrary distinctions. Inappropriate categorizations of people, classes of people, conduct, or things based upon criteria irrelevant to the purpose for which the distinctions are made. For example, a rule intended to regulate the length of time an item may be borrowed should not be based on an irrelevant consideration (arbitrary distinction) such as a personal characteristic of the borrower (e.g., height or age).

censorship. See *challenge.*

challenge. [Note: In 2014 the ALA Intellectual Freedom Committee adopted the following revised definitions to clarify the terminology associated with challenges.]

> ***expression of concern/oral complaint.*** A question asked or objection made informally by an individual about a resource in the library collection that they find objectionable or inappropriate. Expressions of concern sometimes lead to challenges.

> ***challenge.*** An attempt to have a library resource removed or access to it restricted, based on the objections of a person or group. Challenges do not simply involve a person expressing a point of view; rather, they are an attempt to remove material from the curriculum or library, thereby restricting the access of others. Challenges sometimes lead to censorship. There are two types of challenges:

> > ***request for reconsideration***—A formal, written request that the library remove or restrict access to resources, submitted on a form and invoking a formal, standardized review process by the library and/or its governing body.

public challenge—A publicly disseminated statement challenging the value of material, presented to the media and/or others outside the institutional organization to gain public support for further action.

censorship. A decision made by a governing authority or its representative(s) to suppress, exclude, expurgate, remove, or restrict public access to a library resource based on a person or group's disapproval of its content or its author/creator.

child pornography. Images and videos depicting actual children engaged in sexual conduct. Child pornography, *regardless* of whether it is obscene, is not protected by the First Amendment because the production of such materials would not be possible without the abuse of children (*New York v. Ferber* 458 U.S. 747, 1982). For the same reason (involving abuse of children), the possession of child pornography is also illegal. Computer-generated images and the use of adults to portray minors do not fall under the definition of child pornography and are considered affirmative defenses to any charge of possessing child pornography.

CIPA. Acronym identifying the Children's Internet Protection Act (P.L. 106–554). CIPA places restrictions on the use of funding for Internet access that is available through the Universal Service **E-rate** discount program and the Library Services and Technology Act (**LSTA**) available to public schools and public libraries. CIPA requires funding recipients to adopt Internet safety policies and use **filtering software** that blocks or filters certain visual images from being accessed through the Internet.

compelling government interest. A term used by courts when assessing the burden of government regulation or action upon the exercise of a fundamental right such as freedom of speech. For such a rule to withstand constitutional challenge, the government must show more than a merely important reason for the rule. The reason for the rule must be compelling; that is, it must be so important that it outweighs even the most valued and basic freedom it negatively affects.

confidentiality. When personally identifiable information is not shared without the consent of the user or as required by law. In a library setting, confidentiality exists when the library is in possession of personally identifiable information about users and keeps that information private on their behalf.

content-neutral restrictions. See *viewpoint-neutral restrictions.*

COPPA. Acronym identifying the Children's Online Privacy Protection Act (15 U.S.C. § 6501; 16 CFR 312), which includes provisions requiring commercial online content providers who either have actual knowledge that they are dealing with a child under thirteen years of age or who aim their content at children to obtain verifiable parental consent before they can collect, archive, use, or resell any personal information pertaining to that child.

court order. A legal document in which a court tells a person to perform a specific act or prohibits him from performing an act. This includes **search warrants** and preservation of documents orders. It also includes Foreign Intelligence Surveillance Court (FISA) orders for business records authorized by the **USA PATRIOT Act.**

Creative Commons (CC). A nonprofit organization with a mission to increase the number of creative works available for others to build upon legally and to share. The organization provides a variety of free copyright licenses known as Creative Commons licenses. These licenses allow creators to explicitly grant additional uses of copyrighted materials not normally allowed under current copyright law.

data mining. The process of collecting, searching through, and analyzing a large amount of data about individuals in databases to discover patterns or relations.

equal and equitable access to information and services. An approach to operating that ensures that everyone the library serves is entitled to the same level of access to information and services and that all have the opportunity to avail themselves if they so choose. *"Equal"* access refers to uniform access to information and services. *"Equitable"* access refers to just and fair access taking into consideration the facts and circumstances of the individual case. Access to information and services is equal and equitable when there is a level playing field.

E-rate. The Schools and Libraries Program created by the U.S. Federal Communications Commission (FCC) to meet the universal service goals mandated by the Telecommunications Act of 1996. Telecommunications providers are required to supply their services to schools and libraries at discounted rates determined by the FCC. Discounts for support are based on the level of poverty and the urban/rural status of the population served and range from 20 percent to 90 percent of the costs of eligible services. Eligible schools, school districts, and libraries may apply individually or as part of a consortium. Applicants must provide the computers, telephones, and software resources that are necessary to utilize the connectivity provided by the program. Public schools and librar-

Appendixes

ies accepting E-rate funds are subject to **CIPA** and must certify that the institution has adopted an Internet safety policy that includes use of a "technology protection measure"—**filtering software.**

expression of concern. See *challenge.*

expurgation. The excision, alteration, editing, or obliteration of any part(s) of books or other library resources by the library for the purposes of **censorship.**

extra-legal pressure. Threat of legal action or pressure by community members or organized groups that results in the banning of library materials. The term also refers to requests from law enforcement without a proper **court order** and actions taken by persons in positions of authority (e.g., mayors, elected officials, school officials) to remove or restrict access to library materials or services without following library policies and procedures.

fair use. A limitation and exception to the exclusive right granted by copyright law to the author of a creative work. In United States copyright law (17 U.S.C), fair use is a doctrine that permits limited use of copyrighted material without acquiring permission from the rights holders. Courts use a four-part test to determine if a particular use of a work is "fair": (1) the purpose and character of the use, (2) the nature of the copyrighted work, (3) the amount and substantiality of the portion used in relation to the copyrighted work as a whole, and (4) the effect of the use upon the potential market for or value of the copyrighted work. Examples of fair use include commentary, search engines, criticism, parody, news reporting, research, teaching, library archiving, and scholarship.

FERPA. Acronym identifying the Family Educational Rights and Privacy Act (20 U.S. Code §1232g; 34 CFR Part 99), which controls disclosure of a student's educational records and information and gives parents and students the right to inspect and correct their educational records. It applies to all schools that receive funds under an applicable program of the U.S. Department of Education.

filtering software. A "technology protection measure," the use of which is intended to block access to particular kinds of online content. **CIPA** requires public schools and libraries accepting funds for Internet access through the Universal Service **E-rate** discount program and the Library Services and Technology Act (**LSTA**) to certify that the institution has adopted an Internet safety policy that includes use of filtering software to keep adults from accessing visual images online that are obscene or **child pornography**. The filtering software must also block minors' access to images that are **harmful to minors.**

FIPP. Acronym referring to Fair Information Practices Principles developed by the U.S. Department of Health, Education and Welfare in 1973. The principles are Notice/Awareness, Choice/Consent, Access/Participation, and Integrity/Security.

First Amendment. Part of the Bill of Rights of the U.S. Constitution, stating, "Congress shall make no law respecting an establishment of religion, or prohibiting the free exercise thereof; or abridging the freedom of speech, or of the press; or the right of the people peaceably to assemble, and to petition the government for a redress of grievances."

Fourth Amendment. Part of the Bill of Rights of the U.S. Constitution, stating, "The right of the people to be secure in their persons, houses, papers, and effects, against unreasonable searches and seizures, shall not be violated, and no warrants shall issue, but upon probable cause, supported by oath or affirmation, and particularly describing the place to be searched, and the persons or things to be seized."

harmful to minors. Sexually explicit images that adults have a legal right to access but taken as a whole, lack any serious literary, artistic, political, or scientific value for minors. It is illegal to knowingly distribute such materials on the web for commercial purposes on sites available to any minor. Not all states have harmful to minors laws and the coverage varies significantly in states that do.

intellectual freedom. The right of every individual to both seek and receive information from all points of view and all formats without restriction. It provides for free access to all expressions of ideas through which any and all sides of a question, cause, or movement may be explored. **Privacy** is a necessary condition for true intellectual freedom.

intellectual property. Property that results from original creative thought, including works that are patented, copyrighted, or trademarked.

least restrictive means. Narrowly tailored prohibitions or restrictions that are not more restrictive than necessary to serve their objectives.

LSTA. Acronym identifying the Library Services and Technology Act, a federal grant program managed by the Institute of Museum and Library Services (IMLS).

Appendixes

materially interfere. A term used by courts to describe the necessary level of intrusion, inconvenience, or disruption of an accepted or protected activity caused by certain conduct in order to justify regulation of that conduct. A material interference is much more than mere annoyance—it must be an actual obstacle to the exercise of a right.

National Security Letters. Administrative subpoenas issued by the Federal Bureau of Investigation in authorized national security investigations "to protect against international terrorism or clandestine intelligence activities."

NCIPA. Acronym identifying the Neighborhood Children's Internet Protection Act, a subsection of **CIPA** that requires an Internet policy with specific additional required provisions in order to qualify to receive **E-rate** discounts.

Ninth, Tenth, and Fourteenth Amendments. Parts of the Bill of Rights of the U.S. Constitution. The Fourteenth Amendment prohibits states from making or enforcing "any law which shall abridge the privileges or immunities of citizens of the United States" and from depriving "any person of life, liberty, or property, without due process of law"; or denying "to any person within its jurisdiction the equal protection of the laws." The Ninth and Tenth Amendments make it possible for states to provide for persons within their jurisdiction, either by legislative action or citizen initiative, greater rights than provided by the U.S. Constitution and laws.

obscenity. Sexually themed speech or expressive materials that are not protected by the **First Amendment**. The legal test for obscenity includes the following criteria: (1) whether "the average person, applying contemporary community standards" would find that the work, "taken as a whole," appeals to "prurient interest," (2) whether the work depicts or describes, in a patently offensive way, sexual conduct specifically defined by the applicable state law, and (3) whether the work, "taken as a whole," lacks serious literary, artistic, political, or scientific value (see *Miller v. California,* 1973, at www.law.cornell.edu/supremecourt/text/413/15). Only a judge or jury can find that a work is legally obscene.

oral complaint. See *challenge.*

overbreadth doctrine. A principle of judicial review that holds that a law is invalid if it punishes constitutionally protected speech or conduct along with speech or conduct that the government may limit to further a compelling government interest.

personally identifiable information (PII). Information that can be used to distinguish or trace an individual's identity, either alone or when combined with other personal or identifying information that is linked or linkable to a specific individual.

pornography. A colloquial, popular term referring to the representation of sexual behavior in books, pictures, statues, motion pictures, and other media that is intended to cause sexual excitement. In more recent times, the term has been extended to any item or image intended to incite desire (e.g., "food porn"). The decision about what is pornographic is largely subjective and reflects changing community standards and the subjective views of the individual. Imagery that might be considered merely erotic or even religious in one society may be condemned as pornographic in another. Under U.S. law, "pornography" has no legal definition. Courts and legislatures instead identify illegal sexually themed content as **"obscenity,"** which is defined by statute in federal and state law.

privacy. In a library (physical or virtual), the right to privacy is the right to open inquiry without having the subject of one's interest examined or scrutinized by others.

privacy audit. A review of an institution's information-processing procedures to determine if they meet privacy requirements. It examines how information about users is collected, stored, shared, used, and destroyed.

probable cause. Reasonable ground for a belief in a criminal case that the accused was guilty of the crime, or, in a civil case, that grounds for the action existed.

public challenge. See *challenge.*

public forum. A "traditional public forum" is a government-owned place that has been traditionally available for public assembly, speech, and discussion (e.g., parks, sidewalks, and streets). A "designated or limited public forum" is a public place purposefully designated by the government, or established through tradition, as a place dedicated to a particular type of expression. A "nonpublic forum" is a place that is neither traditionally used for expressive activities nor set aside or opened up in a substantial way for expressive activities. Rules about what kinds of restrictions on speech may be legally imposed in a given place are based on the type of forum that has been established.

request for reconsideration. See *challenge.*

Appendixes

RFID. Acronym for radio frequency identification, a technology that uses various electronic devices, such as microchip tags, tag readers, computer servers, and software. It is used by some libraries for circulation, inventory management, and security control.

search warrant. A court order that authorizes law enforcement officers to immediately search a person or place to obtain evidence for presentation in criminal prosecutions. Officers obtain search warrants by submitting affidavits and other evidence to a judge or magistrate to establish that **probable cause** exists to believe that a search will yield evidence related to a crime. If satisfied that the officers have established **probable cause,** the judge or magistrate will issue the warrant.

strict scrutiny. A standard of judicial review for a challenged policy in which the court presumes the policy to be invalid unless the government can demonstrate a **compelling government interest** to justify the policy.

subpoena. A legal order used by a court, grand jury, legislative body, or administrative agency to compel an individual to appear before it at a specified time to give testimony or to provide evidence under a penalty of failure.

substantial objectives. Goals related to the fundamental mission of a government institution and not merely incidental to the performance of that mission. For example, providing free and unrestricted access to a broad selection of materials representing various points of view is a substantial objective of a public library.

time, place, and manner restrictions. Restrictions on the time, place, or manner of expression that are justified when they serve a significant government interest and are neutral or unrelated to the content or viewpoint expressed in the speech. For example, a library's rule forbidding the use of amplified sound by any group using its meeting rooms is an acceptable time, place, and manner restriction because it serves a significant interest (maintaining a quiet environment), applies to all users without discrimination, and is content-neutral.

USA PATRIOT Act. Acronym identifying the Uniting and Strengthening America by Providing Appropriate Tools Required to Intercept and Obstruct Terrorism Act of 2001 (October 26, 2001), which significantly reduced the restrictions on the ability of law enforcement agencies to investigate and gather information and detain and deport people suspected of terrorism.

viewpoint-neutral restrictions. Constitutionally permissible restrictions on expression that apply uniformly to all speech regardless of the point of view expressed by the speaker. Public libraries, like all government agencies, may not silence speakers whom the government opposes or sanction only those whom the government supports, or silence particular speakers because of popular controversy. For example, libraries may not use **filtering software** to block or filter web content favoring same-sex marriage while allowing access to web content opposing or disparaging same-sex marriage.

SELECTED BIBLIOGRAPHY

by Loretta Gaffney

Adams, Helen. *Protecting Intellectual Freedom and Privacy in Your School Library*. Santa Barbara, CA: Libraries Unlimited, 2013.

Alfino, Mark, and Laura Koltutsky, eds. *The Library Juice Press Handbook of Intellectual Freedom*. Sacramento, CA: Library Juice, 2014.

Auguste, Margaret. *VOYA's Guide to Intellectual Freedom for Teens*. Bowie, MD: VOYA, 2012.

Banned Books: Literature Suppressed on Political Grounds, Literature Suppressed on Religious Grounds, Literature Suppressed on Sexual Grounds, and *Literature Suppressed on Social Grounds*. 3rd ed. (4 volumes). New York: Facts on File, 2011.

Batch, Kristen R. "Fencing Out Knowledge: Impacts of the Children's Internet Protection Act 10 Years Later" (Policy Brief no. 5). American Library Association, June 2014. www.ala.org/offices/sites/ala.org .offices/files/content/oitp/publications/issuebriefs/cipa_report.pdf.

Boghosian, Heidi. *Spying on Democracy: Government Surveillance, Corporate Power, and Public Resistance*. San Francisco: City Lights Publishers, 2013.

boyd, danah. *It's Complicated: The Social Lives of Networked Teens*. New Haven, CT: Yale University Press, 2014.

Chmara, Theresa. *Privacy and Confidentiality Issues: A Guide for Libraries and Their Lawyers*. Chicago: American Library Association, 2009.

Crews, Kenneth D. *Copyright Law for Librarians and Educators: Creative Strategies and Practical Solutions.* 3rd ed. Chicago: American Library Association, 2012.

Doyle, Robert P. *Banned Books: Challenging Our Freedom to Read.* Chicago: American Library Association, 2014.

Feldman, Stephen M. *Free Expression and Democracy in America: A History.* Chicago: University of Chicago Press, 2008.

Finan, Christopher M. *From the Palmer Raids to the Patriot Act: A History of the Fight for Free Speech in America.* Boston: Beacon, 2007.

Finkin, Matthew W., and Robert Post. *For the Common Good: Principles of American Academic Freedom.* New Haven, CT: Yale University Press, 2009.

Foerstel, Herbert. *Banned in the U.S.A.: A Reference Guide to Book Censorship in Schools and Public Libraries.* Revised and expanded edition. Westport, CT: Greenwood, 2002.

————. *Refuge of a Scoundrel: The Patriot Act in Libraries.* Westport, CT: Libraries Unlimited, 2004.

————. *Surveillance in the Stacks: The FBI's Library Awareness Program.* New York: Greenwood, 1991.

Griffey, Jason, Sarah Houghton-Jan, and Eli Neiburger. *Privacy and Freedom of Information in 21st-Century Libraries.* Chicago: ALA TechSource, 2010.

Heins, Marjorie. *Not in Front of the Children: "Indecency," Censorship, and the Innocence of Youth.* 2nd ed. New Brunswick, NJ: Rutgers University Press, 2007.

Heins, Marjorie, Christina Cho, and Ariel Feldman. *Internet Filters: A Public Policy Report.* 2nd ed. New York: Brennan Center for Justice, 2006.

Hudson, David L. *Let the Students Speak! A History of the Fight for Free Expression in American Schools.* Boston: Beacon, 2011.

Jones, Barbara M. *Libraries, Access, and Intellectual Freedom: Developing Policies for Public and Academic Libraries.* Chicago: American Library Association, 1999.

————. *Protecting Intellectual Freedom in Your Academic Library: Scenarios from the Front Lines.* Chicago: American Library Association, 2009.

Karolides, Nicholas. *120 Banned Books: Censorship Histories of World Literature.* 2nd ed. New York: Checkmark Books, 2011.

Lane, Frederick S. *American Privacy: The 400-Year History of Our Most Contested Right.* Boston: Beacon, 2009.

LaRue, James. *The New Inquisition: Understanding and Managing Intellectual Freedom Challenges.* Westport, CT: Libraries Unlimited, 2007.

Lesesne, Teri S., and Rosemary Chance. *Hit List for Young Adults 2: Frequently Challenged Books.* Chicago: American Library Association, 2002.

Levine, Judith. *Only a Game: Why Censoring New Media Won't Stop Gun Violence.* New York: Media Coalition, 2013, http://mediacoalition.org/wp-content/uploads/2014/04/Only-A-Game-Why-Censoring-New-Media-Wont-Stop-Gun-Violence.pdf.

Lord, Catherine. *Defending Access with Confidence: A Practical Workshop on Intellectual Freedom.* Chicago: Public Library Association, 2005.

Lukianoff, Greg. *Unlearning Liberty: Campus Censorship and the End of American Debate.* New York: Encounter Books, 2014.

McCord, Gretchen. *What You Need to Know about Privacy Law: A Guide for Librarians and Educators.* Santa Barbara, CA: Libraries Unlimited, 2013.

Morrison, Toni. *Burn This Book: PEN Writers Speak Out on the Power of the Word.* New York: HarperStudio, 2009.

Moshman, David. *Liberty and Learning: Academic Freedom for Teachers and Students.* Portsmouth, NH: Heinemann, 2009.

Nye, Valerie, and Kathy Barco, eds. *True Stories of Censorship Battles in America's Libraries.* Chicago: American Library Association, 2012.

Peters, John Durham. *Courting the Abyss: Free Speech and the Liberal Tradition.* Chicago: University of Chicago Press, 2005.

Pinnell-Stephens, June. *Protecting Intellectual Freedom in Your Public Library: Scenarios from the Front Lines.* Chicago: American Library Association, 2012.

Rabban, David M. *Free Speech in Its Forgotten Years.* Cambridge, UK: Cambridge University Press, 1997.

Richard, Neil M. *Intellectual Privacy: Rethinking Civil Liberties in the Digital Age.* Oxford: Oxford University Press, 2015.

Robbins, Louise S. *Censorship and the American Library: The American Library Association's Response to Threats to Intellectual Freedom, 1939-1969*. Westport, CT: Greenwood, 1996.

_____. *The Dismissal of Miss Ruth Brown: Civil Rights, Censorship, and the American Library*. Norman: University of Oklahoma Press, 2001.

Samek, Toni. *Intellectual Freedom and Social Responsibility in American Librarianship, 1967-1974*. Jefferson, NC: McFarland, 2001.

Scales, Pat R. *Books under Fire: A Hit List of Banned and Challenged Children's Books*. Chicago: American Library Association, 2015.

_____. *Protecting Intellectual Freedom in Your School Library: Scenarios from the Front Lines*. Chicago: American Library Association, 2009.

Solove, Daniel. *Nothing to Hide: The False Tradeoff between Privacy and Security*. New Haven, CT: Yale University Press, 2011.

_____. *Understanding Privacy*. Cambridge, MA: Harvard University Press, 2010.

Stone, Geoffrey R. *Perilous Times: Free Speech in Wartime from the Sedition Act of 1798 to the War on Terrorism*. New York: W. W. Norton, 2004.

Sweeney, Megan. *Reading Is My Window: Books and the Art of Reading in Women's Prisons*. Chapel Hill: University of North Carolina Press, 2010.

CORE INTELLECTUAL FREEDOM DOCUMENTS AND RELATED STATEMENTS

Code of Ethics of the American Library Association (Part I, Chapter 2)

INTERPRETATIONS:

Copyright (part II, chapter 5)

OTHER DOCUMENTS:

Questions and Answers on Conflicts of Interest: An Explanatory Statement of the ALA *Code of Ethics* (ALA website)

Questions and Answers on Enforcement of the *Code of Ethics of the American Library Association* (part I, Chapter 2)

Questions and Answers on Ethics and Social Media: An Explanatory Statement of the ALA *Code of Ethics* (ALA website)

Questions and Answers on Speech in the Workplace: An Explanatory Statement of the ALA *Code of Ethics* (part II, chapter 9)

The Freedom to Read (part I, chapter 2)

Libraries: An American Value (part I, chapter 2)

Library Bill of Rights (part I, chapter 2)

INTERPRETATIONS:

Access to Digital Information, Services, and Networks (part II, chapter 1)

Access to Library Resources and Services for Minors (part II, chapter 3) [formerly titled Free Access to Libraries for Minors; incorporates content from Access for Children and Young Adults to Nonprint Materials]

Access to Library Resources and Services Regardless of Sex, Gender Identity, Gender Expression, or Sexual Orientation (part II, chapter 1)

Access to Resources and Services in the School Library (part II, chapter 3) [formerly titled Access to Resources and Services in the School Library Media Program]

Advocating for Intellectual Freedom (part II, chapter 6) [formerly titled Importance of Education to Intellectual Freedom]

Challenged Resources (part II, chapter 2) [formerly titled Challenged Materials]

Diversity in Collection Development (part II, chapter 4)

Economic Barriers to Information Access (part II, chapter 1)

Evaluating Library Collections (part II, chapter 4)

Exhibit Spaces and Bulletin Boards (part II, chapter 6)

Expurgation of Library Resources (part II, chapter 2) [formerly titled Expurgation of Library Materials]

Intellectual Freedom Principles for Academic Libraries (part II, chapter 1)

Labeling and Rating Systems (part II, chapter 4)

Library-Initiated Programs as a Resource (part II, chapter 6)

Meeting Rooms (part II, chapter 6)

Minors and Internet Activity (part II, chapter 3) [formerly titled Minors and Internet Interactivity]

Prisoners' Right to Read (part II, chapter 1)

Privacy (part II, chapter 7)

Restricted Access to Library Materials (part II, chapter 1)

Services to Persons with Disabilities (part II, chapter 1)

The Universal Right to Free Expression (part II, chapter 1)

Other ALA Statements

Policy on Governmental Intimidation (part II, chapter 8)

Resolution on the Retention of Library Usage Records (part II, chapter 7)

RFID in Libraries (part II, chapter 7)

INDEX

Tribal Library
Saginaw Chippewa Indian Tribe
7070 E. Broadway
Mt. Pleasant MI 48858